WOMEN IN WORLD HISTORY

Volume 1

Readings from Prehistory to 1500

Sources
and
Studies
in World
History

Kevin Reilly, Series Editor

THE ALCHEMY OF HAPPINESS
Abu Hamid Muhammad al-Ghazzali
translated by Claud Field, revised and annotated by Elton L. Daniel

LIFELINES FROM OUR PAST
A New World History
L. S. Stavrianos

NATIVE AMERICANS BEFORE 1492
The Moundbuilding Centers of the Eastern Woodlands
Lynda Norene Shaffer

GERMS, SEEDS, AND ANIMALS
Studies in Ecological History
Alfred W. Crosby

BALKAN WORLDS
The First and Last Europe
Traian Stoianovich

AN ATLAS AND SURVEY OF
SOUTH ASIAN HISTORY
Karl J. Schmidt

THE GOGO: HISTORY, CUSTOMS, AND TRADITIONS
Mathias E. Mnyampala
Translated, introduced, and edited by Gregory H. Maddox

WOMEN IN WORLD HISTORY
Volume 1—Readings from Prehistory to 1500
Volume 2—Readings from 1500 to the Present
Sarah Shaver Hughes and Brady Hughes

WOMEN IN WORLD HISTORY

Volume 1

Readings from Prehistory to 1500

Sarah Shaver Hughes
Brady Hughes

M.E. Sharpe

Armonk, New York
London, England

Library of Congress Cataloging-in-Publication Data

Hughes, Sarah S.
Women in world history / Sarah Shaver Hughes and Brady Hughes.
v.   cm.   —   (Sources and studies in world history)
Includes bibliographical references.
Contents: v. 1. Readings from prehistory to 1500.
ISBN 1-56324-310-5.   —   ISBN 1-56324-311-3 (pbk.)
1. Women—History.   I. Hughes, Brady, 1933–
II. Title.   III. Series.
HQ1121.H93   1995
305.4′09—dc 20   94-23644
CIP

Printed in the United States of America

The paper used in this publication meets the minimum requirements of
American National Standard for Information Sciences—
Permanence of Paper for Printed Library Materials,
ANSI Z 39.48-1984.

∞

BM (c)   10   9   8   7   6   5   4   3   2   1
BM (p)   10   9   8   7

CONTENTS

FOREWORD

Neither world history nor women's history was widely taught a generation ago. Proponents of women's history had to fight the widespread assumption that conventional histories of "man" or "mankind" were universal, that they spoke for the lives of women as well as men. A major problem with such histories was that the preponderance of sources used were written by men. Despite the insistence that "man" stood for women as well as men, students were often left with the distinct impression that history was made by men.

In the last twenty years, scholars of women's history have shown that there were many more important women, more sources written by women, and more sources about women than had previously been assumed. A first stage of scholarship in women's history called for the inclusion of women writers, artists, thinkers, rulers, and public figures.

The recovery of important women, largely from elite families, was a valuable correction. But histories that only added women were still centered on what came to be seen as men's topics: war, diplomacy, statecraft, and industry.

Increasingly, historians became conscious of the degree to which past societies had been divided along sexual lines, expecting different work and preparing different lives for men and women. In this second stage of scholarship, it became obvious that the historical experiences of men and women were different. There was no way that the lives of men could represent those of women. The prior historical division of men's and women's lives had defined the male role as public and political, concerned with city, state, war, and foreign relations. History had been written largely by and for men as a way of understanding and celebrating those male activities.

The second stage of scholarship in women's history has challenged this idea of history. A generation of studies has taught us to see the ways in which men and women are socially and culturally conditioned to certain kinds of behavior. This is why scholars speak now about "gender," the social and cultural behavior that may build upon or ignore biological sexual identity. To see gender in history is to see the ways in which men and women are trained in different (and similar) activities, to explore those diverse realms, and to understand the dynamic of gender interaction. In plain words, this means not just adding a queen for a day but studying kinship as well as kingship, the family as well as the state, domestic relations as well as foreign relations. Activities in which women have played more important roles than men—childrearing, planting, clothing production, local marketing, health care, education—and those, like art and religion, in which women's role has been as great as men's, are as important a part of the human past as the largely male-dominated "outside" activities of traditional history books.

Thus, the new historians of women have opened up vast realms of human activity that were largely ignored in past histories because men did not deem them important. And since men's records of the past are more numerous than women's, they have shown us how to read between the lines of those documents, to find new sources in myths, oral traditions, art and artifact—in short, to develop new methods of investigation and analysis.

It is remarkable that scholars of women's history and allied scholars of what has come to be known as the "new social history" (the study of everyday life, average and marginal people, daydreams, diets, dreads, diseases, hopes, and haircuts) have opened up the past at the same time that world history as a field of study has become established. The field of history has exploded both within and beyond traditional boundaries.

There is no turning back. Just as we cannot ignore the daily lives and inner experiences of women, we cannot ignore the peoples of Asia, Africa, and the Americas. We must know all of ourselves and all of our world.

Sarah and Brady Hughes have set themselves an enormous task. To "gender world history and globalize women's history" is a tall order. But it is a necessary one, and one for which they are especially well qualified. They both have been teaching women's history and world history throughout the recent decades of explosive innovation. They have been leaders in the effort to make world history genuinely inclusive while expanding our knowledge of women in the world. In this book they show us how easy it is to do both at the same time.

Kevin Reilly

PREFACE

This volume of readings (and its sequel covering history since 1500) was prepared to meet dual needs: to gender world history and to globalize women's history. Many world history texts are misnamed, for too often they are histories of the activities of the world's men. The authors seem to be unaware that their portrayal of the historical male emphasizes the aggressive, power-driven, and sadistic aspects of his character. Stirring in a dollop of women's history only contrasts with narratives focused on how powerful empires dominate weaker neighbors. Accurate history demands more than inclusion of fragments of women's history as a gesture toward equity to half of humankind. The social interactions of women and men in the household are a fundamental dynamic of any society, an explanatory factor crucial to understanding other relationships of power between clans, classes, political factions, religions, or nations. Until scholars develop an adequate base of knowledge about gender relationships, our understanding of the structure underlying any society's political, economic, or intellectual history will remained flawed. This book attempts only to suggest how considering the lives of women reveals the complex personal basis of social hierarchies and the family-oriented politics of premodern societies.

Synthesis of women's history generally has been debated within the narrow confines of the Mediterranean region and Western Europe as preludes to the American experience. World history is moving away from such biased investigation. Somewhat tardily following the lead of feminist anthropologists and economists (who have theorized about gender in contemporary societies within a global framework for over twenty years), historians of women have recently begun to examine earlier centuries. Viewing women's earliest history through a wider lens that also encompasses societies of Asia, Africa, and the

Americas reveals a far more complex panorama. Patriarchy did not triumph in the same ways everywhere, and women were not always denied public political or economic roles. Female status in Western civilizations should not be the measure of women's possibilities before 1500. Rather than ignoring women's global history before 1500, historians can find much in the ancient past that is fundamental to constructing modern gender. This volume is only an appetizer, though one which opens up a very promising banquet.

Women in World History is organized on a regional basis, with readings within each chapter placed in chronological sequence. Themes emphasize female agency in the state, religion, literature, economy, and family, as well as oppressive ideologies, laws, and customs. As we attempted to shape a narrative that would be useful to students in world or women's history courses, some hard choices and compromises were necessary. Mesopotamian societies are omitted. But Egypt is well represented in selections that illustrate the continuity of its women's history from ancient pharoanic dynasties to the Roman Mediterranean. Readings on religions that shaped millions of women's spiritual and temporal lives purposely stretch over centuries to compare the beliefs of the founding eras with the practices of later centuries. Women of Southeast Asia, Sub-Saharan Africa, and the Western Hemisphere enter into our history later than those of other continents because of the paucity of available written sources before 800 C.E.

Women's own writings have not been preserved or are poorly preserved from many literate societies. Women in several regions pioneered writing in their vernacular languages because so many were denied education in Latin, Sanskrit, Arabic, or Chinese. These authors are only now beginning to be translated into English. In contrast to the scarcity of female authors, there are an ample number of documents about women, available in English translation, written by men for use by men. This plenitude of sources is due to a long tradition of scholarship in many disciplines. We are indebted to the numerous scholars who have been translating important texts for two centuries and to those who have recently reexamined the past seeking the overlooked and ignored history of our ancestors.

We also have special debts to Kevin Reilly, editor of M.E. Sharpe's

Sources and Studies in World History series, and to Signe Kelker and Diane Kalathas of the interlibrary loan department of Shippensburg University.

On Transliteration

This volume contains a number of words from foreign languages. In order to be consistent and because most of our readers will not be familiar with scholarly systems of translation, we have restricted all spelling to the Roman alphabet and omitted diacritical marks.

Sarah Shaver Hughes
Brady Hughes
March 1995

INTRODUCTION

Gendering World History, Globalizing Women's History

In 1835 the American abolitionist author Lydia Maria Child published a *History and Condition of Women in Various Ages and Nations.* Child's book reflected a need women had long felt, and expressed in their writings in earlier centuries, to understand their place in the world in the broadest historical context. In the 160 years since Child wrote, history has been professionalized, and too often efforts to comprehend the global history of women have been marginalized. There still is no satisfactory general history of all women available in English.

The readings in this volume suggest the richness of women's history beyond North America and Europe and of world history beyond the impersonal, implicitly male story of cities, economies, wars, and empires. The readings are structured within regional chapters to correspond with modern history's geographic/national structure. Selections reveal critical facets of women's lives in particular places and periods. But important themes that cross boundaries of culture and time also appear. For example, a reader may compare how Buddhism, Judaism, Christianity, and Islam affected their female believers or how some of these religions affected women in different times or places. Recurring global themes analyze the political power of women as regents, diplomats, and queens in monarchies; women's fundamental contributions to the production of goods and services necessary to sustain society and to develop economies; enslavement of women; marriage practices and motherhood; and religious and social beliefs that proscribed some women as beyond respectability. Representative samples of literature written by women also appear. In these pages there are some famous women, such as Hatshepsut, Cleopatra, Hortensia, Aisha, and Sei Shonagon, along with many less well known or anonymous ones.

Prehistory

Explaining the asymmetrical relationships of gender is not simple. History does not supply an easy answer to why men subordinated women in so many societies, though women seem never to have dominated men so dramatically. Researchers cannot find convincing universal evidence of a "golden age" of matriarchy (which many nineteenth-century writers, including Friedrich Engels, believed existed before patriarchy's dominion replaced it). Today some feminists posit there was a prehistoric, Neolithic time when the widespread worship of goddesses heralded women's temporal power. Links can be made among female figurines, fertility, the importance of motherhood, and belief in goddesses, but generalizing further to explain a global social structure, or the Neolithic relationships of power between women and men, is contrary to the evidence of decades of research.

The scholarship of archaeologists, anthropologists, and historians illustrates how varied the ways are in which human beings divide social functions by gender, including some that are obscured if we assume only a female/male model. For more than one hundred years Western scientists and social scientists have sought to formulate general explanations for the social differences societies create around issues of gender. Primatologists compare behaviors of various animals with those of humans, seeking the origins of gender differences in distant evolution. Archaeologists look among the ruins and artifacts of lost antiquity. Biologists consider how chromosomes, hormones, reproductive organs, and muscles shape social patterns. Psychologists search for distinctive female behavior patterns, and anthropologists compare how cultures variously construct gender.

The origins of patriarchy have so far defied explanation because there is no simple universal biological, prehistoric, or historical pattern. A trajectory seems clear, even in Western traditions, only when much is omitted. Nor is it even certain that patriarchy has prevailed everywhere, though it is evident in the records of the literate, dominant world civilizations. Conquest, private property, slavery, and subordination of women to men are embedded together in the history of empires in Eurasia, Africa, and the Americas. Although history focuses on these populations, most of the world's women probably have lived outside such cultures in the less hierarchic societies where women's status has often been higher.

The Value of Gender in Historical Analysis

Nevertheless, women in the premodern, literate historical world lived, often with few civil rights, in societies dominated by men. Many women were sold by their fathers to their husbands, abused by them, and legally considered to have no more intellectual capacity than a child. On the other hand, women were loved by their parents, husbands, and children. Women used the lever of family relationships to gain advantages within their social restraints. They negotiated a daily balance of gender power, often ignoring disadvantageous laws or ritual regulations. While applauding small victories, we must also consider the wider meaning of these societies' constructions of gender to favor males. Norwegian historian Ida Blom notes that

> applying gender as an analytical tool—not stopping at analyzing women's oppression but also continuing to locate their strengths and their participation in class, caste and ethnic hierarchies—yields important knowledge as to how societies functioned. Such analysis reveals that every area of society, be it the family, the workplace or the political arena, is gender-structured. Inheritance rules, divisions of work and of authority, beliefs as to psychological characteristics of an individual, even political power relations are structured around dichotomies of gender.*

Particularly striking is women's economic importance. Consider the production of human necessities—food, clothing, and shelter—and think of their immense value to people in preindustrial civilizations. Women's labor in growing, processing, and cooking daily food

---

*Ida Blom, "Global Women's History: Organizing Principles and Cross-Cultural Understandings," in Karen Offen, Ruth Roach Pierson, and Jane Rendall, eds., *Writing Women's History: International Perspectives* (Bloomington: Indiana University Press, 1991), 139.

has been such an accepted reality that it is difficult to find documents describing that essential work. In some societies building and repairing housing has also fallen to women in the division of labor, but almost everywhere making garments to cover bodies and ground was their job. Women have largely produced the clothing of mankind, from harvesting raw fibers or skinning small animals to carrying out all the steps of production to the finished product. Even the poorest person was dependent for clothing on female labor, yet economic development also hinged upon female-produced textiles. Monarchs levied taxes in home-woven fabrics and supported factories where women wove linen or silk to drape the opulent display of court power or to exchange for armed allies. Textiles constituted so much of the value and volume of international trade throughout the premodern era that the topic cannot be discussed without considering them. Usually, however, the value of silk yard goods carried on the Silk Road, calicos of India, batiks of Indonesia, feathered capes of Tenochtitlan, or woolens of Florence is measured without mentioning the women who made them. Under hand manufacture, women always dominated the early stages of producing thread from cotton, flax, hemp, wool, feathers, or silk—the tedious processes of cleaning, carding, and spinning. Weaving the threads was an exclusively male job in some cultures, but more often it has been women's work. Men replaced women at looms often when cash earnings from weaving rose significantly, probably as an economy was monetized. The importance of discerning gender patterns in textile production might seem obvious, but this work, like much of women's labor, is often not even reckoned in counting the wealth or product of an economy.

Americans assume that household labor means what they know of vacuuming, laundry, cookery, and child care. It is hard to imagine the physical effort or the significance of earlier women's domestic labor in gathering and growing crops; processing as well as cooking food; weaving, sewing, and laundering clothes; marketing surpluses; and nursing, educating, and comforting children. It is equally hard to understand personal relationships not based on individual choice— critical differences in the family foundations of societies, varying from how marriages were contracted and ancestry calculated to how property was transferred and classes formed. That women had no public role in classical Athens is relevant to democratic theory and to understanding why American women's demand for voting rights was ridiculed before 1920. Whether considering religion, literacy, health, art, slavery, war, or trade, gender usually mattered.

Differences among Women

Women were not all alike in any society, nor did they act as if they perceived themselves as sisters united against male oppressors. Instead, women divided against one another on the basis of class, family, caste, religion, and respectability. Women policed their own social bounds, as often persecuting as protecting women who disobeyed restrictions on sexuality, dress, or occupation.

Unfortunately, most surviving documents tell about the lives of elite women in civilizations and are seldom adequate to reflect the variations in women's experiences. Within literate societies the least information remains about rural women, working urban women, and slaves. Women's own spaces and cultures are poorly documented either because men were more often literate (except in Southeast Asia) or because men preserved records they perceived as significant. Glimpses of women's romantic love for one another indicate that within the silences of gender-segregated cultures were many possibilities unknown to history. Women in nonliterate societies are least known to historians. The pasts of some can never be retrieved, though more may be recovered as scholars in many fields become sensitive to gender in origin myths, art and architecture, written texts, and oral histories.

In interpreting the known past, a misconception to be avoided is that women's history progresses from a time of unconscious submission to oppression to a liberated twentieth-century West. The readings in this volume present many conditions of women, which varied over time. Were the aristocratic women of the Japanese court in the tenth century C.E. more or less privileged than their modern successors? Why might one argue that the status of women in Thailand, Burma, and Indonesia has declined since 1500? Muslim Arabian women of Muhammad's generation would have been horrified by the restrictions imposed on their sisters under the urban Abbasid empire. Upper-class women in the late Roman Republic lived far more secure lives than sixth-century Frankish women, some of whom were undoubtedly descendants of the Romans.

Searching for Victors as Well as Victims

Within recorded history, women's achievements were normal, not anomalies. But it can be easy to miss this, especially when attention focuses upon the laws of any land. Men, when they dominated public offices, created numerous laws and regulations restricting women's use of space. Sometimes female spaces were confined to the home. Often public debating forums were proscribed, as were some streets, theaters, or temples. Women did internalize these rules and aid in enforcing them. But women also resisted such limitations or ignored them, just as some women overcame the horrors of slavery, exile, and war. Whether it be veiled shoppers in Cairo boldly seizing the streets and gossiping in the bazaar or the Athenian courtesan Neaera bargaining for her freedom, seemingly victimized women demonstrated initiative and courage.

Every chapter in this book contains descriptions of women who broadened the boundaries that sought to restrict them. Few women changed the fate of empires, though Cleopatra tried. Many readings describe women who had the power to influence large and small personal and political decisions. Frequently women used their influence as agents of their families or clans, because in the ancient world most people did not think of themselves as individuals as much as members of the family group. Almost all marriages were arranged with the important objective of allying two families. Young women and men were subordinated to their elders. Although forced marriages of prepubescent girls to elderly men may be shocking, pity does little to further historical understanding. How did these young women survive, to overcome the sacrifice of their youth in the pleasures of motherhood, adultery, widowhood, or spiritual repose? This book emphasizes their successes, as well as their subordination.

Suggested Further Readings

Without question the most useful source for those seeking more information on non-Western women is Cheryl Johnson-Odim and Margaret Strobel, eds., *Restoring Women to History* (Bloomington: Indiana University Press, forthcoming). Its sections on Africa, Asia, Latin America, the Caribbean, and the Middle East contain bibliographies and excellent regional historical summaries from prehistory to the present. *Writing Women's History: International Perspectives* (Bloomington: Indiana University Press, 1991), edited by Karen Offen, Ruth Roach Pierson, and Jane Rendall, surveys women's history broadly, in this case by country. A fine essay by Ida Blom on "Global Women's History" analyzes problems in writing women's history cross-culturally. One of the few books that compare kinship practices in Africa, Asia, and Europe is *The Oriental, the Ancient and the Primitive: Systems of Marriage and Family in the Pre-industrial Societies of Eurasia* (New York: Cambridge University Press, 1990), written by the anthropologist Jack Goody. Gerda Lerner's *The Creation of Patriarchy* (New York: Oxford University Press, 1986) seeks the origins of men's domination of women in Western societies in the ancient history of the Middle East. Bonnie S. Anderson and Judith P. Zinsser in *A History of Their Own: Women in Europe from Prehistory to the Present,* vol. 1 (New York: Harper Collins, 1988), examine, in Part 1, various traditions deriving from European and Mediterranean peoples that shaped the early history of Western women.

–1–
PREHISTORIC WOMEN
Shaping Evolution, Sustenance, and Economy

A 2,000-year-old figurine from a Bronze Age tomb in present-day Iran.
(UPI/Bettmann, photo © 1975 by Andreas Feininger from his book *Roots of Art.*)

When anthropologists and archaeologists explain the origins of human societies, "man the hunter" is the dominant figure. The meat he lugs to the family fire sustains his dependent wife and children. The powerful image of his protective brawn pervades Western culture from cartoons to serious science. A weak, subordinant woman is his implied mate: someone whose dull, repetitive chores need not be discussed because she contributed nothing to culture, history, or civilization. The assumption that the representative human being is male is rooted in nineteenth-century speculation about the beginnings of human cultures. In the past twenty-five years, some scholars have worked from different assumptions. What if "woman the gatherer" returned to camp with most of the family food? What if women's choices were fundamental to human evolution? What if the first great human technological revolution—the discovery of agriculture—was carried out by women? What if the earliest economic development of human societies was based on trade in surplus food and textiles produced by women?

Much of the writing of archaeologists and anthropologists is speculative, so assumptions matter. Stone ruins, burials, broken pots, fragments of cloth, and arrowheads can reveal material cultures of the prehistoric past, but they do not speak directly of the social environment. Who chipped the arrowhead, shaped the clay, wove the cloth, shrouded the body, lifted the stones? Usually there is no way to know the answers to these questions. Scientific analysis has transformed the study of prehistory in the past fifty years: radiocarbon dating and physical and chemical studies of trace elements in pottery shards, human bones, and ancient seeds have solved many old puzzles about when settlements were built and what botanical and mineral resources were available.

Less progress has been made in gendering the prehistoric past. The gender and age of skeletons are routinely considered today when graves are opened, and it is possible to determine by carbon isotope values and chemical analysis whether men or women, adults or children, were fed better during their lifetimes. Until new techniques permit analyses to determine the sex of fingerprints or other molecular residues, no one can tell us whether women or men created the baskets, pottery, cloth, or metal artifacts of a prehistoric people. Even when that is known, interpretation and assumptions will guide teasing out the motivations underlying a social structure. New techniques and more evidence may fail to yield a better understanding of prehistoric peoples unless there is an acknowledgment of present androcentric biases.

1.1 Women in the "Gatherer-Hunter" Phase

Before we can confidently say what gender had to do with human accomplishments in any prehistoric period or place—or how gender patterns may have changed over many thousands of years—we need to free our minds from stereotypes of "man the hunter," as Adrienne Zihlman illustrates.

About 5 million years ago forest-ranging, knuckle-walking apes— very much like living chimpanzees—evolved through the process of natural selection into the earliest humans, the hominids, who walked upright on two legs, used tools, and lived and gathered food on the African savannas. Females, so long ignored in evolutionary reconstructions, must have played a critical role. Influencing the evolutionary direction of the species, they invested tíme and energy in their offsprings' survival (maternal investment) and chose as their mates those males more protective and willing to share food than the average male ape (sexual selection). Whereas male apes depart from their mothers and siblings at puberty, male hominids were integrated along with the females into their mothers' kin group and contributed to the survival of long-dependent young (kin selection). These relatively sociable males probably became the preferred sexual partners of females in neighboring groups, and, in this way, reinforced the evolutionary process by changing human males through sexual selection.

The presently popular "hunting hypothesis" of human evolution argues that hunting as a technique for getting large amounts of meat was the critical, defining innovation separating early humans from their ape ancestors. This view of "man the hunter" has been used to explain many features of modern Western civilization, from the nuclear family and sexual division of labor to power and politics. But as more and more data have accumulated in recent years, and as approaches to them have changed, the notion that early "man" was primarily a hunter, and meat the main dietary item, has become more and more dubious. Consequently, interpretations of early human social life and the role of each sex in it must be reevaluated. The usual question in most interpretations of human prehistory is "What were the women and children doing while the males were out hunting?" Here I ask instead, "How did human males evolve so as to complement the female role?"

Even without fossil evidence, Darwin deduced that bipedalism and tool using must have been early characteristics of the human line which originated in Africa. Evidence supporting his hypothesis began turning up in South Africa in the 1920s. In the past two decades, hundreds of hominid fossils and thousands of stone tools have been unearthed in both East and South Africa. Our early ancestor, *Australopithecus,* "southern ape," was neither ape nor exclusively southern. It had a brain size that was a little larger than that of the apes, but was entirely bipedal, with small unapelike canine teeth and large molar and premolar teeth—similar to those of plant-eating, not meat-eating animals. . . . During the past decade, new fossils, dating between 1 and 4 million years old, have been coming to light in Africa at a rapid rate. The time span of these fossils is consistent with the biochemically estimated divergence of humans from African apes about 5 million years ago. . . .

The African savanna, where all these fossils have been found, consisted then as now of grasslands, low bush, and riverine forests— a mosaic of vegetation types. . . . The diversity of plant, and consequently animal, life on the savanna presented an opportunity to the evolving and omnivorous hominids for exploiting these abundant resources.

We cannot escape the evolutionary implication that, to some extent, we are what our ancestors ate. Among the hominids, social organization would have been different if the diet was mostly vegetarian than if the diet was primarily one of meat acquired through hunting. The importance of plant food in the diet of early hominids has long been acknowledged, but its significance tended, until recently, to be obscured by the overemphasis on meat and hunting. The fallacious picture of early hominids as a newly emerging meat-eating primate is refuted not only by their omnivore-like masticatory system but also by numerous observations on predation and meat-eating in chimpanzees and baboons—a confirmation of the principle of evolutionary continuity. Studies of living peoples who gather and hunt reveal that throughout the world, except for specialized hunters in arctic regions, more calories are obtained from plant foods gathered by women for family sharing than from meat obtained by hunting. Due to the relative durability of bone as opposed to plant refuse, the archaeological record may exaggerate the amount of meat in the early hominid diet.

Adrienne L. Zihlman, "Women in Evolution, Part II: Subsistence and Social Organization among Early Hominids," *Signs* 4 (1978): 4–7. Reprinted by permission of the publisher, the University of Chicago. © 1978 by the University of Chicago.

Part of the "man the hunter" argument was based on the numerous collections of animal and hominid bones found together in African sites. Archaeologists who have examined the bones more carefully have argued that they are not the hominid hunter's trash pile but the predator's garbage. And the hominid remains in the piles are those of the victims, not the victors.

Although there is no direct evidence for australopithecine predation or for bone and stone toolmaking before about 2 million years ago, it is likely that, continuing the ape ancestral pattern, they engaged in predation and making tools, albeit of organic materials. Tools for digging and carrying food meant that greater quantities could be collected for sharing. Large carnivores posed a real danger on the savanna. Therefore part of the food-getting process had to include the ability of hominids to protect themselves. Their small canine teeth, integral to the food-grinding mechanism, also imply that they used means other than physical prowess in predator defense. Both females and males could deal with predators in a variety of ways: by avoiding them and being active during the day; by traveling, sleeping and getting food in the company of several other individuals and so finding safety in numbers; or, in the event that a confrontation occurred, throwing objects as part of threatening, noisy displays not unlike the bipedal, branch waving and object throwing of chimpanzee displays.

The hominid way of life, which relied on bipedalism and tool using, required a long period for the young to learn and develop associated motor patterns before they were completely independent, perhaps not before eight or ten years of age.

Adrienne L. Zihlman, "Women in Evolution, Part II: Subsistence and Social Organization among Early Hominids," *Signs* 4 (1978): 7–8. Reprinted by permission of the publisher, the University of Chicago. © 1978 by the University of Chicago.

Human children must be carried for three to five years, and they lack the endurance to take long walks at the adult's pace until they are eight at least. Furthermore, they probably cannot master the use of even simple tools before they are five years old.

The early hominids, whose way of life depended upon making and using tools both for obtaining and preparing food and for using objects in defense, must have required even more time to learn such skills. A long dependency prior to walking long distances and mastering tools meant a major investment by mothers in each offspring—in time and energy and in physical, social, and economic efforts.

There is no evidence that, at this early time in prehistory, australopithecine "campsites" or "home bases" existed where the young could be left by mothers and cared for by other group members, as is typical of Kalahari gatherer-hunters today. The burden of child care could only have been possible, I propose, if care was shared by other group members who, at this stage, were close kin. Males who were brothers and sons of the females were regular members of the kin group. Their roles in socialization and care of the young, defense, obtaining meat, sharing food, and, perhaps, collecting raw materials, were significant contributions to the group as a whole. Thus male and female kin contributed to the survival of their young relatives. With this support, mothers could have another offspring before the previous one was entirely independent. Without this involvement of kin—a social solution to a physical problem—birth spacing would have to be extended to more than three or four years, leaving little time for reproduction in a species whose life span may have been little more than twenty years.

Australopithecine females and males had similar-size canine teeth and no more than moderate differences in body size, that is, minimal sexual dimorphism. The degree of sexual dimorphism in canine teeth and body sizes, within the many monkey and ape species studied, correlates with behavioral differences in predator defense and social roles. The small canine teeth in early hominids must be related to three things: diet and mastication, predator defense, and mating patterns. First, the reduced canines in both sexes of early hominids . . . function as part of the biting and grinding mechanism. Second, large male canine teeth and body size differences, as in baboons, function as part of the species' defense system. For the hominids, predator defense would have little anatomical basis. Both sexes probably engaged in a variety of antipredator behaviors. Finally, and perhaps most importantly, the small canines of male hominids suggest that they were more sociable and less aggressive in their interactions with other males and with females. They probably competed with each other for mating with females in agreeable ways rather than by overt fighting or dominance behavior as monkeys and apes do. Hominid male sociable behavior would be advantageous, and indeed necessary, for integration initially into their kin groups and, subsequently, into larger social groupings. Females most frequently chose sexual partners from among the sociable males outside the immediate kin group. . . . Sexual behavior then, as now, was only one expression of social bonds between females and males.

Adrienne L. Zihlman, "Women in Evolution, Part II: Subsistence and Social Organization among Early Hominids," *Signs* 4 (1978): 8–10. Reprinted by permission of the publisher, the University of Chicago. © 1978 by the University of Chicago.

In this model the formation of sharing food networks and family units should be clarified.

Sharing food among the nonhuman primates is infrequent and is of social, rather than nutritional, significance. The new and fundamental elements in the human way of life included food sharing as a matter of survival, regular sharing between mother and offspring, and the expansion of sharing networks to include adult females giving to adult males. This latter kind of sharing may have developed initially within the kin group: mothers gave to their young male offspring and continued to do so when they grew up and stayed with the mother-centered group. Females also shared with their male siblings. Later these behaviors would be a basis for generalizing the sharing with adult males outside the immediate kin group.

Adrienne L. Zihlman, "Women in Evolution, Part II: Subsistence and Social Organization among Early Hominids," *Signs* 4 (1978): 10. Reprinted by permission of
the publisher, the University of Chicago. © 1978 by the University of Chicago.

In the "man the hunter" hypothesis, both economic and reproductive functions occur in the nuclear family, just as they do
today.

I propose, alternatively, that among the australopithecines the economic units were primarily the smaller kin groups that shared plant
and animal foods and cared for the young. Sexual behavior and the
"reproductive units" occurred within the larger associations of unre-
lated individuals who came together in their kin groups at food and
water sources and sleeping places. These two units became linked
much later in time and, even then, only in some societies.

A picture then emerges of a cooperative, sociable kin group of both
females and males learning to make and use tools; opportunistically
gathering food of many plant types covering a large range on the savanna; sharing plant and animal foods; and defending themselves in
conjunction with other kin groups more or less effectively against the
lions, leopards and hyenas which were even more abundant then. The
presence of males, unencumbered by infants, would have enhanced the
survival of such a group. They could range farther in search of food,
help care for the young, and contribute to defense against predators.

Adrienne L. Zihlman, "Women in Evolution, Part II: Subsistence and Social Organization among Early Hominids," *Signs* 4 (1978): 10–11. Reprinted by permission
of the publisher, the University of Chicago. © 1978 by the University of Chicago.

1.2 Who Invented Farming?

The first representatives of our genus, *Homo habilis,* appeared
perhaps about 2.5 million years ago. They also lived in gatherer-
hunter bands. In time several species of the genus spread out
across Africa and Eurasia. All of them lived in gatherer-hunter
bands, although with improved hunting potential. Our own species, *Homo sapiens sapiens*, arose about 500,000 years ago in
Africa. Margaret Ehrenberg considers the transition from gathering to farming.

From the point of view of the lives of women, the Neolithic period [beginning about 7000 B.C.E.] is perhaps the most important phase of prehistory. . . . At the end of the [earlier] Palaeolithic and Mesolithic, women enjoyed equality with men. They probably collected as much, if not more, of the food eaten by the community and derived equal status from their contribution. But by about four thousand years ago, in the Bronze Age, many of the gender roles and behaviour typical of the Western world today had probably been established. The implication is that the crucial changes must have taken place during the Neolithic period.

The chief characteristic of the Neolithic was the establishment of agriculture in south-west Asia [the Middle East] and south-east Europe, perhaps around the seventh millennium BC or earlier. . . . Numerous other inventions and adaptations in lifestyle seem to have occurred more or less at the same time. These include the change from a nomadic to a sedentary settlement pattern, the invention of pottery and the use of polished stone tools. . . .

One of the most momentous changes in the history of the human species was surely the domestication of plants and animals—the invention of agriculture. . . . The transition from foraging to farming would have made profound differences to nearly all aspects of the lifestyle of prehistoric women and men. Rather than moving around in search of food, the discovery of agriculture allowed, or perhaps necessitated, a sedentary lifestyle. It would also have given rise to, or perhaps was precipitated by, an increase in the size of the population. . . . The discovery of farming techniques has usually been assumed to have been made by men, but it is in fact very much more likely to have been made by women. On the basis of anthropological evidence for societies still living traditional foraging lifestyles and those living by simple, non-mechanical farming, taken in conjunction with direct archaeological evidence, it seems probable that it was women who made the first observations of plant behaviour, and worked out, presumably by long trial and error, how to grow and tend crops. . . .

How may we imagine the discovery of agriculture was made? By analogy with present-day foraging societies . . . it was almost certainly women who were responsible for gathering plant foods, which . . . make up the bulk of the diet in nearly all traditional societies. They would therefore have been aware of the most likely place to find a certain plant growing: for example, one plant food may have grown beside a river, another under the shelter of trees. After a lifetime of watching plants growing, these women would have understood a great deal about the complicated business of plant biology; they would have recognized the young seedlings which had become fully grown crops when they returned to the same place later in the year. They would soon have realized that if there was less rain or less sunshine than usual the plants would not be so big and there would be less to eat, and they would have realized also that the seeds needed to fall to the ground if more of that food was to grow in the same place next year. If the whole plant was pulled up or eaten, none would grow there the next season, but if some of the seeds were dropped or sprinkled somewhere else then that plant might grow there instead. Undoubtedly many thousands of foraging women would have realized this, but to most there would not have seemed to be any advantage in controlling the places where the food grew. . . . Many present-day foragers, for example the !Kung of the Kalahari desert, are well aware that their neighbours practice agriculture, and even of how it works, but they choose to retain their traditional, easy practices: "why bother to grow crops when there are so many mongongo nuts in the world. . . ."

Around 10,000 BC women all over Europe and south-west Asia would have spent part of their days gathering the crops and plants which grew around them. . . . When women thought a plant growing some way from home would be getting ripe, or the men noticed that there were fewer and fewer animals nearby, they would take their small collection of belongings and move perhaps a few miles, perhaps many, till they came to a better source of supply. How often such a move was necessary would vary tremendously. . . . The foods that were actually eaten, of course, varied from area to area, and some would have been more obvious candidates for domestication than others. In the mountain valleys of south-west Asia there grew a number of grasses, the seeds of which, it was discovered, could be boiled or ground into flour, and were particularly tasty and nutritious. These grasses, which we know as the cereals wheat and barley, were only found in the mountain valleys, but other foods eaten in the area seem to have grown on lower land, near the river valleys. Cereals only ripen once a year, but the seeds could be kept and eaten in a later season. Foragers do not as a rule carry food around with them, but some of the women gathering these cereals may have found that they could easily gather enough food in a few days to last for some time; some people would probably have stayed where the seeds were harvested, while others may have preferred to carry them some distance to other places, where perhaps other foods were to be found.

These discoveries would probably have had two important consequences: firstly a change from a nomadic lifestyle to sedentism, and secondly a significant increase in population. In the first place it would have been difficult to carry heavy bags full of cereals around; and if they were left somewhere, with the intention of returning to them later, someone or some animal would be very likely to find them, and eat them before the harvesters came back. For these reasons, therefore, it would soon have been discovered that it was best to leave at least some of the group guarding the grain stores. . . . If sufficient grain was collected to last for a considerable part of the year, it may have become easier to stay in one place for many months, provided that some other sources of food were also available nearby. When the cereal grain was moved from its storage place to where it was to be eaten, some seeds would inevitably have dropped on the ground, and some may eventually have germinated. If the group was still living in, or had returned to, the same place the next spring, some of the women would no doubt have noticed the new plants of wheat and barley growing there. Some particularly observant women, or perhaps even a child, may have watched as the seed lying on the ground sprouted, and gradually grew bigger and bigger, until it was recognizable as a cereal plant. This would happen year after year in many different settlements around the natural sources of wheat and barley. However, it would have been a major and significant step deliberately to drop or sprinkle some precious seeds near the homebase and to be confident that new plants would grow there. On the other hand, once this step had been taken, it would have saved the trek to the place where the cereal was normally harvested. It would then have been important to remain nearby while the young plants were growing in order to ward off scavenging animals and people. And once the ripe grain had been harvested, it would have had to be carefully stored and protected while it was gradually being eaten over the winter. So, without any original intent, the group would have had to remain in the same place all year round; at no season could the whole community have easily moved away. From a nomadic foraging society the group would thus have become sedentary horticulturalists.

From *Women in Prehistory* by Margaret Ehrenberg, 77–8, 84–6. © 1989 by Margaret Ehrenberg. Reprinted by permission of the University of Oklahoma Press.

1.3 Women's Carding, Spinning, and Weaving

Before the Neolithic period, both women and men were capable of performing any of the tasks needed by the group. Men were usually hunters and women gatherers, but most other tasks were not identified with one gender. By the end of the Neolithic period much more routine work was assigned to only one gender. Scholars naturally wondered what reasoning was used to assign some jobs to women and others to men. Judith Brown* made an interesting suggestion based on the observation that women were customarily in charge of raising their children.

E.J.W. Barber has used Brown's suggestion in her explanation of women's production of textiles.

Why should the making of textiles be so predominantly a female occupation in early societies? Under what circumstances was it not? What, in fact, are the socioeconomic factors at work on textile production?

To begin with, in an article on basic subsistence activities, Judith Brown points out that one obtains a much higher degree of predictability in the division of labor by sex on the basis of one particular observation than on any other factor that has been proposed. That observation is that "nowhere in world is the rearing of children primarily the responsibility of men, and in only a few societies are women exempted from participation in subsistence activities. If the economic role of women is to be maximized, their responsibilities in child care must be reduced or the economic activity must be such that it can be carried out concurrently with child care." After elaborating her data she summarizes by

---

*Judith Brown, "A Note on the Division of Labor by Sex," *American Anthropologist* 72 (1970): 1073–8.

saying that certain "societies are able to draw on womanpower because their subsistence activities are compatible with simultaneous child watching. Such activities have the following characteristics: they do not require rapt concentration and are relatively dull and repetitive; they are easily interruptable and easily resumed once interrupted; they do not place the child in potential danger; and they do not require the participant to range very far from home." Subsistence activities that fall under these categories include such typically, though not exclusively, female activities as "gathering, hoe agriculture, and [local] trade." They do *not* include "the herding of large animals, the hunting of large game, deep-sea fishing, or plow agriculture." It is not that women are incapable of such activities—societies can be cited in which women participate in any one of these, just as societies can be cited in which men gather, trade locally, etc. But because none of them can be accomplished safely with tots underfoot, societies do not *depend* for them on its [*sic*] women alone.

The model gives equally accurate predictions outside the realm of direct subsistence activities. The mine, with its deep holes and falling rocks, and the smithy, with its flying hammers and sparks, are hardly safe play-grounds for little ones. On the other hand, domestic spinning, weaving, fiber preparation, etc. have been found the world around to be ideal for women's chores: they are not dangerous to children, they can be done at home, and they are repetitious and simple enough to be interrupted and resumed easily around the frequent little crises of child-raising. . . .

So Brown's observation predicts, and in an intuitive satisfying way, that textile production will generally be women's work. But how, then, are we to understand those recorded cases in which the men were weaving? Are they random flukes, is the model wrong, or are there subsidiary principles of socioeconomics that explain them.

Consider the men we see weaving in Egypt. Throughout the Middle Kingdom, for all the many representations of weaving, it is always women who are shown at the task, using the ancient ground-loom. Then, well into the New Kingdom, we begin to see a few depictions of men weaving—and weaving on a newly introduced vertical loom. The two go together—new loom and new type of weaver. . . .

Male weavers existed in classical Athens, too, in this case working in small, private shops in order to sell the resulting clothing in the market, while the women made cloth and clothing for home and personal use. . . .

We have not far to go for predictive principles. In both cases the womanpower is still being used maximally in the home, where the children are, and for basic subsistence purposes. But the men, who in each case are weaving *in addition* to the women, are weaving either for the luxury of their masters (if they are slaves) or for their own profit (if they are free).

E.J.W. Barber, *Prehistoric Textiles: the Development of Cloth in the Neolithic and Bronze Ages with Special Reference to the Aegean* (Princeton, NJ: Princeton University Press, 1991), 289–90.

In additional examples, Barber gives instances of men weaving for subsistence and women weaving for luxury or the market. Still, women dominated textile production then and now. As Barber concludes, "Clothes may make the man, but women spent their lives making the clothes" (298).

1.4 Cooking: Women's Work in the Division of Labor

Anthropologist Jane Guyer challenges claims that the "natural" division of labor between women and men originated in the biological fact of women's childbearing and nursing of infants. Guyer develops her argument on the basis of comparative anthropological data on the division of labor by gender in 185 societies, compiled from the World Ethnographic Survey by George P. Murdock and Caterina Provost.*

Of the fifty technological activities studied, fourteen are almost exclusively male in the pre-industrial societies compared; a further nine are predominantly assigned to men, twenty are what is termed "swing activities" which vary in sex specificity, seven are predominantly female and none are exclusively female. . . . The male activities tend to require relatively great physical strength, and are performed at a greater distance from the home base. . . . [Some scholars accept Judith Brown's

---

*George P. Murdock and Caterina Provost, "Factors in the Division of Labor by Sex: A Cross-Cultural Analysis," *Ethnohistory* 12 (1973): 203–25.

suggestion] that "simultaneous child care responsibilities" limit women to relatively safe, interruptable, home-bound work. . . .

An alternative hypothesis, which I put forward here, seems equally plausible. . . . Childbearing and nursing are unambiguously female activities, but if one searches through Murdock's tables there is one technological task which comes close to being universally assigned to women, namely cooking. Thinking carefully about cooking as one task in a set of fifty, one is increasingly struck by the limitations of the "task" approach. Cooking is a true universal; it is different in kind from other tasks. Cooking must be one of the earliest manifestations of the superior imagination of homo sapiens. It exists in every known society, regardless of the general level of technical and social complexity, and the nature of the resource base. Without a shadow of a doubt cooking as a task must be the greatest single consumer of human time, effort and routine attention, even in the most technologically advanced of societies. If work were to be graphed in terms of time allocation, many of the tasks on Murdock and Provost's list— bone-setting, collection of wild honey, lumbering, and bodily mutilation, for example—would simply disappear next to cooking. Further, as a consumer of female labor time it surely outstrips nursing and child care since cooking is a life-long occupation regardless of childbearing status. Girls often take part in cooking before puberty, childless women are not exempt, and cooking does not become a redundant activity at menopause.

In terms of combinability with a variety of occupations outside the domestic sphere, caring for a baby who is still exclusively at the breast poses hardly any of the logistical problems involved in ensuring an adequate and regular food supply for weanlings and for the rest of the family. This is particularly true for work requiring travel at a distance from home. What brings a mother home quickly is not the nursling strapped to her back or side, but the small child who is too heavy to carry along, the man returning from work or the old people unable to provide for themselves. . . .

One might argue, however, that cooking is a simple extension of nursing and is therefore subsumed by the child care and nurturing argument. On the contrary, I would argue that, while they appear to be related on the ideological level, they are much more difficult to combine in practice than the functional arguments suggest.

It is neither convenient nor safe for a woman to cook and care for small children at the same time. Doing it is nerve-wracking, and one only has to observe it during field-work to see that every child's first experience of the categorical imperative [No!] takes place in its mother's kitchen, and one of its earliest comprehended words is "hot." Of course, the situation is managed, usually by having older children or other adults to do the strict surveillance necessary. But as soon as one admits that the social context of child care is important in allowing mothers to do dangerous tasks, like tending the cooking fire or moving pots of boiling water and oil, then a whole range of other activities become theoretically possible to combine with child care.

One is inclined to argue that cooking is assigned to women *in spite of* child care. . . .

Jane I. Guyer, "The Raw, the Cooked, and the Half-Baked: A Note on the Division of Labor by Sex," working paper no. 48, 1–6, African Studies Center, Boston University, 1981.

Guyer completes her case for cooking by noting that among the 185 societies, men did most of the cooking in only two and shared the task equally with women in another two.

Guyer's speculation is based on ethnographic evidence collected by anthropologists from modern cultures. Both she and Judith Brown believe that prehistoric gender patterns might resemble those most common among nonindustrialized world societies nearly 8,000 years later.

Why do scholars bother theorizing about what we may never know? They do so because assumptions and speculation shape the interpretation of the writings at the beginning of history, just as they do the evidence from prehistoric periods. Consider, for instance, what gendering prehistoric and ancient economic history means in thinking about the origins of human civilizations.

At the most fundamental level, increasing social complexity rests on the generation of surplus products. What seem to have been predominantly male activities like hunting and mining played a role in creating a surplus, but the spread of agriculture is generally assumed to have been the critical factor in expanding productivity. If men sowed and harvested the grain, while boys herded and sheared the sheep, then women and girls disappear from the economy into the home. If women sowed and reaped, while girls herded geese, sheep, and goats, the basis of economic growth shifts. If, as many later cultures will demonstrate, women also "owned" their products and sold them in the local market, trade was also complicated by gender.

Another key product of early societies was textiles. Humans, lacking enough protective hair to withstand cold, needed synthetic skins of leather; animal fur; or cloth made from tree bark, plant fibers, or animal hairs. Whatever the process, wherever the society in historic times, women have produced most clothing. The methods derive from prehistory—whether tanning leather; sewing fur; spinning thread; or making cloth by knotting, knitting, weaving, or felting. Because women have traditionally made fabrics to clothe the living and shroud the dead in their families, their labor is often regarded as "housework." Too often its economic importance to their societies is disregarded. Kings and priests from the ancient Mediterranean to Incan Peru understood the value of the textiles they appropriated to support their rule. Perhaps women's textiles were the most important item of local and world trade from prehistoric times to the age of industrialization.

Suggested Further Readings

Readings in Sandra Morgen, ed., *Gender and Anthropology: Critical Reviews for Research and Teaching* (Washington, DC: American Anthropological Association, 1989) are a good introduction to the literature on gender and primates, evolution, and archaeology. Articles in Frances Dahlberg, ed., *Woman the Gatherer* (New Haven, CT: Yale University Press, 1981) present case studies of contemporary foraging societies in the Philippines, Canada, Australia, and Zaire. Margaret Ehrenberg, in *Women in Prehistory* (Norman: University of Oklahoma Press, 1989), presents a balanced and readable review of anthropological and archaeological evidence about prehistoric women in Europe. Karen Sacks, in *Sisters and Wives: The Past and Future of Sexual Equality* (Westport, CT: Greenwood Publishing Group, 1979), reviews the history of anthropology's hypotheses about gender and argues against the theory of women's universal subordination by using comparative evidence from many societies.

Those interested in women's production of textiles should read Elizabeth W. Barber, *Women's Work: The First 20,000*

Years: Women, Cloth, and Society in Early Times (New York: W.W. Norton, 1994). Two discussions of the critical place studies of ancient Greek peoples had in setting the parameters of Western thought about women are Nicole Loraux's "What Is a Goddess?" and Stella Georgoudi's "Creating a Myth of Matriarchy," in Georges Duby and Michelle Perrot, eds., *A History of Women*, vol. 1, *From Ancient Goddesses to Christian Saints* (Cambridge: The Belknap Press of Harvard University Press, 1992).

THE WOMEN OF ANCIENT EGYPT

Girl musicians, a detail from a wall painting in the tomb of Nakht at Thebes, Egypt.
(Photograph by Egyptian Expedition, The Metropolitan Museum of Art.)

Egypt is a North African Mediterranean society with written records spanning almost 2,500 years of ancient history. It is possible to trace a continuity of state throughout most of those years down to Alexander's conquest in 332 B.C.E. After his death a Macedonian dynasty, the Ptolemaic, ruled by developing a synthesis of Egyptian and Greek culture known as Hellenistic.

Ancient civilizations were almost always ruled by men, and Egypt fits that pattern. Nevertheless, it had several female pharaohs. Two of its female rulers are famous: Hatshepsut, who reigned from about 1473 B.C.E. to 1458 B.C.E.; and Cleopatra, who lived from 69 B.C.E. to 30 B.C.E. Successful women monarchs tend to be determined, intelligent, and capable. Frequently they come to power during a period when national traditions of administration have been under stress because the nation has experienced a trauma such as a revolutionary change in government or a foreign occupation. In other words, the people feel they have lived through momentous and dangerous times.

In the case of Cleopatra, the Roman Empire had de facto control of most of the weaker states surrounding the Mediterranean. The trauma was the impact on those states of the difficult transformation of the Roman empire from a republic to a monarchy. Julius Caesar was the first of the Roman emperors, and Cleopatra sought an alliance with him, but he was assassinated in 44 B.C.E. She replaced Caesar with Mark Antony in her quest to maintain Egyptian autonomy. During these years the whole empire was in turmoil. Different factions maneuvered their armies around the Mediterranean, seeking resources, mainly money, and support.

In Hatshepsut's era, the trauma was the expansion of Egypt after its domination by a foreign invader. The northern part of Egypt had been occupied by the Hyksos for about 150 years. During that time, the southern part was a tributary state of the occupiers. A famous pharaoh from the south, Ahmose I, drove out the invaders and ushered in a period when Egypt conquered neighboring countries and became quite wealthy. Historians have called this period the New Kingdom, and some consider it the high point of Egyptian history.

2.1 Hatshepsut's Reign, 1473–1458 B.C.E.

Hatshepsut's genealogy was an important bulwark supporting her claim to power. She was the sole surviving grandchild of Queen

Ahmose-Nefertari. Queen Nefertari's husband was Pharaoh Ahmose I, the founder of the eighteenth dynasty. That dynasty gave more respect to their queens than most others. This tradition began with King Ahmose's mother, who had been a leader in the resistance to the Hyksos. As pharaoh, Ahmose created a special title for his wife, God's Wife of Amon-Re, which reflected the popular belief that the god Amon-Re inhabited the king's body and impregnated the queen with divine seed.

Hatshepsut was also the sole surviving royal daughter of her father, Pharaoh Tutmose I, a great general. His successor, a concubine's son, was married to Hatshepsut. They had no sons, so when her husband died, one of his concubine's sons was made pharaoh, but he was a child. As Chief Royal Wife, Hatshepsut accepted her role as regent for the young pharaoh. The expectation was that she would relinquish control of the country when he was an adult. But something undocumented happened, and she ruled directly even after he became an adult. There has been scholarly controversy over the nature of her relationship with her stepson, the pharaoh. Either she engineered a coup, or they ruled jointly; a majority of the scholars favor a coup as the explanation of her long reign. Her stepson, the young pharaoh, was given a military command and became a very successful general. As such he was in an excellent position to organize an army revolt against Hatshepsut, but he did not. When she died, he began a long and notable career as pharaoh.

When Hatshepsut ruled, she was publicly portrayed as a male. Male pronouns were used and statues depicted her with a beard and dressed in a male kilt, although with breasts. Evidently she had to become a cross-dresser on official occasions. This engendering a female ruler as male is frequently found in societies when female political authority is an anomaly.

In the twenty-two years of her reign, Hatshepsut proved to be an exceptionally competent ruler whose policies were designed to increase her support among key groups of Egyptians. As God's Wife of Amon-Re, she won the backing of the priests, who accepted her claim that her father was the god Amon-Re. Furthermore, she restored and staffed abandoned temples. For the army, she conducted four successful military campaigns, mostly in Nubia, or modern Sudan, where her soldiers acquired as booty a share of the plunder in slaves and conquered land. The treasury was increased by the output of the gold mines in Nubia. And for the manufacturers, she sent expeditions to Punt, probably modern Somalia, to bring back tree stock that was used in making incense. Well could she boast on a temple inscription:

Hear ye, all people and the folk as many as they may be, I have done these things through the counsel of my heart. I have not slept forgetfully, [but] I have restored that which had been ruined. I have raised up that which had gone to pieces *formerly,* since the Asiatics [the Hyksos] were in the midst of Avaris of the Northland, and vagabonds were in the midst of them, overthrowing that which had been made. They ruled without Re, and he did not act by divine command down to [the reign of] my majesty. [Now] I am established upon the thrones of Re. I was foretold for the limits of the years as a born conqueror. I am come as the uraeus-serpent of Horus, flaming against my enemies. I have made distant those whom the gods abominate, and earth has carried off their foot[prints]. This is the precept of the father of [my] fathers, who comes at his [appointed] times, Re, and there shall not occur damage to what Amon has commanded. My [own] command endures like the mountains, [while] the sun disc shines forth and spreads rays over the formal titles of my majesty and my falcon is high above [my] name-standard for the duration of eternity.

James B. Pritchard, ed., *Ancient Near Eastern Texts Relating to the Old Testament* (Princeton, NJ: Princeton University Press, 1969), 231.

Egyptian women were fortunate in having more equality with men than the average woman of Eurasia. Perhaps it is not coincidental that they also manufactured vital products for domestic consumption and export. However, even though they had legal equality with men and produced products with significant economic importance, women in Egypt shared with their sisters in the ancient world exclusion from direct participation in the political system.

In the ancient period most Eurasian women had few legal rights. They were usually treated as legal dependents whose every legal act had to be authorized by a male guardian such as a father or husband. In contrast, Egyptian women had the same legal rights as Egyptian men. On their own they could buy, sell, inherit, and will property both immovable (land) and movable. They could sue and be sued. They could sign contracts, even those of their own marriages. At that time, these legal rights for women were remarkable. Even though Egyptian women had the right to take legal action, in reality most legal acts were taken by men.

Socially women enjoyed considerable freedom, being able to leave their homes to visit or to conduct business freely. Egyptian parties had both male and female guests. In contrast, Athenian women were not even supposed to leave their houses without an escort. The legal and social position of Egyptian women can be compared to that of women in the late twentieth century.

Why were they so fortunate? One explanation points to the different way Egyptians determined descent and kinship—through the females. An Egyptian man identified himself by his mother's name, not his father's: for example, Hay, son of the woman Hener.

2.2 A Brother–Sister Marriage

The principle of female inheritance in ancient Egypt was important for the royal family. When a pharaoh or king died, his male replacement did not necessarily have to be his son. But whoever was chosen sought to marry a royal heiress, who then became the queen. Marriage to a royal heiress, though not necessary, legitimized the king's claim to the throne. Sometimes this meant that the king married his full sister, or even his own daughter. The Egyptians did not consider close marriages improper or incestuous. Still, historians have found few examples of brother–sister royal marriages before the Ptolemaic dynasty. The story of Naneferkaptah and Ahwere illustrates one example. In this romantic version a woman's desire, rather than legitimacy, appears to be the issue.

In the reading, Princess Ahwere refers to her time of purification. Women in much of the ancient world were considered unclean during menstruation. At the end of their period, they were required to undergo religious cleansing, usually involving rituals as well as bathing. By ceasing to perform the ritual, a woman indicated that she was pregnant.

Ahwere's story was written during the Ptolemaic period but is set in an early dynasty. Ahwere narrates the story. She and Naneferkaptah were sister and brother and the only children of

King Mernebptah. They were in love and wanted to marry. But their father, the pharaoh, wanted them to marry outside the family to secure powerful allies. Ahwere asked the steward of the pharaoh's palace to plead with her father for the brother–sister marriage. When Mernebptah heard the steward's argument, he was upset. The steward asked why, and the pharaoh replied:

"It is you who distress me. If it so happens that I have only two children, is it right to marry the one to the other? I will marry Naneferkaptah to the daughter of a general, and I will marry Ahwere to the son of another general, so that our family may increase!"

When the time came for the banquet to be set before Pharaoh, they came for me and took me to the banquet. But my heart was very sad and I did not have my former looks. Pharaoh said to me: "Ahwere, was it you who sent to me those foolish words, 'Let me marry [Naneferkaptah, my] elder [brother]'?"

I said to him: "Let me marry the son of a general, and let him marry the daughter of another general, so that our family may increase!" I laughed and Pharaoh laughed.

[When the steward of the palace came] Pharaoh said to him: "Steward, let Ahwere be taken to the house of Naneferkaptah tonight, and let all sorts of beautiful things be taken with her."

I was taken as a wife to the house of Naneferkaptah [that night, and Pharaoh] sent me a present of silver and gold, and all Pharaoh's household sent me presents. Naneferkaptah made holiday with me, and he entertained all Pharaoh's household. He slept with me that night and found me [pleasing. He slept with] me again and again, and we loved each other.

When my time of purification came I made no more purification. It was reported to Pharaoh, and his heart was very happy. Pharaoh had many things taken [out of the treasury] and sent me presents of silver, gold, and royal linen, all very beautiful.

Miriam Lichtheim, ed., *Ancient Egyptian Literature*, vol. 3, *The Late Period* (Berkeley: University of California Press, 1980), 127–8.

Ahwere had a son. King Mernebptah had not objected to his children's marriage on moral grounds. His objection was political, for if his son and daughter married into other families, his dynasty's influence would be broader. Yet his daughter's unhappiness swayed him to approve a love match instead.

2.3 Women's Work

The materials made by Egyptian women were important to the Egyptian economy. Historians have generally ignored the labor of women, assuming it to be merely "domestic," even though they discuss men's work as economically "productive." In ancient civilizations this division of labor into women's production for the household and men's production for the market is misleading. Adults of both sexes, free and slave, produced necessities of family consumption, and women's work could be as commercial as men's. In the sophisticated ancient Egyptian economy this was especially true. The variety of female occupations extended far beyond those tasks traditionally associated with domestic life.

Barbara Lesko describes the many jobs of Egyptian women:

The tomb paintings show women harvesting and winnowing wheat and handpicking flax for the linen that all Egypt wore. It was hard hot labor, and the wall scenes show long lines of heavily ladened female as well as male basket bearers carrying produce from field to storehouse.

While there is, admittedly, no glory in drudgery, it is gratifying to note that there is evidence from the household accounts of an Egyptian farm in 2000 B.C. that *all* members of one family were paid in proportion to the work they did, *independent of age or sex.*

Men and women worked side by side at jobs indoors as well. Innumerable tomb scenes show kitchen staffs of male and female servants grinding wheat, brewing beer and baking bread. Both male and female servants waited on guests at banquets to which both men and women were invited. Women guests were not segregated off in their own quarters, but intermingled with the male guests at social events. . . .

No excessive prudery seems to have existed among the Egyptians. Scenes of women workers stripped to the waist or totally without their confining slim-line skirts are not unusual. Likewise, the members of the all-women bands—always in demand for festive occasions—often dressed in transparent, filmy garments, while the dancers they accompanied appeared nude. At the other end of the scale, there is little to differentiate the fashions for wealthier men and women in the empire period of the New Kingdom when both donned voluminous robes and jewelry. Eyepaint was used by both sexes throughout the ages.

Certain occupations seem to have been dominated by women. Judging from tomb art, dancers and acrobats were almost always female while musicians very frequently were. Written sources yield titles of women in supervisory positions in commerce and industry such as "Mistress of the Wig Workshop" or "Mistress of the Dining Hall." Most important of all were the state textile factories and perfume manufactures, both staffed and supervised by women almost exclusively. These were major state industries occupying a central role in Egypt's economy. The textile industry was Egypt's largest industry after agriculture, producing everything from the coarsest, most utilitarian weave (for the sails of ships) through various grades of lighter fabrics used as bedlinens and clothing, down to the finest cambrics ever produced, for those who desired the very best. This last, known as "royal linen," was used for royal gifts and temple offerings. Although the basic Egyptian wardrobe was all white, it could be accented by border trims and sashes of brightly colored fabrics. Good clothing and even the sails of yachts were often completely embroidered with an array of colorful designs.

Fragrant oils and perfumes were a necessity for both men and women in the hot, dry climate of Egypt—hence the importance of this industry. Like the textile mills, the perfume houses often were associated with the Chief Royal Wife's estates, those in the area near the Fayum lake in particular. Teams of women picked and pressed lilies to extract their essences. The fragrances extracted were added to oils used to rub into the skin after bathing. Even statues of gods were anointed in the daily temple ritual, and the fragrant oils were so sought after and valuable that they are generally among the precious things recorded already in antiquity as stolen by tomb robbers.

Barbara S. Lesko, *The Remarkable Women of Ancient Egypt* (Berkeley, CA: B.C. Scribe Publications, 1978), 15–7. © 1978 by Barbara S. Lesko.

The importance of wig making is not apparent to us, since today wigs are seen as an occasional fashion accessory. Egyptian tomb art shows both men and women wearing wigs from the earliest periods on. Men either shaved their heads or cut their hair short. To avoid sunstroke or sunburn they wore wigs outdoors. Women used wigs to supplement thinning hair, but mostly as a decoration. There were changes in fashion from curls to braids, and ornaments, sometimes of gold, were worn on the wigs. Some wigs were so valuable that they were mentioned in wills or carefully placed in their special box and put into the owner's tomb.

2.4 Cleopatra, 69–30 B.C.E.

Fourteen hundred years after Hatshepsut's reign, another of history's most famous queens, Cleopatra VII, sat on Egypt's throne. She, as a Hellenistic monarch, sought to restore the power and glory Egypt had enjoyed during the Eighteenth Dynasty. Cleopatra was eighteen in 51 B.C.E. when her father died and she was made Queen of Egypt. It was hardly the time or place to launch a career that would bring lasting fame. Rome dominated the Mediterranean and most of the bordering countries, including Egypt. The Roman republic itself was struggling with the civil wars that led to its collapse. A small group of ambitious Roman generals, including Pompey and Caesar, were competing with each other for enormous political power.

Egypt was a wealthy client-kingdom. Rome increasingly interfered with its internal affairs. Cleopatra's father, Ptolemy XII, had to bribe Caesar with 6,000 talents (bars of silver usually weighing 57 pounds) for confirmation by the Roman senate of his right to the Egyptian throne. When he returned to Alexandria the people rebelled, and he fled back to Rome seeking aid. The Romans sent an army, which made the Egyptians take him back. In gratitude he appointed a Roman, Rabirius, minister of finance. Rabirius made so much money out of his appointment that a mob sought to kill him before he escaped to Rome. Roman interference was bad enough; worse was the possibility that Egypt might become a Roman province under a Roman governor. While Ptolemy XII was disgraced and exiled in Rome, his two daughters, Cleopatra VI and Berenice IV, were recognized as Egypt's joint sovereigns; when Cleopatra VI died, her sister Berenice ruled alone. Her father was finally able to resume the throne only by assassinating her. At his death, power passed to his younger children, who reigned as Cleopatra VII and Ptolemy XIII.

The Ptolemies, who believed that royal brother-sister marriages were an Egyptian tradition, practiced such unions with a frequency that belied any custom of ancient Egypt. Cleopatra VII became queen when she married her brother Ptolemy XIII, who was only ten years old. Although three guardians had been appointed to rule for the three years before he reached maturity, they allowed Cleopatra to reign. This was not unusual, for the older sisters or mothers of male Ptolemaic heirs often exercised power for the underaged pharaohs, sometimes retaining sovereignty themselves even after the heirs attained maturity. At least seven queens of the Ptolemaic dynasty before Cleopatra had ruled in a span of only some 225 years. As the time approached when her brother might take over the government, his relatives and friends forced her to flee Egypt. Her administration had been successful, so she was able to assemble an army to reconquer Egypt. As her brother moved his army to oppose her, events took an unexpected turn.

The Roman civil war was the source of the renewed interference in Egypt. Caesar had defeated Pompey, who then sailed to Alexandria to get money and aid while he regrouped. Ptolemy XIII and his advisors were uncertain how to greet the fugitive. They chose what they thought was the safe plan—to kill Pompey and wait for a reward from Caesar. When Caesar arrived, also seeking money, and was presented with Pompey's head and signet ring, he burst into tears. Then he ordered the royal pair to cease their controversy, dismiss their forces, and submit to his arbitration. Her brother was determined to keep Cleopatra away from Caesar and sought to deny all avenues of approach. Historian Hans Volkmann takes up the story:

Only one thing counted for her now: the crown of Egypt was at stake. This crown her fraternal consort and his partisans denied her: and this Roman was going to give it to her.

The daring plan was as daringly executed. She left her camp and managed to reach Alexandria, where a single confidant, the Sicilian Appollodorus, conveyed her in a boat through the darkness of the night into the Great Harbour, without anything being noticed from the hostile guard-posts. On the steps of the royal palace she had herself rolled up in a carpet. Her companion carried the carefully-corded bale past the sentries to Caesar's apartment. The bale was opened and the twenty-one-year-old Queen of Egypt stood before the astonished Roman and conquered. And then a miracle befell. The brief interview, the result of cool political calculation, ended in no fleeting sensual fit, but inaugurated a deeper bond, in which personal inclination and political reflection were indistinguishably fused.

For her sake Caesar interrupted his victorious career for six months, and set at hazard all he had gained. For during this time the Pompeians reassembled, and collected new forces against him. It is the privilege of the poet to look deep into the heart of man, but we too may divine what fettered Caesar to this royal woman. As a woman, indeed, she was no beauty: the extant coin-portraits show her with a long hooked nose and a large mouth. Of course she knew how to improve her appearance with every fashionable device of the toilet customary at court in this cosmopolitan city. . . .

Cleopatra's contemporaries were already aware that the unique power of enchantment which she wielded lay rather in her mental gifts and her manner of behaviour. While not one of her predecessors in the dynasty had been able to overcome a reluctance to learn Egyptian, and some of them even neglected the Macedonian dialect spoken in their homeland, Cleopatra's genius for language was conspicuous. In addition to the tongues mentioned and, of course, the standard Greek, she enjoyed a command of the dialects and languages of the Ethiopians, Arabians and Trogodytes, not to mention those of the peoples of hither Asia, including Syrian, Median, Parthian and Aramaic. With this linguistic versatility, which permitted her to dispense with interpreters, went dexterity and address in personal intercourse. "Her society had an irresistible attraction; her form, together with the persuasiveness of her conversation and the style of her behaviour had an almost magical effect. It was a delight to listen to the sound of her speech. Her voice was like a lyre of many strings, which she could use for any language with equal ease." For Caesar, a master of style, who pondered over the "elegentia summa scribendi," and was as knowledgeable in art and science as in politics, her company must have been enchanting. Here was a woman mentally alive, a woman about whom gleamed the aura of the Ptolemaic crown, and who bravely pursued a policy of her own. She appealed to Caesar's bent for gaming and adventure. . . . His political interests had fallen into line with his human inclinations. Love and politics—often antagonists—had struck a bargain.

The sudden arrival of Cleopatra and her attempt to obtain the support of the Roman power immediately kindled the wrath of the Alexandrians. When on the following day Ptolemy XIII was summoned, so that he could be reconciled with his sister, he no sooner set eyes on her than he flew off to the masses in a rage and tore the diadem from his head. The throng surged on the palace. To calm the people down, Caesar had to grant material concessions. At a solemn ceremony he announced his decision. Ptolemy XIII and Cleopatra were to rule jointly in Egypt, in accordance with their father's will. Their younger brother Ptolemy XIV and younger sister Arsinoe were to rule over Cyprus, likewise jointly. The conquering Roman, who had recently been named dictator in Rome and was now performing his first official act in that capacity, thus gave away without a struggle a piece of Roman imperial territory annexed only ten years previously. Cleopatra, on the other hand, enjoyed her first triumph: the Ptolemaic Empire had been halted on its backward course. Would it be her mission to restore it to its ancient glory?

Hans Volkmann, *Cleopatra: A Study in Politics and Propaganda*, trans. T.J. Cadoux (New York: Sagamore Press, 1958), 66–8. © 1958 by Elek Books Ltd.

The Alexandrians revolted, and the Egyptian army joined in the attack on Caesar's small force. Ptolemy XIII and the younger sister Arsinoë were leaders of the Egyptians. Caesar put down the revolt, with Ptolemy XIII dying in battle and Arsinoe being taken prisoner. Caesar left after marrying Cleopatra to her eleven-year-old brother Ptolemy XIV.

Once again Cleopatra's destiny was kind to her, and drew closer the bonds between Caesar and herself. In the summer of 47 she bore a son. From the moment of its birth she deliberately pressed the child into the service of her political propaganda. She gave him the proud names of Ptolemy and Caesar. . . . The babe was not only to be a prince, like Ptolemy, progenitor of the dynasty, but should also feel that he was Caesar's heir: for, since the death of his beloved daughter Julia, Caesar was childless. . . .

An important official character [coins issued with his image] was thus bestowed on the birth of Caesarion [Caesar's child]. This fact, together with the surname of Caesar given him by his own mother, is comprehensible only if Caesar was really his father. For Caesar to have allowed his name to be borne by the son of some unknown man becomes all the more improbable when we learn that in the summer of 46 he actually allowed the Queen to come to Rome.

Hans Volkmann, *Cleopatra: A Study in Politics and Propaganda*, trans. T.J. Cadoux (New York: Sagamore Press, 1958), 74–7. © 1958 by Elek Books Ltd.

Cleopatra moved into Caesar's garden outside the walls of Rome with her husband and child. Unfortunately, when her patron Caesar was assassinated eighteen months later (March 15, 44 B.C.E.), his will recognized his grandnephew Octavian as his heir. Soon Octavian made an alliance with Antony and Lepidus, the other triumvirs, against Caesar's murderers. Realizing that in the ensuing civil war Egypt would be a valuable prize, Cleopatra returned to Alexandria to protect Egypt if possible. Soon after their arrival Ptolemy XIV died. To strengthen her position she married her three-year-old son Ptolemy XV Caesar.

Egypt suffered one of its periodic famines, and Cleopatra distributed food from the government warehouses. A terrible plague caused many deaths. In the midst of these problems Cassius, one of the murderers, attacked some of the forces loyal to Caesar in Syria. Cleopatra did not want to aid Cassius, but both her military and her naval commanders supported him. She refused to provide anything from Egypt itself, pleading the effects of the famine and plague.

By 42 B.C.E. Caesar's murderers were dead.

The fate of the Roman Republic was sealed: the victorious triumvirs divided the Empire between them. Italy was declared their common possession, Spain assigned to Octavian and northern Africa to Lepidus. Antony, the most powerful of the three, received as his portion the whole of the East, in addition to Gaul in the West. To the East he now betook himself, with a view to restoring tranquillity and raising money to pay for the war.

Antony in the East was the right man in the right place. Of sanguine temperament, and with something magnificent about him, he was better fitted for the brilliant pomp of a Hellenistic monarch's court than for the type of public life which the Romans had inherited from their remote ancestors. The Antonii, as custom was, traced their descent back to a divine ancestor, in this case Heracles. Antony was now a man of forty. With his bulky but powerful frame and the thick neck revealed by his coins he felt himself to be in very truth a second Heracles. He even copied the hero's outward appearance. He strutted about in a heavy war-cloak, with his tunic hitched up, and was girt with a large sword: he also wore a full curly beard. A dazzling cavalry officer, he had opened the road to Alexandria for Cleopatra's father and had later proven himself under Caesar. . . . While the dictator was detained in Egypt by Cleopatra's affairs, Antony headed the administration in Italy as his master of horse and principal representative. Conscious of his power, he seized this opportunity to taste life and its pleasures to the full. A mighty toper like Heracles, on one occasion he drank so heavily that he was obliged to vomit in the Forum when about to deliver a speech. Another time he drove through the narrow streets of Rome in a coach drawn by two lions, accompanied by the fashionable actress Cytheris. . . . In his jests he was blunt and coarse, though always ready for a laugh against himself; generous with his friends, chivalrous to his enemies. . . .

It was an exceptional stroke of good luck for Cleopatra that fate brought this particular man to the East. He immediately won the sympathy of the Athenians. . . . Then as he moved from festival to festival, the dynasts of the Orient thronged about him. . . . At Ephesus . . . Antony was welcomed by the customary procession, not however as a victorious general, but as a god, as the "New Dionysus.". . . . They hailed him as Dionysus "the giver of joy," "the gracious one." The Roman can hardly have realized the full political significance of the honours thus heaped on him.

Cleopatra, on the other hand, who had grown up amid the jargon of political propaganda, and whose father had also been hailed as a "New Dionysus," did not fail to perceive that Antony's reception in the East offered unique possibilities. She might use this "New Dionysus" to further her political plans; she might form a permanent tie with him under the form of the ruler-cult. As a "New Dionysus" Antony stepped right into the Ptolemaic tradition: it was only necessary to make him conscious of this, and bring it to fulfillment in the sight of the world.

When the opportunity came, she made striking use of it. At first she had held aloof from the doings of the various local rulers in Antony's court. Then in 41 he invited her to appear before his tribunal to answer for her equivocal conduct during the civil wars that had recently ended . . . Cleopatra agreed to go. . . . Antony and his friends were already making repeated enquiries about her arrival, when at last she came.

Antony was in the city of Tarus in Cilicia. . . . One day he was sitting in the market-place dispensing justice, when the throng of people round him suddenly fell into a commotion and rushed off to the harbour on the river-bank. He found himself alone. "A saying ran through the crowd, that Aphrodite was to come to revel with Dionysus for the good of Asia." This message was a masterpiece of diplomacy, whose seductive appeal and manifold significance could only be appreciated in full by those who lived in the world of the Hellenized East, with its disappointments and hopes. Cleopatra, the new Aphrodite-Isis, invited Antony, the new Dionysus, to serve the good of Asia. All the resentment of the ransacked East against the rule of Rome . . . all the prophesies uttered by the Sibylline oracle about the coming triumph of Asia over the unrighteousness and greed of Rome—all re-echoed in this promise. Was this the beginning of a new and better age?. . . .

Cleopatra went to meet Antony with the dignity that befitted an exalted goddess. She rejected his invitation to dinner, and summoned him to eat with her on board her ship. He went: and the soldier, habituated to coarse pleasures, saw displayed for his benefit the tasteful and refined table-luxury of the royal court.

Light streamed from all sides, reflected by an array of mirrors. All the table-ware was of gold studded with jewels and adorned with exquisite work by the best artists. Purple tapestries, embroidered with gold, covered the walls. Twelve dining-couches stood ready to receive the triumvir and his retinue. Antony expressed his surprise at the magical speed with which this splendid reception had been prepared. The Queen replied with a smile that he must make shift with what had been done, and pardon the deficiencies due to the haste of her arrival. She would know how to make them good if he would consent to dine again with her on the morrow. She also invited him to accept from her, as a gift, everything he saw. . . .

He was utterly carried away by this enchanting queen of twenty-eight years. "Everything that Cleopatra asked for was done, irrespective of whether it was just, or in accordance with divine law.". . . At her wish Antony had the hapless Arsinoe [Cleopatra's younger sister] killed. . . . A man who had pretended to be Ptolemy XIII, the older of Cleopatra's two brothers, who had fallen in battle by the Nile, likewise lost his life. . . .

It was Cleopatra who made these decisions; and it was Cleopatra who decided when these days of revelry were to end. . . . She had taken this Roman by storm: would she be able to hold him permanently? Risking the experiment, she suddenly returned to Egypt alone in the autumn 41: and the event justified her.

All over the East pressing tasks waited for Antony's attention. . . .

These considerations, however, troubled Antony but little. With the utmost haste he discharged only the most urgent of his duties. Then he hurried to Alexandria to join Cleopatra. He said to himself perhaps that, after all, Egypt would be his most important source of help in the coming war with the [Parthian] empire that threatened from the East, and that therefore it now behoved him to go there himself and see the land with its treasures and marvels.

If he did entertain such political notions, they receded from his mind throughout the winter of 41/0 which he spent in Egypt. This winter was entirely devoted to pleasurable living: it was one long Bacchanalian feast. . . .

Hans Volkmann, *Cleopatra: A Study in Politics and Propaganda*, trans. T.J. Cadoux (New York: Sagamore Press, 1958), 94–100. © 1958 by Elek Books Ltd.

In the spring of 40 B.C.E. Antony left Cleopatra and was involved in affairs in Italy. He drew closer to Octavian (who later assumed the title Caesar Augustus), and their alliance was strengthened by Octavian giving his sister to Antony in marriage. Cleopatra was eclipsed. In 39 B.C.E. and 38 B.C.E. his subordinates successfully campaigned against the Parthians, but Antony stopped the war before a total victory was achieved. Then, in the winter of 37–36 B.C.E., Antony prepared to take personal direction of the Parthian campaign. He sent his pregnant Roman wife to Italy and invited Cleopatra to join him in Antioch:

Antony summoned the Queen to come to him at the moment when he was embarking on the war with Parthia [present day Iran], and to a place suitable for the necessary preparations. Time and place, then, give this encounter a markedly political stamp.

To Antony, in fact, Cleopatra was the queen and ruler of a land which because of its wealth had an important part to play in the Roman system of defence in the East. Whereas, in the West, the Roman Empire was divided into provinces, administered directly by Roman governors armed with all necessary authority, and Roman troops protected the frontiers, the eastern half of the Empire exhibited an entirely different structure, owing to its historical development. Provincial administration of the usual type was to be found in the provinces of Macedonia, Asia, Bithynia and Syria: but elsewhere this system yielded place to various local forms, such as the independent city or princedom, enjoying self-government subject only to the general supervision of Rome. The aim of Roman policy was to pass the burden of defending the eastern frontiers of the Empire to these client-states. . . . The rulers of these territories naturally felt more closely attached to the Roman statesman or general who had for the time being secured them in their position, or had originally granted it, than to the Roman Empire as such. . . .

Some scholars, indeed, think that Antony could have exploited the wealth of Egypt for his purposes independently of Cleopatra; and that in case of need he could have deposed her. . . .

To whom could Antony have more safely entrusted the government of this important country than to the woman who was devoted to him? His great master Caesar, on whose plan of a Parthian expedition he meant to improve, had also entrusted Egypt to the care of his mistress. Again, it was not merely love, but political sagacity, which induced Antony to enlarge the Ptolemaic Empire by gifts of territory. The client-states of the East, being very numerous as well as diverse in form, were easily sundered by any shock, as the Parthian invasion had shown. When Antony looked about for some clamp to hold these unequal forces together, it seemed an obvious step to go back to the traditional form of union—that is, to the Ptolemaic Empire. Extended to its old frontiers, and with its long tradition of rule and administration, it offered a solid basis for a great empire of the East such as he dreamed of ruling. And his claim to do so was legitimized by his marriage with Cleopatra.

The eastern policy, on which Antony, led by the Queen, had now decided, thus led him inevitably to Egypt, the political centre of gravity of the East.

Hans Volkmann, *Cleopatra: A Study in Politics and Propaganda,* trans. T.J. Cadoux (New York: Sagamore Press, 1958), 124–6. © 1958 by Elek Books Ltd.

The Parthian expedition of 36 B.C.E. was a horrible failure. Antony lost approximately one-third of his forces in a disastrous retreat. When he finally returned, Cleopatra brought him money and supplies to rearm his forces. His next campaign did not begin until 34 B.C.E. When he captured Armenia, on the Parthian border, he returned to Alexandria to proclaim his Empire of the East in a triumphal celebration.

In the spacious halls of the gymnasium a gigantic throng of people witnessed the solemn proclamation of the Empire of the East. Antony and Cleopatra took their places on golden thrones raised on a platform of silver. At their feet sat the royal children. . . . Then Antony divided the lands of the East between Cleopatra and her children. . . .

It was a signal triumph for Cleopatra. None of the Ptolemies had ever wielded the sceptre over such extensive domains as Antony had now placed under her and her children. . . .

As yet, however, things were still in the stage of development. This is shown by the somewhat ambiguous position assigned to Antony in the new imperial system. By the side of Isis-Cleopatra he was the god Dionysus-Osiris. . . . He was the 'God and Benefactor', as an inscription names him. But he did not take the final constitutional step. He did not assume the diadem or the title of King. . . .

Hans Volkmann, *Cleopatra: A Study in Politics and Propaganda,* trans. T.J. Cadoux (New York: Sagamore Press, 1958), 147–50. © 1958 by Elek Books Ltd.

The proclamation of the Empire of the East was Cleopatra's greatest triumph. After this high point, destiny seems to have turned against her. Rome could not ignore the plan to divide the Roman empire into two parts, and the Senate declared war on Cleopatra in 32 B.C.E. The ensuing war was decided the next year in one famous sea battle at Actium. Cleopatra and Antony escaped to Egypt only to wait for the victorious Octavian's arrival. The two committed suicide there in 30 B.C.E.

Cleopatra's subsequent fame can be credited primarily to dramatists, although other authors and painters have contributed. Some of the best-known plays in English were written about Cleopatra, by such greats as William Shakespeare, George Bernard Shaw, and Thornton Wilder. Her character has been played by Sarah Bernhardt, Theda Bara, Vivian Leigh, and Elizabeth Taylor. Most of these dramatizations draw upon the contemporary propaganda of her enemies in portraying her as malevolently using her sexual wiles to entrance Caesar and Antony. While this narrative resonates powerfully within cultures that presume political power is a male prerogative, it lacks historical accuracy in representing Cleopatra's real motives as queen of Egypt.

Suggested Further Readings

The history of Egyptian women during the first three millennia of the Egyptian empire, prior to the invasion of Alexander, is the topic of Gay Robins's *Women in Ancient Egypt* (Cambridge: Harvard University Press, 1993). She has written a fine survey in which she discusses royal women, marriage, family, work, law, and religion. For the Hellenistic period, Sarah B. Pomeroy's *Women in Hellenistic Egypt: From Alexander to Cleopatra* (New York: Schocken Books, 1984) is the authoritative text. Pomeroy's focus is on Greek women in Egypt, rather than on Egyptian women, so she underestimates the impact of Egyptian customs in the changes attributed to Hellenistic influences.

–3–

INDIA
Women in Early Hindu and Buddhist Cultures

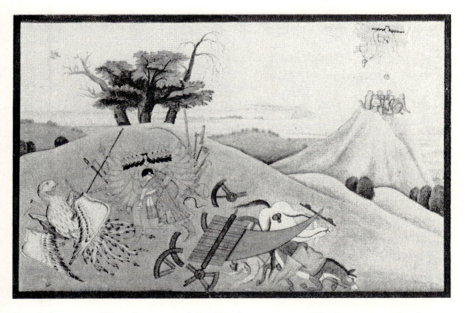

The abduction of Sita, heroine of the Hindu epic poem *The Ramayana,* by the ten-headed demon king, Ravan. Ravan has killed the giant bird, Jatayu, who tried to to rescue Sita. An eighteenth-century painting by an unknown Indian artist. (The Brooklyn Museum, anonymous gift.)

Hinduism, the dominant religion of India, arose in a nation of cattle herders called Aryans, who migrated from the Plateau of Iran into the northwest region of India about 1700 B.C.E. and slowly spread across much of the subcontinent. They adopted the farming practices of the peoples they conquered, cleared the forests, and settled in villages. Originally illiterate, between 700 and 500 B.C.E. Hindu Indians began writing in Sanskrit. Sacred ancient Vedic verses and the *Mahabharata* and *Ramayana,* two epic poems, portray their beliefs.

Aryans divided society into four categories, or *varnas:* warriors and administrators; priests and teachers (Brahmans); merchants, artisans, and farmers; and the servants of the upper *varnas.* Over the centuries each *varna* subdivided into many castes, then further subdivided into *jatis. Jati* members had to remain in the occupation of the *jati* of their parents and to marry within specific groups. Below the *varnas* were people isolated from the castes, the "outcastes," or "untouchables," whose work and status made their very "touch" dangerous to the spiritual purity of those higher in rank. Midwives, who handled women's polluting blood and afterbirth, were among the lowest of the untouchables. For Hindus, all human emissions and materials involved in human or animal deaths contaminated any person who touched them. Women, with monthly bleeding and periodic childbirth, were potentially threatening to themselves and to the men of their families. As the Hindu caste system, developing complexity over time, became India's most distinctive social characteristic, women's status was entwined in its strictures.

Brahmans supported themselves by performing rituals and purification ceremonies derived from sacred Vedic texts. About 600 B.C.E. a female scholar, Gargi Vacaknavi, publicly debated Vedic philosophy at King Janaka's court. A century later that would be impossible, for the Brahmans had solidified their dominance over the other groups, in part by strictly enforcing caste rules and subordinating women. The priests forbade women to learn—or even hear—the sacred verses of the Vedas and excluded them from sacrifices. Thenceforth the practice of Hindu Sanskrit rites was reserved for male Brahmans, though women might emotionally worship the god Vishnu through pure love. Hindu religious beliefs grew in continuing interaction with non-Aryan cultures, a process that provided another avenue for women's religious expression. Although goddesses were relatively unimportant in the

Aryan pantheon, several powerful ones were incorporated into Hindu beliefs from non-Aryan religions. Three female personifications of belief in an ultimately feminine universe were the mother goddess Devi; the powerful Durga; and the embodiment of death and destruction, Kali.

Among the reform movements that arose in response to the Brahmans was that of the Buddha, born Siddhartha Gautama (ca. 560–480 B.C.E.). Like Hindus, Buddhists believe in reincarnation. Right living and right actions in a balanced life, Buddhists believe, lead to reincarnation or rebirth on a higher level. Instead of preaching the concept of reincarnation as a justification of the caste system, the Buddha said that human desires cause the suffering inevitable in life. Seeking Nirvana, or the renunciation of all desire and action, a person might escape further reincarnation by ceasing to exist as an individual essence. Buddhists opposed the Brahman priesthood, the caste system, and animal sacrifices. Stressing self-education and self-discipline, they accepted men and women of all castes as well as outcastes as candidates for spiritual enlightenment.

The classic cultural age of India occurred in the 700 years between 300 B.C.E. and 400 C.E., spanning the eras of the Maurya and Gupta empires. Buddhism spread in India and abroad, eventually becoming the prevalent religion of East and Southeast Asia, though languishing within India by the medieval period. Hinduism, capable of absorbing many local beliefs, developed as the dominant religion of India, with no serious rivals until the Muslim invasions of about 1200 C.E. During this classic period, the versions of the *Mahabharata* and the *Ramayana* known today emerged, as did a codification of Hindu legal concepts about women, called the Laws of Manu. Compiled between 200 and 400 C.E. from traditional social practices, these laws express the Brahman males' ideal of female subservience.

3.1 The Laws of Manu

In childhood a female must be subject to her father, in youth to her husband, when her lord is dead, to her sons; a woman must never be independent [Laws of Manu, bk. 5, law 148].

A wife, a son, and a slave, these three are declared to have no property; the wealth which they earn is [acquired] for him to whom they belong [Laws of Manu, bk. 8, law 416].

A man, aged thirty years, shall marry a maiden of twelve who pleases him, or a man of twenty-four a girl of eight years of age; if [the performance of] his duties would [otherwise] be impeded, [he must marry] sooner [Laws of Manu, bk. 9, law 94].

Manu, *The Laws of Manu,* trans. G. Buhler (Dehli: Motilal Banarsidass, 1964), 195, 326, 344.

The Laws of Manu were written over three centuries, with the earliest composed in the second century C.E. to give religious and secular instruction to the Hindu community. Brahmans were expected to follow these rules more closely. The expectations for others, especially those with little status, were lower; they could bend or break the rules for practical reasons. For example, poor men of lower castes might marry women nearer their own age because they needed the labor of an adult woman.

Obviously there were many widows in India, since brides were often sixteen to eighteen years younger than their husbands. Although the Laws of Manu were harsh regarding women, they did not require widows to commit ritual suicide, or *sati.* Although the earliest documented instance of *sati* was in 316 B.C.E., it was an infrequent practice during the classical period. The spectacle of a widow climbing up the funeral pyre of her husband and burning to death was seldom seen. The Laws of Manu disapproved of widow remarriage in any form, and the status of widows without sons was often little different from that of a servant to her in-laws.

A virtuous wife who after the death of her husband constantly remains chaste, reaches heaven, though she have no son, just like those chaste men [Laws of Manu, bk. 5, law 160].

But a woman who from a desire to have offspring violates her duty towards her [deceased] husband, brings on herself disgrace in this world, and loses her place with her husband [in heaven] [Laws of Manu, bk. 5, law 161].

Manu, *The Laws of Manu,* trans. G. Buhler (Delhi: Motilal Banarsidass, 1964), 197.

Although she was expected to remain chaste, a widow in a wealthy family might be pressured to adopt a son. The preferred adoption was from her husband's family so that her property would remain within that family.

Laws can describe the limits that society would like to place on behavior. By their nature these laws generally present a negative view of a society—what people should not do. To find out what people actually did, with the approval of their neighbors, other sources must be used. Folk tales can be a very useful and dramatic form of evidence.

3.2 The Carpenter's Wife

India has a long tradition of folk stories. While the telling of folk tales has died out in Europe and the United States, it still survives in India. The stories are transmitted orally from generation to generation. In the repetitive storytelling minor points are changed but the central theme is kept. Because they reflect the day-to-day lives of the listeners, these stories provide evidence of how people lived.

Women are usually important characters. They are depicted as either good or bad. One of the common "bad" characters is the adulterous wife who is obsessed with sex. "The Carpenter's Wife" is an example, with the deceived husband portrayed as a foolish object of community ridicule.

In a small town there was a carpenter whose lovely wife was as unfaithful as the carpenter's friends and family reported. In order to determine the truth of these rumors, the carpenter said to his wife one day, "My dear, there is a palace to be constructed in a distant city and I must go there to work. I will leave tomorrow and will spend a number of days there. Please make some food for my journey." The carpenter's wife joyfully prepared the provisions her husband requested. Early in the morning while it was still dark, the carpenter took his knapsack of provisions and said to his wife, "I am going, my dear, please lock the door." Instead of leaving, the carpenter circled his house, came in the back door and situated himself and his apprentice under his own bed.

The carpenter's wife was overjoyed at the thought that she could meet her paramour with no fear of being caught by her husband. She quickly summoned her lover through a close friend and the lovers ate and drank a meal together as though they were children freed from parental guidance. When they climbed into bed the wife's foot brushed against her husband's knee as he lay coiled up under the bed. Terrified, the wife thought, "Without a doubt, that must be my husband! What can I do?" Just then her lover asked, "Tell me dear, whom do you love more, me or your husband?"

The quick-witted wife responded, "What a silly question to ask. As you know, we women are accused of being immoral creatures who resort to all kinds of activities to satisfy our natural longings. In fact, some men would claim that we women would eat cow dung if we did not have noses to smell. But I would die on the spot if I should hear of any harm coming to my dear husband."

The carpenter was deceived by the lying words of his shameless wife, and he said to his apprentice, "Long live my beloved and fully devoted wife! I will praise her before all the people of the town." As he spoke, the carpenter rose up with the bed on his back, bearing his wife and her lover through the streets of the town proclaiming his wife to be devoted and honorable. And all of the people of the town laughed at the foolish carpenter.

From *Lustful Maidens and Ascetic Kings: Buddhist and Hindu Stories of Life*, 27–8, by Roy C. Amore and Larry D. Shinn. © 1981 by Oxford University Press, Inc. Reprinted by permission.

3.3 Sita, the Ideal Hindu Wife

In the "good" wife tales, the heroine faces a series of extraordinary tasks. Sita, the wife of Rama, is generally presented as the appropriate image of an ideal Hindu wife.

Sita of Videha is the heroine of the famous Hindu epic poem *The Ramayana*. There are many different versions of this tale. Through approximately 24,000 couplets, she survived a remarkable series of disasters. Always faithful, obedient, devoted, and loyal to her husband, the hero Rama, Sita received few rewards for her exemplary conduct.

Rama's father wanted to make his son regent and designated heir but was forced to banish him to the forest for fourteen years. Sita chose to accompany him. She was kidnapped by Ravan, a king from Sri Lanka. When Rama discovered what had happened

to Sita, he organized an army and defeated Ravan. Finally Rama
and Sita met, but instead of celebrations they had a confrontation:

> For she dwelt in Ravan's dwelling,—Rumor clouds a woman's fame—
> Righteous Rama's brow was clouded, saintly Sita spake in shame:

> "Wherefore spake ye not, my Rama, if your bosom doubts my faith,
> Dearer than a dark suspicion to a women were her death!

> Wherefore, Rama, with your token came your vassal o'er the wave,
> To assist a fallen women and a tainted wife to save,

> Wherefore with your mighty forces crossed the ocean in your pride,
> Risked your life in endless combats for a sin-polluted bride?

> Hast thou, Rama, all forgotten?—saintly Janak saw my birth,
> Child of harvest-bearing furrow, Sita sprang from Mother Earth,

> As a maiden true and stainless unto thee I gave my hand,
> As a consort fond and faithful roved with thee from land to land!

> But a woman pleadeth vainly when suspicion clouds her name,
> Lakshman, if thou lov'st thy sister, light for me the funeral flame,

> When the shadow of dishonor darkens o'er a women's life,
> Death alone is friend and refuge of a true and trustful wife,

> When a righteous lord and husband turns his cold averted eyes,
> Funeral flame dispels suspicion, honor lives when woman dies!"

> Dark was Rama's gloomy visage and his lips were firmly sealed,
> And his eye betrayed no weakness, word disclosed no thought
>   concealed,

> Silent heaved his heart in anguish, silent drooped his tortured head,
> Lakshman with a throbbing bosom funeral pyre for Sita made,

> And Videha's sinless daughter prayed unto the Gods above,
> On her lord and wedded consort cast her dying looks of love!

> *"If in act and thought," she uttered, "I am true unto my name,*
> *Witness of our sins and virtues, may this Fire protect my fame!*

If a false and lying scandal brings a faithful woman shame,
Witness of our sins and virtues, may this Fire protect my fame!

If in lifelong loving duty I am free from sin and blame,
Witness of our sins and virtues, may this Fire protect my fame!"

Fearless in her faith and valor Sita stepped upon the pyre,
And her form of beauty vanished circled by the clasping fire,

And an anguish shook the people like the ocean tempest-tost,
Old and young and maid and matron wept for Sita true and lost,

For bedecked in golden splendor and in gems and rich attire,
Sita vanished in the red fire of the newly lighted pyre!

Rishis and the great *Gandharvas,* Gods who know each secret deed,
Witnessed Sita's high devotion and a woman's lofty creed,

And the earth by ocean girdled with its wealth of teeming life,
Witnessed deed of dauntless duty of a true and a stainless wife!

Slow the red flames rolled asunder, God of Fire incarnate came,
Holding in his radiant bosom fair Videha's sinless dame,

Not a curl upon her tresses, not a blossom on her brow,
Not a fibre of her mantle did with tarnished lustre glow!

Witness of our sins and virtues, God of Fire incarnate spake,
Bade the sorrow-stricken Rama back his sinless wife to take:

"Ravan in his impious folly forced from thee thy faithful dame,
Guarded by her changeless virtue, Sita still remains the same,

Tempted oft by female Rakshas in the dark and dismal wood,
In her woe and in her sadness true to thee hath Sita stood,

Courted oft by royal Ravan in the forest far and lone,
True to wedded troth and virtue Sita thought of thee alone,

Pure is she in thought and action, pure and stainless, true and meek,
I, the witness of all actions, thus my sacred mandate speak!"

Rama's forehead was unclouded and a radiance lit his eye,
And his bosom heaved in gladness as he spake in accents high:

"Never from the time I saw her in her maiden days of youth,
Have I doubted Sita's virtue, Sita's fixed and changeless truth,

I have known her ever sinless,—let the world her virtue know,
For the God of Fire is witness to her truth and changeless vow!

Ravan in his pride and passion conquered not a woman's love,
For the virtuous like the bright fire in their native radiance move,

Ravan in his rage and folly conquered not a faithful wife,
For like ray of sun unsullied is a righteous woman's life,

Be the wide world now a witness,—pure and stainless is my dame,
Rama shall not leave his consort till he leaves his righteous fame!"

In his tears the contrite Rama clasped her in a soft embrace,
And the fond forgiving Sita in his bosom hid her face!

Ramesh C. Dutt, *The Ramayana & The Mahabharata* (New York: J.M. Dent & Sons Ltd., 1966 [1910]), 138–40.

Rama and Sita returned to the kingdom of his birth, his fourteen-year exile over. He was given the crown and accepted as king. However, rumors continued, expressing doubts that Sita had been faithful, and Rama banished her to the forest again. There she gave birth to twins, whom Rama eventually recognized as his sons. Then Rama had the nerve to bring Sita back and ask her forgiveness. Sita wasn't tempted into submitting to an emotional whiplashing again. She called upon the Earth Mother to take her back—the earth yawned and granted her request. Today those Hindus wishing to follow a traditional life-style still consider Sita the ideal wife.

After reading classical Indian literature, it is easy to pity the women of India as powerless dependents of jealous male relatives. But that is not the whole story. Customs provided wives with some protection and security.

When a Hindu father agreed to his daughter's marriage, he may have said, "I give my daughter to" the groom, as if she were a present. In wealthy families expensive wedding presents were also exchanged, some of which were consumed during the wedding ceremony; others eventually ended up in the household of the newlyweds. The bride had a claim on these gifts, since in a divorce her family could demand that part of the presents should be returned to them.

At the wedding, the bride wore her jewelry and might bring expensive clothes and money with her. These objects were kept in a locked box in the bedroom—a box to which she had the only keys. During a family crisis, a husband could ask for some of her jewelry for sale or pawn. If she gave him any, he was obligated to replace or return it when normality returned. In a divorce, the contents of the box were hers and went with her.

After marriage, a woman continued to visit her natal family. If she had an abusive husband or was treated inappropriately, she might appeal to her father and brothers for help.

3.4 Psalms of the Buddhist Nuns

By 600 B.C.E. increasing caste discrimination, ritualization, and the Brahman priests' domination of Hinduism led to dissatisfaction among the people of India. New religions avoided these problems. Buddhism and Jainism, two of the most successful, both offered women more opportunities than Hinduism, although neither offered equality.

The Buddha was ambivalent about the spiritual role of women and was reluctant to change their traditional inferior status. A crisis arose among Buddhists over the question of whether women could become nuns. Buddhist monks were active in spreading the new religion. They were not supposed to own anything and had to beg for food and all their other needs. Except during the rainy season, monks were homeless. They did not lie and they abstained from sex. Conventional wisdom stated that women were incapable of learning religious teachings and maintaining ascetic discipline.

The Buddha had been raised by his aunt, and she asked him if women could become nuns; he responded negatively. Then his favorite male disciple, Ananda, asked the same question three times with the same result. Ananda realized that there was a contradiction in the refusal. The Buddha proclaimed enlightenment was possible for all, but at the same time he denied women the opportunity to take an essential step in reaching enlightenment. Those seeking enlightenment had to renounce their homes, live in a homeless state, and study to gain control of mind and body. The men who lived this way were monks. So Ananda asked the Buddha whether women were capable of reaching enlightenment, and the answer was yes. Realizing the contradiction in his denial of the state of nun to women while urging everyone to seek enlightenment, the Buddha reluctantly allowed women to become nuns.

The Buddha recognized nuns grudgingly, for they had to follow not only all the rules for monks but eight special additional rules. These additional rules forced the nuns into a status inferior to that of the monks. For example, any nun, even though she might be 100 years old, had to stand up and show respect to any monk, even the youngest. Initially the nuns had very little control over their religious ceremonies, which were performed by monks. The nuns opposed this practice and sought to create separate female communities, distinct from male monasteries.

Using various strategies, the nuns achieved this goal. One technique they employed was to publicly embarrass the monks. In India, priests were expected to be married, and Brahmans were encouraged to have sex with their wives. Nuns exploited this aspect of their culture by stopping monks in public, kneeling before them, and openly performing the religious rituals of respect the Buddha had required. Non-Buddhist observers interpreted this performance as a ceremony between husbands and wives and thought the monks and nuns were later having sex. The Buddha then changed the rules to allow religious ceremonies to be conducted by designated nuns. Through a series of similar episodes the nuns achieved practical self-government.

Poems written by nuns at the time of their enlightenment have been preserved under the title *Therigatha* (Psalms of Nuns). The poems and an accompanying commentary were passed down orally until they were put into written form in 80 B.C.E. An analysis of the psalms and commentary explains why women became nuns. The explanations fall into two categories. First, many women wanted to leave a hard life. Some were widows, others had suffered a series of misfortunes. For example, all members of their family might have died, or they might have been worn down by the "Five Woes of Women": leaving their parents' home when young to live with strangers; menstruation; pregnancy; giving birth; and having to wait on men (father, husband, and possibly their own sons) all their lives. Second, some women, through study and practice, were already well along in the process of reaching enlightenment.

Sumangala's mother was born into a poor family and was married to a rush plaiter, who mistreated her. Her first son became an influential monk. When she received enlightenment, she was able to master her emotions. She reflected upon her married life and composed the following poem:

O woman well set free! How free am I,
How thoroughly free from kitchen drudgery!
Me stained and squalid 'mong my cooking-pots
My brutal husband ranked as even less
Than the sunshades he sits and weaves always.

Purged now of all my former lust and hate,
I dwell, musing at ease beneath the shade
Of spreading boughs—O, but 'tis well with me!

C.A.F. Rhys Davids, *Psalms of the Early Buddhists,* vol. 1, *Psalms of the Sisters* (London: Luzac, 1964 [1909]), *Therigatha,* XXI, 25.

The Buddha advised women who wished to become nuns, but who still had obligations to infirm parents or husbands who depended on them, to fulfill their familial responsibilities first. Applicants were told to obtain the permission of the male who controlled them. Hence many women were not able to pursue a spiritual life until they were old, as was Mettika when she composed her poem:

Though I be suffering and weak, and all
My youthful spring be gone, yet have I come,
Leaning upon my staff, and clomb aloft
The mountain peak.

My cloak thrown off,
My little bowl o'erturned: so sit I here
Upon the rock. And o'er my spirit sweeps

The breath of Liberty! I win, I win
The Triple Lore! The Buddha's will is done!

C.A.F. Rhys Davids, *Psalms of the Early Buddhists*, vol. 1, *Psalms of the Sisters* (London: Luzac, 1964 [1909]), *Therigatha*, XXIV, 28.

As nuns became absorbed in their religious experience, they lost concern with their physical appearance. Ambapali was one of several courtesans who became nuns. Her poem emphasizes the law of impermanence by reflecting on her inevitable loss of beauty in an aging body.

Glossy and black as the down of the bee my curls once clustered.
They with the waste of years are liker to hempen or bark cloth.
Such and not otherwise runneth the rune, the word of the Soothsayer
    [the Buddha].

Fragrant as casket of perfumes, as full of sweet blossoms the hair of me.
All with the waste of the years now rank as the odor of hare's fur.

Dense as a grove well planted, and comely with comb, pin, and parting.
All with the waste of the years dishevelled the fair plaits and fallen.

Glittered the swarthy plaits in head-dresses jewelled and golden.
All with the waste of the years broken, and shorn are the tresses.

Wrought as by sculptor's craft the brows of me shone, finely pencilled.
They with the waste of years are seamed with wrinkles, o'erhanging.

Flashing and brilliant as jewels, dark-blue and long-lidded the eyes
    of me.
They with the waste of years spoilt utterly, radiant no longer. . . .

Gleamed as I smiled my teeth like the opening buds of the plantain.
They with the waste of the years are broken and yellow as barley.

Sweet was my voice as the bell of the cuckoo through woodlands
    flitting.
Now with the waste of the years broken the music and halting. . . .

Beauteous of yore were my soft hands with rings and gewgaws
    resplendent.
They with the waste of the years like roots are knotted and scabrous.

Full and lovely in contour rose of yore the small breast of me.
They with the waste of years droop shrunken as skins without water. . . .

Such hath this body been. Now age-weary and weak and unsightly.
Home of manifold ills; old house whence the mortar is dropping.

C.A.F. Rhys Davids, *Psalms of the Early Buddhists,* vol. 1, *Psalms of the Sisters*
(London: Luzac, 1964 [1909]), *Therigatha,* LXVI, 121–5.

The nun Subha describes how a man stopped her in the forest
and tried to seduce her. She pointed out to him the many bad
effects of sensual pleasures and why she had renounced them,
but he only saw the beauty of her eyes. She replied:

"What is this eye but a little ball lodged in the fork of a hollow tree,
Bubble of film, anointed with tear-brine, exuding slime-drops,
Compost wrought in the shape of an eye of manifold aspects?"
Forthwith the maiden so lovely tore out her eye and gave it to him:
"Here, then! take thou thine eye!" Nor sinned she, her heart unob-
    structed.
Straightway the lust in him ceased and he her pardon imploring:
"O that thou mightest recover thy sight, thou maid pure and holy!
Never again will I dare to offend thee after this fashion.
Sore hast thou smitten my sin; blazing flames have I clasped to my
    bosom;
Poisonous snake have I handled—but O! be thou heal'd and forgive me!"

C.A.F. Rhys Davids, *Psalms of the Early Buddhists,* vol. 1, *Psalms of the Sisters*
(London: Luzac, 1964 [1909]), *Therigatha,* LXXI, 154–5.

Subha went on her way, and when she was in the Buddha's
presence her eye was restored.

Women were able to create new careers as nuns after nunneries were established that were largely staffed by women. These
careers offered opportunities that had not existed before and that
gave them a rough equality with monks. But lay women also had
a vital role in the support of Buddhism on a daily basis. Since

both nuns and monks were homeless, they had to beg daily for food and other necessities. It was women to whom they naturally turned, for women were the cooks and in charge of household goods. Wealthy women, including numerous queens, supported both nuns and monks with endowments of land and monasteries.

One of the personalities famous for her support was the courtesan mentioned above, Ambapali, who was very wealthy. Because her son was a Buddhist elder, she built a monastery in her garden. She became interested in the religion, so when she heard the Buddha was nearby, she went to see him. After he had finished teaching, they had a religious discussion. She invited him and his accompanying monks to dinner at her home the next night, and he accepted. Soon afterward the local prince invited him also, but the Buddha declined. The next night the prince came to Ambapali's with his gorgeous chariots, but the Buddha preferred the courtesan's home. Eventually Ambapali gave her mango grove to the Buddha and became a nun.

Buddhist nuns remained an important minority among Indian women for more than a thousand years. They last appear in records in the ninth century C.E.

Suggested Further Readings

Two older books on women of India, both with an emphasis on women's helpless dependency, are A.S. Altekar, *The Position of Women in Hindu Civilization* (Delhi: Motilal Banarsidass, 1963 [1938]), a twentieth-century classic; and I.S. Hoerner, *Women under Primitive Buddhism: Laywomen and Almswomen* (Delhi: Motilal Banarsidass, 1975 [1930]). Note: these books are not easy to read. Romila Thapar has written an excellent short essay on Indian women in ancient times, called "Looking Back in History," in *Indian Women* (New Delhi: Ministry of Information and Broadcasting, Government of India, 1975), edited by Devaki Jain. The superb anthology of literature, *Women Writing in India: 600 B.C. to the Present*, vol. 1, *600 B.C. to the Early Twentieth Century* (New York: Feminist Press, 1991), edited by Susie Tharu and K. Lalita, includes mostly writings of non-Hindu women in the early centuries. The editors' introductions are particularly informative.

For women in the Hindu religion, a good source is Julia Leslie, "Essence and Existence: Women and Religion in Ancient Indian Texts," in Pat Holden, ed., *Women's Religious Experience* (Totowa, NJ: Barnes and Noble Books, 1983). And for women in the Buddhist religion, there are Janice D. Willis, "Nuns and Benefactresses: The Role of Women in the Development of Buddhism," in Yvonne Yazbeck Haddad and Ellison Banks Findley, eds., *Women, Religion and Social Change* (Albany, NY: State University of New York, 1985); Nancy Falk, "An Image of Woman in Old Buddhist Literature: The Daughters of Mara," in Judith Plaskow and Joan Arnold, eds., *Women and Religion,* rev. ed. (Missoula, MT: Scholars Press, 1974); and Diana Y. Paul, *Women in Buddhism: Images of the Feminine in Mahayana Tradition,* 2d ed. (Berkeley, CA: University of California Press, 1985).

–4–

ISRAEL

Jewish Women
in the Torah and the Diaspora

Scenes from the story of Adam and Eve as depicted in a *haggadah,* or commentary on the Torah, from fourteenth-century Spain. The scenes should be "read" in the following sequence: top right, top left, bottom right, and bottom left. They show, respectively, bliss, temptation, shame and expulsion from the Garden of Eden, and the requirement to work. This haggadah is known as the Sarajevo Haggadah because it has been in the Sarajevo National Museum since 1894.

Patriarchal cultures dominated nearly all of the ancient Mediterranean world. The earliest Hebrews were not unique in delegating to fathers unlimited powers of life or death; freedom or slavery; and love or exile over their wives, sons, daughters, servants, and slaves. It was the patriarchal God of Judaism that set the Jews apart from Babylonians, Assyrians, Persians, and Greeks.

While other peoples worshiped a pantheon of gods and goddesses, those who claimed descent from Abraham and Sarah had covenanted their obedience to only one male deity. Though the numbers of Jews were small, their vision of God the Father was ultimately persuasive. When transmitted from Judaism to Christianity and Islam, it became the prevailing form of monotheism in the world. In the Mediterranean, shrines to Ishtar, Isis, Demeter, and Vesta disappeared, as did their human priestesses.

Judaism embodied the religious, cultural, and legal traditions of Hebrew societies. The oldest scriptures are the Mosaic laws of the first five books of the Bible, or the Torah. Scholars believe that the Torah, the later books of the Prophets, and the books of writings were composed between the twelfth and third centuries B.C.E. Jewish society underwent drastic changes through those centuries. After the exodus from Egypt to Israel (about 1250 B.C.E.), the Hebrew people lived a seminomadic existence organized in clans and tribal leagues that were governed by elders. Then gradually the Israelis turned more and more to agriculture. Towns sprang up and eventually a nation was formed under a monarchy. After civil wars divided the land into the kingdoms of Israel and Judah, the Jews were repeatedly conquered by West Asian neighbors until their land became a Roman province in 63 B.C.E. Jewish families migrated throughout the Mediterranean, seeking new opportunities and fleeing repression after revolts against the Romans, until by the end of the fifth century C.E. the kingdoms of Israel and Judah were only a memory in the communities of the diaspora.

Patriarchal power dimmed as the social environment changed from nomadic tribes to sedentary villages and towns. Fathers heading farm and town households had less control over their dependents as communal rules governing marriage and children were modified. Change was circumscribed, however, by Mosaic law, for the essence of Judaism is daily obedience to God's laws in rituals, ethics, and morality.

4.1 Eve's Purpose and Her Sin in Genesis

Woman's place in the society was established when God created Eve from Adam's rib.

The Lord God formed man from the dust of the earth. He blew into his nostrils the breath of life, and man became a living being.

The Lord God planted a garden in Eden, . . . and placed there the man whom He had formed. And from the ground the Lord God caused to grow every tree that was pleasing to the sight and good for food, with the tree of life in the middle of the garden, and the tree of knowledge of good and bad. . . .

And the Lord God commanded the man, saying, "Of every tree of the garden you are free to eat; but as for the tree of knowledge of good and bad, you must not eat of it; for as soon as you eat of it, you shall die."

The Lord God said, "It is not good for man to be alone; I will make a fitting helper for him." . . . So the Lord God cast a deep sleep upon the man; and, while he slept, He took one of his ribs and closed up the flesh at that spot. And the Lord God fashioned the rib that He had taken from the man into a woman; and He brought her to the man.

Then the man said,

"This one at last
Is bone of my bones
And flesh of my flesh.
This one shall be called Woman,
For from man was she taken."

Hence a man leaves his father and mother and clings to his wife, so that they become one flesh.

The two of them were naked, the man and his wife, yet they felt no shame.

Genesis 2:7–9, 16–8, 21–5, *Tanakh: A New Translation of the Holy Scriptures According to the Traditional Hebrew Text* (Philadelphia: The Jewish Publication Society, 1985), 5–6.

It was the action of this woman—whether because of creative initiative or fatal curiosity—that, according to the Bible, caused the expulsion of Adam and Eve from the Garden of Eden and subjected women to the rule of men.

Now the serpent was the shrewdest of all the wild beasts that the Lord God had made. He said to the woman, "Did God really say: You shall not eat of any tree of the garden?" The woman replied to the serpent, "We may eat of the fruit of the other trees of the garden. It is only about fruit of the tree in the middle of the garden that God said: 'You shall not eat of it or touch it, lest you die.' " And the serpent said to the woman, "You are not going to die, but God knows that as soon as you eat of it your eyes will be opened and you will be like divine beings who know good and bad." When the woman saw that the tree was good for eating and a delight to the eyes, and that the tree was desirable as a source of wisdom, she took of its fruit and ate. She also gave some to her husband, and he ate. Then the eyes of both of them were opened and they perceived that they were naked. . . .

The Lord God called out to the man and said to him, "Where are you?" He replied, "I heard the sound of You in the garden, and I was afraid because I was naked, so I hid."

Then He asked, "Who told you that you were naked? Did you eat of the tree from which I had forbidden you to eat?" The man said, "The woman You put at my side—she gave me of the tree, and I ate." And the Lord God said to the woman, "What is this you have done!" The woman replied, "The serpent duped me, and I ate."

Genesis 3:1–7, 9–13, *Tanakh: A New Translation of the Holy Scriptures According to the Traditional Hebrew Text* (Philadelphia: The Jewish Publication Society, 1985), 6.

Relenting from his original threat of death for eating the fruit of the tree of knowledge, God decreed separate punishments for Adam and Eve before he drove them out of the Garden of Eden.

And to the woman He said,

"I will make most severe
Your pangs in childbearing;

In pain shall you bear children.
Yet your urge shall be for your husband,
And he shall rule over you."

To Adam, He said, "Because you did as your wife said and ate of
the tree about which I commanded you, 'You shall not eat of it,'

Cursed be the ground because of you;
By toil shall you eat of it
All the days of your life. . . ."

Genesis 3:16–7, *Tanakh: A New Translation of the Holy Scriptures According to the Traditional Hebrew Text* (Philadelphia: The Jewish Publication Society, 1985), 7.

4.2 Marriage and Childbirth among Eve's Descendants

If bearing children was woman's painful duty, not bearing any
was worse in cultures that deemed motherhood to be her purpose in life. Barren or infertile women appear again and again in
the lives of Adam and Eve's descendants. One of those was
Jacob's wife Rachel. Jacob's father sent him to Laban, Jacob's
mother's brother, to find a wife. When Jacob arrived he first saw
Rachel, Laban's younger daughter, who tells her father of Jacob's
appearance.

On hearing the news of his sister's son Jacob, Laban ran to greet him;
he embraced him and kissed him, and took him into his house. . . .
    When he had stayed with him a month's time, Laban said to
Jacob, "Just because you are a kinsman, should you serve me for
nothing? Tell me, what shall your wages be?" Now Laban had two
daughters, the name of the older one was Leah, and the name of the
younger one was Rachel. Leah had weak eyes; Rachel was shapely
and beautiful. Jacob loved Rachel; so he answered, "I will serve you
seven years for your younger daughter Rachel." Laban said, "Better
that I give her to you than that I should give her to an outsider. Stay
with me." So Jacob served seven years for Rachel and they seemed
to him but a few days because of his love for her.
    Then Jacob said to Laban, "Give me my wife, for my time is

fulfilled, that I may cohabit with her." And Laban gathered all the people of the place and made a feast. When evening came, he took his daughter Leah and brought her to him; and he cohabited with her—Laban had given his maidservant Zilpah to his daughter Leah as her maid.—When morning came, there was Leah! So he said to Laban, "What is this you have done to me? I was in your service for Rachel! Why did you deceive me?" Laban said, "It is not the practice of our place to marry off the younger before the older. Wait until the bridal week of this one is over and we will give you that one too, provided you serve me another seven years." Jacob did so; he waited out the bridal week of the one, and then he gave him his daughter Rachel as wife.—Laban had given his maidservant Bilhah to his daughter Rachel as her maid.—And Jacob cohabited with Rachel also; indeed, he loved Rachel more than Leah. And he served him another seven years.

The Lord saw that Leah was unloved and he opened her womb; but Rachel was barren. Leah conceived and bore a son. . . .

Genesis 29:13–32, *Tanakh: A New Translation of the Holy Scriptures According to the Traditional Hebrew Text* (Philadelphia: The Jewish Publication Society, 1985), 44–5.

Leah eventually had four sons, each time expecting that her husband would love her, but he did not. The story continues:

When Rachel saw that she had borne Jacob no children, she became envious of her sister; and Rachel said to Jacob, "Give me children, or I shall die." Jacob was incensed at Rachel, and said, "Can I take the place of God, who has denied you fruit of the womb?" She said, "Here is my maid Bilhah. Consort with her, that she may bear on my knees and that through her I too may have children." So she gave him her maid Bilhah as a concubine, and Jacob cohabited with her. Bilhah conceived and bore Jacob a son. And Rachel said, "God has vindicated me; indeed, He has heeded my plea and given me a son."

Genesis 30:1–6, *Tanakh: A New Translation of the Holy Scriptures According to the Traditional Hebrew Text* (Philadelphia: The Jewish Publication Society, 1985), 45–6.

Rachel appropriated Bilhah's son from his mother, but that did not end the competition between Rachel and Leah. Leah gave her maid Zilpah to Jacob as a concubine; then she claimed Zilpah's two sons as her own. After Leah herself had three more children, "God remembered Rachel . . . and opened her womb" [Genesis 30:22].

Rachel's story illustrates how barren wives longed to escape their guilt and social stigmatization. It also shows how privileged legal wives were in comparison to slave concubines. Bilhah and Zilpah had no choice about cohabiting with Jacob or yielding their children to his wives. Inequality and jealousy was rampant in Jacob's family. Sons were what counted in the competition between Leah and Rachel, not daughters.

Female children were less desirable than males. A Jewish woman was always under the legal control of a male: as a child, her father; as a wife, her husband; and as a widow, a male relative. In the Hebrew culture of the Torah, even when a woman's husband died, she could not be independent of male authority. The Jewish custom of levirate marriages, also found in other ancient civilizations, meant that a widow without a male child would have to wed one of her husband's brothers, who was expected to father her child. If the child were male, it would carry her first husband's name and would be given her first husband's property. The story of Judah and Tamar is about a woman shamed when her brothers-in-law rejected her. Judah had three sons: Er, Onan, and Shelah.

Judah got a wife for Er his first-born; her name was Tamar. But Er, Judah's first-born, was displeasing to the Lord and the Lord took his life. Then Judah said to Onan, "Join with your brother's wife and do your duty by her as a brother-in-law, and provide offspring for your brother." But Onan, knowing that the seed would not count as his, let it go to waste whenever he joined with his brother's wife, so as not to provide offspring for his brother. What he did was displeasing to the Lord and He took his life also. Then Judah said to his daughter-in-law Tamar, "Stay as a widow in your father's house until my son Shelah grows up"—for he thought, "He too might die like his brothers." So Tamar went to live in her father's house.

A long time afterwards . . . the wife of Judah died. When his period of mourning was over, Judah went up to Timnah to his sheepshearers, together with his friend Hirah the Adullamite. And Tamar was told, "Your father-in-law is coming up to Timnah for the sheepshearing." So she took off her widow's garb, covered her face with a veil, and wrapping herself up, sat down at the entrance to Enaim, which is on the road to Timnah; for she saw that Shelah was grown up, yet she had not been given to him as wife. When Judah saw her, he took her for a harlot; for she had covered her face. So he turned aside to her by the road and said, "Here let me sleep with you"—for he did not know that she was his daughter-in-law. "What," she asked, "will you pay for sleeping with me?" He replied, "I will send a kid from my flock." But she said, "You must leave a pledge until you have sent it." And he said, "What pledge shall I give you?" She replied, "Your seal and cord, and the staff which you carry." So he gave them to her and slept with her, and she conceived by him. Then she went on her way. She took off her veil and again put on her widow's garb.

Judah sent the kid by his friend the Adullamite, to redeem the pledge from the woman; but he could not find her. He inquired of the people of that town, "Where is the cult prostitute, the one at Enaim, by the road?" But they said, "There has been no prostitute here." So he returned to Judah and said, "I could not find her; moreover, the townspeople said: There has been no prostitute here." Judah said, "Let her keep them, lest we become a laughingstock. I did send her this kid, but you did not find her."

About three months later, Judah was told, "Your daughter-in-law Tamar has played the harlot; in fact, she is with child by harlotry." "Bring her out," said Judah, "and let her be burned." As she was being brought out, she sent this message to her father-in-law, "I am with child by the man to whom these belong." And she added, "Examine these: whose seal and cord and staff are these?" Judah recognized them, and said, "She is more in the right than I, inasmuch as I did not give her to my son Shelah." And he was not intimate with her again.

Genesis 38:6–26, *Tanakh: A New Translation of the Holy Scriptures According to the Traditional Hebrew Text* (Philadelphia: The Jewish Publication Society, 1985), 60–1.

———————

Why did Tamar trick Judah? Most commentators on marriage customs argue that the obligation of a widow to marry one of her dead husband's relatives rested upon the desire of his family to retain her dowry and her labor. She would have inherited nothing else; she didn't even have a claim on their home. Judah's sons' refusal to marry Er's widow is not explained, but their contempt for her is implicit in the story. Tamar risked much in retaliating for the humiliation Judah and his sons caused her. Women's subordination did not render Tamar passive, nor is her initiative condemned.

4.3 The Rites of Jewish Women

The meaning of the actions of Leah, Rachel, or Tamar may be open to interpretation as symbolic, cautionary, or representative of women's dilemmas in ancient Jewry. Elsewhere, Mosaic law of the Torah was unambiguous in specifying women's obligations in the ceremonies of daily life and religion.

Among Jews, ritual cleanliness was critical to the pursuit of holiness. Women and men washed their hands each morning before donning clothes appropriate to their gender. Whenever men or women emitted body fluids they were considered to be polluted beyond immediate cleansing. Then they were avoided, as was anything they touched. After every menstrual period and each birth, a woman required purification by a priest.

When a man has an emission of semen, he shall bathe his whole body in water and remain unclean until evening. All cloth or leather on which semen falls shall be washed in water and remain unclean until evening. . . .

When a woman has a discharge, her discharge being blood from her body, she shall remain in her impurity seven days; whoever touches her shall be unclean until evening. Anything that she lies on during her impurity shall be unclean; and anything that she sits on shall be unclean. Anyone who touches her bedding shall wash his clothes, bathe in water, and remain unclean until evening; and anyone who touches any object on which she has sat shall wash his clothes, bathe in water, and remain unclean until evening. Be it the bedding, or be it the object on which she has sat, on touching it he shall be unclean until evening. . . .

When she becomes clean of her discharge, she shall count off seven days, and after that she shall be clean. On the eighth day she shall take two turtle doves or two pigeons, and bring them to the priest at the entrance of the Tent of Meeting. The priest shall offer the one as a sin offering and the other as a burnt offering; and the priest shall make expiation on her behalf, for her unclean discharge, before the Lord.

Leviticus 15:16–30, *Tanakh: A New Translation of the Holy Scriptures According to the Traditional Hebrew Text* (Philadelphia: The Jewish Publication Society, 1985), 179.

When a woman birthed a boy, she was unclean for seven days and required thirty-three days for purification. When she had a girl, both times were doubled. Maintaining her own purity while undertaking the onerous laundering to maintain that of her family was a heavy obligation. Women were also responsible for their family's observance of dietary laws regarding what foods might be eaten and how they should be cooked.

The ancient laws of the Torah harshly condemned sexual crimes. Adulterers merited death. A girl who committed "fornication while under her father's authority" was stoned to death at the entrance of her house [Deuteronomy 23: 20–22]. Parents of a married woman kept the bloody cloth that proved her bridal virginity in case they might later need to defend her before the elders.

Written scriptures form part of the Judaic tradition. By the sixth century B.C.E., when the Temple in Jerusalem was rebuilt, another tradition of biblical interpretation by priests and scholars began. Rather than relying only on literal readings of the ancient texts, commentaries reconciling passages in the Bible were developed through authoritative interpretations and collected in the Talmud. As Jews were expelled or emigrated from Israel, differing scholarly traditions arose. But there was general agreement in this period that thrice-daily prayer was a male obligation, that a ritual religious community was composed of ten men, and that only males could perform sacred rituals in the temple or synagogue. Women were usually segregated from men in public prayer.

Though public Judaism was male, women remained its essential conduit. Following the precedent of God's ruling when Abraham had sons by both his wife Sarah and his Egyptian concubine Hagar, which was that only his heirs by his Jewish wife would count among the chosen, children born to Jewish fathers and non-Jewish mothers remained outside the Judaic community. Rabbinic exegesis allowed the peoples of the Diaspora to adapt to living as minorities in many countries of Asia, Africa, and Europe, as well as to change their practices of marriage, divorce, and inheritance to keep pace with their circumstances.

4.4 Marriage in the Diaspora: Medieval Egypt

Jewish women's lives were changed as they migrated from Israel to lands where they lived as minorities. Those living in the city of Fustat, Egypt, from the eleventh through thirteenth centuries C.E. gained some legal rights. Fustat, the capital of Egypt during most of the period, was an important commercial center not only for Egypt but also for international trade with North Africa, Europe, and later with the lands bordering the Indian Ocean. Fustat Jews numbered over 3,000 in 1170 C.E. Families of merchants left the bulk of the surviving personal documents that reveal women's status.

Marriage contracts were written to provide protection for the bride. At the time of the marriage the groom gave the bride an "immediate gift," usually cash, which became her sole property, and promised her a "delayed gift," also in cash. The immediate payment varied with the wealth of the groom but represented about one year of his income. The "delayed gift" was insurance for the bride in case of a divorce or the death of her husband. Normally three or more times larger than the immediate payment, it was seldom actually paid.

Few wedding contracts have been preserved, but several engagement contracts specify the final terms of the marriage. The following extracts summarize clauses protecting the bride's interests.

That he was not permitted to take a second wife, or to acquire a maidservant his wife disliked;

that his wife was regarded as trustworthy in all matters concerning food and drink;

and that no oath, grave or light, could be imposed on her in this matter;

and that "the equal shares" be observed, meaning, God forbid, that if after entering the bridal chamber Sitt al-Turaf [the bride] died without producing a living child, male or female, one-half of her bridal outfit would return to her heirs from her father's house;

and that the domicile was according to her wishes; and she could not be forced to live where she did not like to. . . .

S.D. Goitein, *A Mediterranean Society: The Jewish Communities of the Arab World, as Portrayed in the Documents of the Cairo Geniza,* vol. 3, *The Family* (Berkeley: University of California Press, 1978), 67.

———————

Although the medieval Fustat Jewish community still accepted polygamy, individual women demanded monogamy as a condition of marriage. Further, women who, as wives, would be responsible for managing household expenditures and the observance of Jewish ritual dietary rules demanded acceptance as "trustworthy" adults. The bridal outfit was the dowry, consisting of her jewelry, clothes, furniture, copper utensils, and other household goods. It usually was valued at about ten times the amount of the husband's immediate gift. It was partly bought by her father and partly given to her from her mother's or grandmother's dowries. Her husband was legally responsible for replacing items that wore out, especially the bride's clothes, an expensive obligation because apparel was costly. A wife who bore children retained her dowry if divorced or widowed. For Jewish women of the Diaspora, the right to remain near their own families was important.

Some brides could demand more, as the following contract shows.

1. Should separation occur, the document freeing Sitt al-Dalal ("Lady Bold") will be produced by her husband without delay.
2. She is trustworthy in her statements concerning everything and no oath of any kind may be imposed on her.
3. He will not marry another wife [nor keep a slave girl disliked by her].
4. He will not beat her.
5. He will not leave Fustat and travel anywhere [except with her consent].

6. Before setting out on a journey he will write her a conditional bill of divorce and deposit the delayed installment of her marriage gift as well as the sums needed for her maintenance during his absence.

7. The young couple will live in her parents' house. The husband owes a yearly rent of 6 dinars and will never be late in paying it.

8. He will not separate her from her parents, as long as the latter are alive, and cannot force her to live anywhere else.

9. A fine of 50 dinars is imposed on him in case he fails to fulfill any . . . of the preceding conditions.

S.D. Goitein, *A Mediterranean Society: The Jewish Communities of the Arab World, as Portrayed in the Documents of the Cairo Geniza,* vol. 3, *The Family* (Berkeley: University of California Press, 1978), 144.

————————————

This contract was framed to protect a woman whose husband was expected to be absent for months, as his trading carried him to distant cities. Travelers on sea or land were in considerable danger. Attacks by bandits, pirates, even fellow travelers could result in death, imprisonment, or slavery. If her husband was only going to nearby towns and villages, his wife expected him to honor his sexual obligations to her. At this time it was customary for couples to have sex on Fridays, before the Jewish sabbath began. Remembering that menstruation created a period of nearly two weeks of impurity out of every four, a wife could be insistent that the scheduling of short trips not interfere with her available Fridays.

The purpose of contracts was to secure married women's emotional, physical, sexual, and economic welfare. These documents indicate that medieval women expected love and personal satisfaction, as well as economic support, from marriage. In contrast to the situation in ancient Israel, when couples lived in patrilineal and patriarchal multigenerational households, Fustat women remained close to their own protective parents and siblings. A woman without a family was severely disadvantaged, but she might be independent and determined to protect herself.

S.D. Goitein tells of such a woman. Her story comes from legal inquiries submitted to Moses Maimonides, a famous Jewish legal scholar, and his decisions in reply.

It was a fantastic story, in many respects characteristic of prevalent social conditions and notions. It begins with a child marriage, arranged in order to keep a property together, but certainly also with a view of providing a home for an orphan. A woman arranged the marriage of an orphaned relative, nine years old, who had a share in the house in which she and her sons lived, to one of her sons, promising to maintain the young couple for ten years. After seven years she declared that she was no longer able to keep up her obligations. At about that time, the girl gave birth to a son. When the child was about nine months old, the husband vanished, traveling to Palestine, Damascus, and other places. He absented himself for three years without leaving his wife money "sufficient for one supper." When he came back, he did not earn a penny, but sired another son. He was so poor that sometimes his brother and sometimes his young wife or his mother had to pay the poll tax for him—otherwise he would have been thrown into prison. As an indication of his utter penuriousness the letter indicates that he never lighted a lamp for his wife ("not even with linseed, let alone with olive oil"). If she wished to see light, she had to visit the apartments of her [husband's] mother, or brother-in-law, who, we remember, lived in the same house. A year and half after the birth of his second son the man disappeared again and roamed the world for another three years.

Meanwhile, the young wife had reached the age of twenty-five years. In one respect she had made good use of her loafer of a husband: she had learned from him how to read the Bible, and perfected her knowledge during his absence. Her brother, a school teacher, accepted her as partner, and this arrangement lasted six years. Then her brother left town, and she ran the school alone for four years, employing her elder boy, who by then was seventeen, as her associate. This she did, as the letter is careful to stress, "so that he could talk to the fathers of the schoolchildren, while she would take care of the mothers."

During the years she taught school her husband stayed with his mother. When he happened to have some money, he would spend it on himself and his mother, but never on her and the children. He never provided them with clothing ("not even shoes"), bedding, school fees, or the poll tax. All he bought for the household during twenty-five years of marriage was—a mat. She stayed with her boys on the school premises, which she rented for 14 dirhems (per month).

The law suit reflected in the two letters to Maimonides started at that juncture and probably went on for some time. The good-for-nothing complained, (a) that it injured his dignity for his wife to be a school mistress, and (b) that he had no one to serve him. She should give up her teaching and stay with him; otherwise, he should be permitted to take an additional wife. To this she retorted that she could not leave the school to her son "even for one day," for the parents sent their boys to her school because of her, not because of him. If her husband agreed with this, she was prepared to live with him, either in her own apartment in the family house or on the school premises, and if the latter she would permit him to take for himself the rent on the apartment belonging to her. She was also ready to accept a divorce. The idea of a second wife was preposterous.

From the letter in favor of the husband it becomes evident why he preferred a second wife to a divorce. Naturally, nothing is said of his inability or unwillingness to maintain his family. We read only that during his repeated travels (on business, of course) his wife became a school mistress, with the result that she had constantly to meet with the fathers of her pupils, which he abhorred, "both in his own interest and in hers." He further complains that she failed to provide him with the services expected from a wife (including the conjugal duties) and that she neglected her children. He was unable to divorce her because of her share in the family home; she would "take it with her" and marry another man, whereupon his sons might lose their inheritance.

To this Maimonides replies that the husband was not permitted to marry someone else without the consent of his wife. But the school mistress should be instructed by the local judge in the strongest possible terms that the demand of her husband that she desist from teaching was endorsed by the law and therefore could never be a claim for divorce.

The answer to the letter in favor of the wife was different in tone and emphasis, but essentially the same in substance. If a husband did not support his wife, he would be forced to set her free and to pay her the delayed marriage gift. On the other hand, he had the right to forbid her to teach, whether a craft or "reading." The way for her to get free was a declaration that she could not live with him, in which case she would lose her marriage gift (which she had little prospect of receiving anyway). As a divorcee, Maimonides concludes, "she would have disposition over herself, she could teach what she liked and do what she liked."

S.D. Goitein, *A Mediterranean Society: The Jewish Communities of the Arab World, as Portrayed in the Documents of the Cairo Geniza*, vol. 3, *The Family* (Berkeley: University of California Press, 1978), 344–6.

Suggested Further Readings

For those interested in the early history of Jewish women, the best start would be to read some of their stories in the Torah. Phyllis Trible wrote a short essay with numerous references to the relevant stories in the Torah; the essay is found in the *Interpreter's Dictionary of the Bible; Supplementary Volume*, edited by Keith R. Crim et al., under the entry "Women in the Old Testament" (Nashville, TN: Abingdon Press, 1976). A more detailed study, "Images of Women in the Old Testament," by Phyllis Byrd, can be found in a useful anthology, *Religion and Sexism: Images of Women in the Jewish and Christian Tradition*, edited by Rosemary Radford Ruether (New York: Simon and Schuster, 1974). Judith Hauptman, in "Images of Women in the Talmud," also found in *Religion and Sexism*, discusses how the Rabbinic legal tradition affected later women. Gerda Lerner analyzes the early history of Hebrew women in *The Creation of Patriarchy* (New York: Oxford University Press, 1986), which includes a bibliography of secondary sources. Also see Leonie Archer, "Virgin and Harlot in the *Writings of Formative Judaism*," *History Workshop* 24 (autumn 1987): 1–16; S.J.D. Cohen, "Women in Synagogues in Antiquity," *Conservative Judaism* 34 (1980): 23–9; Ross S. Kraemer, "Monastic Jewish Women in Greco-Roman Egypt: Philo Judeaus on the Therapeutrides," *Signs* 14 (winter 1989): 342–70; and Ivan G. Marcus, "Mothers, Martyrs and Moneymakers: Some Jewish Women in Medieval Europe," *Conservative Judaism* 38 (spring 1986): 34–45.

–5–
GREECE
Patriarchal Dominance in Classical Athens

Women working wool on a Greek vase from the sixth century B.C.E.
(The Metropolitan Museum of Art, Fletcher Fund, 1931.)

Classical Greece, 500–338 B.C.E., has long been admired by Westerners for its political theories, philosophy, science, and the arts. Generally ignored are aspects of Greek civilization that show a darker side. Slavery and subordination of women are topics once dismissed as insignificant but now recognized as important to understanding the culture. In the classical period, there were actually many Greeces, with distinct societies developing in separate city-states such as Thebes, Sparta, and Athens. Gender patterns varied considerably among these cities.

From the island of Lesbos, Sappho's lyric lines speak of women's love for one another. In the sixth century B.C.E., she expressed her emotions on parting from a friend:

"'The truth is, I wish I were dead.' She left me, whispering often, and she said this, 'Oh what a cruel fate is ours, Sappho, yes, I leave you against my will.'

And I answered her: 'Farewell, go and remember me, for you know how we cared for you. . . .'"

These rare fragments of the feminine voice from an outer Greek island have no counterpart in Sparta or Athens. Sparta's women were often left alone to acquire wealth and some autonomy when their mercenary husbands soldiered elsewhere. To Athenian men like Aristotle, Spartan women were despicable, licentious, and greedy. Ascribing Sparta's decline to them, Aristotle wrote: "What difference does it make whether women rule, or the rulers are ruled by women?"*

Aristotle and other Athenian men dominate the discourse of gender from classical Greece. Male descriptions, such as Xenophon's of an ideal wife, brag of how Athenian society secluded elite women, denigrated them, exploited them, and made them legal dependents of men. Most records reveal the lives of privileged women, yet many were slaves. Athenian enslavement of females was exceptional in its concentration on prostitution. Perhaps the large numbers of slave sex workers can be explained by the Athenians' desire to attract sailors and merchants to their port. Marginal women, such as sex workers, are almost universally ignored in ancient writings. Court transcripts telling Neaera's story provide a rare glimpse into the underclass and

---

*Quotations from Sappho and Aristotle in Mary R. Lefkowitz and Maureen B. Fant, *Women's Life in Greece and Rome: A Source Book in Translation* (Baltimore: Johns Hopkins Press, 1982), 5, 65.

must represent thousands of similar unknown women of the ancient world. Her biography indicates that even with the severest initial handicaps, some strong women did take control of their lives, notwithstanding the continuous danger of an enforced return to slavery.

5.1 The Reign of Phallocracy

The following descriptions are more detailed and graphic than can be found for other civilizations. We are fortunate to know so much about this period of Greek history. In fact, the domination of women by men was so thorough in Athens that Eva Kuels coined the term "phallocracy" to identify it.

In the case of a society dominated by men who sequester their wives and daughters, denigrate the female role in reproduction, erect monuments to the male genitalia, have sex with the sons of their peers, sponsor public whorehouses, create a mythology of rape, and engage in rampant saber-rattling, it is not inappropriate to refer to a reign of the phallus. Classical Athens was such a society. . . .

First of all, what is "phallocracy"? Literally meaning "power of the phallus," it is a cultural system symbolized by the image of the male reproductive organ in permanent erection, the phallus. It is marked by, but is far more particular than, the dominance of men over women in the public sphere. In historic times, at least, such dominance has been almost universal. Nor does phallocracy refer simply to the worship of the male organ, a practice considered bizarre by most Westerners but common in many parts of the world, especially in conjunction with worship of the female counterpart. Although cultures that revere sexuality are, like others, generally dominated by men, much of their art and rituals presents the phallus as a symbol of generativity and of union with, rather than dominance over, the female. Furthermore, phallocracy does not allude to male dominance solely within a private sphere of sexual activity. Instead, . . . the concept denotes a successful claim by a male elite to general power, buttressed by a display of the phallus less as an organ of union or of mutual pleasure than as a kind of weapon: a spear or war club, and a scepter of sovereignty. In sexual terms, phallocracy takes such forms as rape, disregard of the sexual satisfaction of women, and access to the bodies of prostitutes who are literally enslaved or allowed no other means of support. In the political sphere, it spells imperialism and patriarchal behavior in civic affairs. . . .

The reign of the phallus comprised nearly every aspect of Athenian life. Once alert to its implications, we can see it reflected in architecture, city planning, medicine and law. In the public sphere of men, buildings were massive and surrounded by phallic pillars, whereas private dwellings, largely the domain of women, were box-like, enclosed, and modest. In law, we can trace the origins of the syndrome back to Solon, a founder of Athens and a father of its democracy. In the early sixth century B.C., the great legislator not only overhauled the Athenian political system but also instituted many controls over sexual and family life. He originated the principle of the state-controlled and price-controlled brothel, and passed, or singled out for perpetuation, "Draconian" laws for safeguarding the chastity of citizen women, including the notorious statute that a father could sell his daughter into slavery if she lost her virginity before marriage. He also may have instituted the Women's Police (gynaikonomoi), not securely attested in Athens until the post-Classical age but probably much older. At any rate, enough domestic legislation goes back to Solon to consider him a codifier of the double standard of sexual morality.

Eva C. Keuls, *The Reign of the Phallus: Sexual Politics in Ancient Athens,* 2d ed. (Berkeley: University of California Press, 1993), 1–5.

––––––––––

5.2 The Perfect Wife at Home

In ancient Athens, women in wealthy families were confined inside their homes all their lives. Even within the home they spent most of their time in the women's quarters. Of course, women in other families worked outside; a common occupation was selling goods in the marketplace. Although wealthy women seldom went out, and then only with a companion, they could attend religious festivals where they might mingle with the crowd.

While marriage was the most important event in a woman's life, it could also be a lifelong prison. Developing companionship with her new husband was difficult for the bride. She had not chosen him and might not have seen him before the marriage. He was much older than she. Customarily in a first marriage the bride was in her midteens, and the groom was roughly twice as old. Her family would have provided a dowry sufficient to feed and clothe her. As a result she was entitled to lifetime maintenance. Everyone knew that she was expected to provide a heir, but until she produced a male child she would not be fully accepted into her husband's family. At night her husband might lock up all the females in the house, including his wife, for fear of pregnancies by another male. Her husband thought of and treated his wife as a child. Greeks thought men and women had different characteristics: men were brave and logical, and women were fearful and illogical.

The following conversation between the philosopher Socrates and Ischomachos, a wealthy Athenian, illustrates some of the young bride's problems from a male perspective. It was written by Socrates's student, Xenophon. Ischomachos describes how he trained his young bride. He is proud and smug about how eager she is to follow his instructions. Ischomachos needed a wife to manage the complicated operations of his home and to be responsible for the valuable resources stored there—something he would be reluctant to entrust to slaves. She trained the house slaves (called "servants"), thereby increasing their value. The bride's name is never mentioned. Socrates is the narrator.

Seeing him then one day sitting in the colonnade of Zeus the Deliverer, I went over to him, and as he seemed to be at leisure, I sat down with him and spoke. "Why are you sitting like this, Ischomachos, you who are so unaccustomed to leisure? For I mostly see you either doing something or at least hardly at leisure in the market place."

"Nor would you see me now, Socrates," said Ischomachos, "if I hadn't made an appointment to meet some foreigners here."

"When you aren't doing this sort of thing," I said, "by the gods, how do you spend your time and what do you do?" . . .

"As to what you asked me, Socrates," he said, "I never spend time indoors. Indeed," he said, "my wife is quite able by herself to manage the things within the house."

"It would please me very much, Ischomachos," I said, "if I might also inquire about this—whether you yourself educated your wife to the way she ought to be, or whether, when you took her from her mother and father, she already knew how to manage the things that are appropriate to her."

"How, Socrates," he said, "could she have known anything when I took her, since she came to me when she was not yet fifteen, and had lived previously under diligent supervision in order that she might see and hear as little as possible and ask the fewest possible questions? Doesn't it seem to you that one should be content if she came knowing only how to take the wool and make clothes, and had seen how the spinning work is distributed among the female attendants? For as to matters of the stomach, Socrates," he said, "she came to me very finely educated; and to me, at any rate, that seems to be an education of the greatest importance both for a man and a woman."

"And in other respects, Ischomachos," I said, "did you yourself educate your wife to be capable of concerning herself with what's appropriate to her?" . . .

And Ischomachos replied: "Well, Socrates," he said, "when she had got accustomed to me and had been domesticated to the extent that we could have discussions, I questioned her somewhat as follows, 'Tell me, woman, have you thought yet why it was that I took you and our parents gave you to me? That it was not for want of someone else to spend the night with—this is obvious, I know, to you too. Rather, when I considered for myself, and your parents for you, whom we might take as the best partner for the household and children, I chose you, and your parents, as it appears, from among the possibilities chose me. Should a god grant us children, we will then consider, with respect to them, how we may best educate them; for this too is a good common to us—to obtain the best allies and the best supporters in old age; but for the present this household is what is common to us. As to myself, everything of mine I declare to be in common, and as for you, everything you've brought you have deposited in common. It's not necessary to calculate which of us has contributed the greater number of things, but it is necessary to know this well, that whichever of us is the better partner will be the one to contribute the things of greater worth.' To this, Socrates, my wife replied: 'What can I do to help you?' she said. 'What is my capacity? But everything depends on you: my work, my mother told me, is to be moderate.' 'By Zeus, woman,' I said, 'my father told me the same thing. But it's for moderate people—for man and woman alike—not only to keep their substance in the best condition but also to add as much as possible to it by fine and just means.' 'Then what do you see,' said my wife, 'that I might do to help in increasing the household?' 'By Zeus,' I said, 'just try to do in the best manner possible what the gods have brought you forth to be capable of and what the law praises.'. . .

"'Since, then, work and diligence are needed both for the indoor and for the outdoor things, it seems to me . . . that the god directly prepared the woman's nature for indoor works and indoor concerns. For he equipped the man, in body and in soul, with a greater capacity to endure cold and heat, journeys and expeditions, and so has ordered him to the outdoor works; but in bringing forth, for the woman, a body that is less capable in these respects, the god has, it seems to me, ordered her to the indoor works. But knowing that he had implanted in the woman, and ordered her to, the nourishment of newborn children, he also gave her a greater affection for the newborn infants than he gave to the man. Since he had also ordered the woman to the guarding of the things brought in, the god, understanding that a fearful soul is not worse at guarding, also gave the woman a greater share of fear than the man. And knowing too that the one who had the outdoor works would need to defend himself should someone act unjustly, to him he gave a greater share of boldness. But because it's necessary for both to give and to take, he endowed both with memory and diligence in like degree, so that you can't distinguish whether the male or the female kind has the greater share of these things. As for self-control in the necessary things, he endowed both with this too in like degree; and the god allowed the one who proved the better, whether the man or the woman, to derive more from this good. Since, then, the nature of each has not been brought forth to be naturally apt for all of the same things, each has need of the other, and their pairing is more beneficial to each, for where one falls short the other is capable.'. . .

"'It will be necessary,' [Ischomachos] said, 'for you [his wife] to remain indoors and to send out those of the servants whose work is outside; as for those whose work is to be done inside, these are to be in your charge; you must receive what is brought in and distribute what needs to be expended, and as for what needs to be set aside, you must use forethought and guard against expending in a month what was intended to last a year. When wool is brought to you, it must be your concern that clothes be made for whoever needs them. And it must be your concern that the dry grain be fine and fit for eating. There is one thing, however,' I said, 'among the concerns appropriate to you, that will perhaps seem less agreeable: whenever any of the servants become ill, it must be your concern that all be attended.' 'By Zeus,' said my wife, 'that will be most agreeable, at least if those who have been well tended are going to be grateful and feel more good will than before.' I admired her reply," said Ischomachos, "and spoke: ... 'Other private concerns will prove pleasant for you, woman,' I said, 'as when you take someone who knows nothing of spinning and make her knowledgeable, so that she is worth twice as much to you; or when you take someone who knows nothing of housekeeping or waiting and make her a knowledgeable, trusted, and skilled waiting maid, worth any sum; or when you're allowed to treat well those who are both moderate and beneficial to your household, and to punish anyone who looks to be wicked. But the most pleasant thing of all: if you look to be better than I and make me your servant, you will have no need to fear that with advancing age you will be honored any less in the household, and you may trust that as you grow older, the better a partner you prove to be for me, and for the children the better a guardian of the household, by so much more will you be honored in the household.' ...

"And yet once, Socrates," he said, "I saw she had applied a good deal of white lead to her face, that she might seem to be fairer than she was, and some dye, so that she would look more flushed than was the truth, and she also wore high shoes, that she might seem taller than she naturally was. 'Tell me, woman,' I said, 'would you judge me more worthy to be loved as a partner in wealth if I showed you our substance itself, didn't boast of having more substance than is really mine, and didn't hide any part of our substance, or if instead I tried to deceive you by saying I have more substance than is really mine and by displaying to you counterfeit money, necklaces of gilt wood, and purple robes that lose their colour, and asserting they are genuine?' She broke in straightway. 'Hush,' she said; 'don't you become like that; if you did, I could never love you from my soul.' 'Haven't we also come together, woman,' I said, 'as partners in one another's bodies?' 'Human beings say so, at least,' she said. 'Would I then seem more worthy to be loved,' I said, 'as a partner in the body, if I tried to offer you my body after concerning myself that it be healthy and strong, so that I would really be well complexioned, or if instead I smeared myself with vermilion, applied flesh colour beneath the eyes, and then displayed myself to you and embraced you, all the while deceiving you and offering you vermilion to see and touch instead of my own skin?' 'I wouldn't touch vermilion with as much pleasure as I would you,' she said, 'or see flesh colour with as much pleasure as your own, or see painted eyes with as much pleasure as your healthy ones.' 'You must believe, woman, that I too am not more pleased by the colour of white lead or dye than by your colour, but just as the gods have made horses most pleasant to horses, oxen to oxen, and sheep to sheep, so human beings suppose the pure body of a human being is most pleasant. Such deceits may in some way deceive outsiders and go undetected, but when those who are always together try to deceive one another they are necessarily found out. For either they are found out when they rise from their beds and before they have prepared themselves, or they are detected by their sweat or exposed by tears, or they genuinely are revealed in bathing.'"

"By the gods," I said, "what did she reply to this?"

"What else," he said, "was her reply, if not that she never did anything of the sort again and tried always to display herself suitably and in a pure state. At the same time she asked me if I could not advise her how she might really come to sight as fine and not merely seem to be. I advised her, Socrates," he said, "not always to sit about like a slave but to try, with the gods' help, to stand at the loom like a mistress, to teach others what she knew better than they, and to learn what she did not know as well; and also to examine the breadmaker, to watch over the housekeeper in her distribution of things and to go about and investigate whether each kind of thing is in the place it should be. In this way, it seemed to me, she could both attend to her concerns and have the opportunity to walk about. And I said it would be good exercise to moisten and knead the bread and to shake out and fold the clothes and bedcovers. I said that if she exercised in this way, she would take more pleasure in eating, would become healthier, and so would come to sight as better complexioned in truth. And a wife's looks, when in contrast to a waiting maid she is purer and

more suitably dressed, become attractive, especially when she grati-
fies her husband willingly instead of serving him under compulsion.
On the other hand, women who always sit about in pretentious solemnity lend themselves to comparison with those who use adornments and deceit. And now, Socrates," he said, "know well, my wife
still arranges her life as I taught her then and as I tell you now."

From Leo Strauss: *Xenophon's Socratic Discourse: An Interpretation of the
Oeconomicus,* 29–46. Translation of the *Oeconomicus* by Carnes Lord. © 1970 by
Cornell University. Used by permission of the publisher, Cornell University Press.

5.3 Athenian Slavery

In Athens a large number of women were slaves. The possibility
of enslavement was always in every woman's mind, since all the
women and children in a defeated Greek city-state might be sold
into slavery by the victors. That is what the Athenians did with
the inhabitants of the island of Melos during the Peloponnesian
War. However, as Eva Keuls explains, most slaves were not
Greeks.

One of the most revealing aspects of Athenian society was the simi-
larity of the positions of women and slaves: a considerable number of
references and symbols connect the two categories. The legal term
for wife was *damar,* a word derived from a root meaning "to subdue"
or "to tame." When the bride arrived at the groom's house, a basket
of nuts was poured over her head for good luck, a treatment also
extended to newly purchased slaves. This was called the *kata-
chysmata* or "downpourings." Like a slave, a woman had virtually no
protection under the law except insofar as she was the property of a
man. She was, in fact, not a person under the law. The dominance of
male over female was as complete during the period in question as
that of master over slave. As a result, the lives of Athenian women
have been nearly excluded from the record. The women of the age of
eloquence were silenced, and deprived of the form of immortality
that Greek men prized above all others: that of leaving a record of
their achievements. . . .

But men sat uneasily on the victor's throne. For there was a vital
difference between women and slaves in the minds of the men who

owned them. Slaves and their agonies could be excluded from one's consciousness, like the sufferings of animals, but women are men's mothers, wives, sisters, and daughters, and the battle of the sexes had to be fought over again in the mind of every male Athenian. . . .

Judged by the ideals of modern Western society, life in the ancient world in general was brutal. Slavery brought the gruesome implications of man's victories over his fellow men into every home. Even so, household and other urban slaves were a privileged elite. What went on in the mines, quarries, and treadmills (with which the masters of [Greek] comedy constantly threaten their slaves) must largely be filled in from imagination. . . .

Some Classicists argue that the ancient Athenians were mild masters to their slaves, thus echoing Aristotle, who wrote of the "customary gentleness of the Athenian people." Such evidence as we have, however, suggests that slavery was more unmitigated in Athens than in many other ancient societies. A telling detail of their customs was the use of an object called a "gulp preventer" *(pausikape),* a wooden collar closing the jaws, which was placed on slaves who handled food to keep them from eating it. The tortures of Tantalus were mirrored in everyday life.

A practice exclusive to Athens among Greek cities (with the possible exception of the Asian city of Miletus) was the routine torture of slaves in legal proceedings. A slave's testimony was admissible in court only if he gave it under torture, a provision that shows contempt for his character and disregard for his well-being. An owner could refuse to surrender his slaves to the opposition for questioning, but this would obviously cast a suspicion of guilt on him. If the slave was permanently injured during torture, the owner was entitled to damages. The state maintained a public torture chamber for legal purposes *(basanisterion).* The interrogations there were a form of popular entertainment: "Whenever someone turns over a slave for torture, a crowd of people gathers to hear what is said," Demosthenes reports. The Athenians were, in fact, inordinately proud of their practice of examination by torture, considering it, as one orator put it, "the justest and most democratic way" (Lycurg. 29).

Sexually, as in all other ways, slaves were at the mercy of their owners. Slaves, whether owned by public and private brothels or by individuals, provided men's habitual sex outlets, a circumstance which in itself must have generated an equation of sex with domination. Those slaves who were also women carried a double burden of oppression and were the most defenseless members of society. . . .

Whether or not a master could legally kill a slave at will is debated, but an owner could certainly inflict everything short of outright death on his property. The mere suspicion of a crime was sufficient cause for execution of a slave, as is revealed in Antiphon's speech *Against the Stepmother:* a slave prostitute, who had been an unwitting accessory to alleged murder, is routinely tortured and executed, apparently without any legal process.

Eva C. Keuls, *The Reign of the Phallus: Sexual Politics in Ancient Athens,* 2d ed. (Berkeley: University of California Press, 1993), 6–9.

5.4 Neaera, a Courtesan

Many slaves were prostitutes, and almost all prostitutes were slaves. They suffered triple degradation as females, slaves, and prostitutes. Athens and its port Piraeus were known for the quality and quantity of their prostitutes. Only Corinth had more. Most of the women were employed in brothels, but some were streetwalkers who congregated at the city gates and in the marketplace. The business was quite open. After the reforms of Solon, the city controlled prices in both city-owned and privately owned brothels. There were also male homosexual prostitutes, but that is another story.

In Athens and many other ancient civilizations, a small number of prostitutes were courtesans, women who had been trained in singing and dancing, and were hired at higher rates. In Greek, courtesans were called *hetaera.* They most frequently worked at private parties, which were called symposiums.

Symposiums were held in the male section of private homes, with the host's wife providing the food. The guests were all men, invited by the host. Wives never attended in person, since proper Athenian women did not eat and drink in public. Female slaves did the serving. Eva Keuls described the symposium as a "unique gathering, dedicated to a varying blend of eating, drinking, games of all sorts, philosophical discourse, and public sex with prostitutes, concubines, and other men, but never with wives" (160). Fortunately we know the life story of an Athenian *hetaera,*

Neaera, written in the latter part of the fourth century B.C.E. Very few accounts exist of the lives of women like Neaera, who lived on the margin of society.

The story is recorded in the court record of the trial of Neaera, who was accused by Apollodorus and his son of concealing her past as a slave, a prostitute, and a *hetaera*. They make it clear that they are really attacking Stephanus, who had passed himself off as Neaera's husband. The trial was also an effort to weaken the group of Athenians, which included Stephanus, who were supporters of Philip of Macedonia. It was written for a male jury.

She was one of seven little girls bought when small children by Nicarete, a freedwoman who had been the slave of Charisius of Elis, and the wife of Charisius' cook Hippias. Nicarete was a clever judge of beauty in little girls, and moreover she understood the art of rearing and training them skillfully, having made this her profession from which she drew her livelihood. She used to address them as daughters, so that she might exact the largest fee from those who wished to have dealings with them, on the ground that they were freeborn girls; but after she had reaped her profit from the youth of each of them, one by one, she then sold the whole lot of them together, seven in all: Anteia, Stratola, Aristocleia, Metaneira, Phila, Isthmias, and the defendant Neaera.

Now who were their respective purchasers, and how they were set free by those who bought them from Nicarete, I will explain in the course of my speech, if you wish to hear, and if I have enough time. But the fact that the defendant Neaera did belong to Nicarete and worked as a prostitute open to all comers—this is the point to which I wish to return.

Lysias the professor of rhetoric was the lover of Metaneira. He decided that in addition to the other expenses he had incurred for her, he would like to get her initiated. He thought that the rest of his expenditure went to her owner, but whatever he spent on her over the festival and initiation ceremony would be a present for the girl herself. He therefore asked Nicarete to come to the Mysteries and bring Metaneira so that she could be initiated and he promised to instruct her himself in the Mysteries.

When they arrived, Lysias did not admit them to his house, out of respect for his own wife, who was the daughter of Brachyllus and his own niece, and for his mother, who was somewhat advanced in years and lived in the same house. Instead, he lodged them—that is, Metaneira and Nicarete—with Philostratus of Celonus, who was still a bachelor and also a friend of his. The women were accompanied by the defendant Neaera, who was already working as a prostitute, though she was not yet of the proper age. . . .

On a later occasion, gentlemen, Simos the Thessalian brought Neaera here to the Great Panathenaic Festival. Nicarete also accompanied them, and they put up at the house of Ctesippus son of Glauconidas. The defendant Neaera drank and dined with them in the presence of a large company, as a courtesan would do. . . .

After that, she worked openly at Corinth as a prostitute, and became famous. Among her lovers were Xenoclides the poet and Hipparchus the actor, who had her on hire. . . .

After that, she acquired two lovers, Timanoridas of Corinth and Eucrates of Leucas. These men found Nicarete's charges excessive, as she expected them to pay all the daily expenses of her household; so they paid down to Nicarete 30 minas as the purchase-price of Neaera, and bought her outright from her mistress, according to the law of that city, to be their slave. They kept her and made use of her for as long as they wished. Then, being about to get married, they informed her that they did not wish to see the woman who had been their own mistress plying her trade in Corinth nor kept in a brothel: they would be glad to receive less money for her than they had paid, and to see her also reaping some benefit. They therefore offered to allow her, towards the price of her freedom, 1,000 drachmas, that is, 500 each; as for the 20 minas remaining, they told her to find this sum herself and repay it to them.

Neaera, on hearing these propositions from Timanoridas and Eucrates, sent messages to a number of her former lovers, asking them to come to Corinth. Among these was Phrynion, an Athenian from Paeania, the son of Demon, and the brother of Demochares, a man who was living a dissolute and extravagant life, as the older of you remember. When Phrynion arrived, she told him of the proposition made to her by Eucrates and Timanoridas, and handed him the money which she had collected from her other lovers as a contribution towards the purchase of her freedom, together with her own savings, asking him to make up the amount to the 20 minas, and pay it to Eucrates and Timanoridas, so that she should be free.

Phrynion was delighted to hear this proposition of hers. He took the money which had been contributed by her other lovers, made up the deficit himself, and paid the 20 minas to Eucrates and Timanoridas as the price of her freedom and on condition that she would not practice her profession in Corinth. . . .

When they arrived here at Athens, he kept her and lived with her in a most dissolute and reckless way. He took her out to dinner with him wherever he went, where there was drinking; and whenever he made an after-dinner excursion, she always went too. He made love to her openly, anywhere and everywhere he chose, to excite the jealousy of the onlookers at his privilege. Among the many houses to which he took her on an after-dinner call was that of Chabrias of the suburb Alexone when the latter had won the victory at Delphi with a four-horse chariot team which he had bought from the sons of Mitys the Argive, and on his return from Delphi was celebrating victory down at Colias. On that occasion, many men made love to Neaera when she was drunk and Phrynion was asleep, including even some of Chabrias' servants. . . .

However, finding herself treated with the most outrageous brutality by Phrynion, instead of being loved as she had expected, or having attention paid to her wishes, she packed up the goods in his house, including all the clothes and jewellery which he had provided for her personal adornment, and taking with her two servants, Thratta and Coccalina, ran away to Megara.

This happened when Asteius was Chief Magistrate at Athens, . . . during your second war against Sparta. Neaera spent two years in Megara; but her profession did not produce sufficient income to run her house, as she was extravagant, and the Megarians are mean and stingy, and there was no great foreign colony there because it was war-time, and the Megarians favored the Spartan side, but you were in command of the seas. She could not go back to Corinth because the terms of her release by Eucrates and Timanoridas were that she should not practice her profession there.

However, peace came. . . . It was then that our opponent Stephanus visited Megara. He put up at her house, as that of a prostitute, and became her lover. She told him her whole life-story and of her ill-treatment at the hands of Phrynion. She longed to live in Athens, but was afraid of Phrynion, because she had done him wrong and he was furious with her. She knew the violence and arrogance of his character. She therefore made the defendant Stephanus her protector, and while they were still in Megara, he talked encouragingly and filled her with hope, saying that Phrynion would be sorry for it if he laid hands on her, as he himself would take her as his wife, and would introduce the sons she already had to his clansmen as being his own, and would make citizens of them. No one on earth, he said, should do her any harm.

And so he arrived here at Athens from Megara with her and her three children, Proxenus, Ariston, and a daughter, who now bears the name of Phano. He took her and the children to the little house which he owned, alongside the Whispering Hermes. . . .

He had two reasons for bringing her here: first, that he would have a handsome mistress without expense; second, that her profession would provide him with the necessaries of life and keep the household, for he had no other source of income, except what he picked up by occasional blackmail.

When Phrynion heard that she was in Athens and living with the defendant, he took some young men with him and went to Stephanus's house to get her. Stephanus asserted her freedom, according to law, and Phrynion thereupon summoned her before the Polemarch, under surety. . . .

When she had thus been bailed out by Stephanus and was living with him, she carried on the same profession no less than before, but she exacted a larger fee from those who wished to consort with her, as having now a certain position to keep up and as being a married woman. Stephanus helped her by blackmail; if he caught any rich unknown stranger making love to her, he used to lock him up in the house as an adulterer caught with his wife, and extract a large sum of money from him—naturally, because neither Stephanus nor Neaera had anything, not even enough to meet their daily expenses, but their establishment was large. There were himself and herself to keep, and three small children—the ones she brought with her to him—and two maids and a man-servant; and above all, she had acquired the habit of good living, as formerly it had been others who had provided her with all necessaries. . . .

To continue: Phrynion began his law-suit against Stephanus, on the grounds that Stephanus had robbed him of the defendant Neaera and made a free woman of her, and that Stephanus had received the goods of which Neaera had robbed him when she left. However, their friends brought them together and persuaded them to submit the dispute to arbitration. The arbitrator who sat on Phrynion's behalf was Satyrus of Alopece, the brother of Lacedaemonius, and on Stephanus' behalf, Saurias of Lampra; they chose as umpire Diogeiton of Acharnae. These three met in the temple, and after hearing the facts from both the litigants and also from the woman herself, they gave their judgment, which was accepted by the litigants: namely that the woman should be free and her own mistress, but that the goods which Neaera had taken from Phrynion when she left should all be returned to Phrynion, except the clothes and jewellery and maid-servants which had been bought for Neaera herself; further, that she should spend the same number of days with each of them; but that if they agreed to any other arrangement, this same arrangement should hold good; that the woman's upkeep should be provided by the person with whom she was living at the time; and that for the future the litigants should be friends and should bear no malice. . . .

When the business was over, the friends of each party, those who had assisted them at the arbitration and the rest, did as I believe is usual in such cases, especially when a mistress is in dispute: they went to dine with each of them at the times when he had Neaera with him, and she dined and drank with them as mistresses do. . . .

I have now outlined the facts about Neaera, and have supported my statements with evidence: that she was originally a slave, was twice sold, and practised the profession of a prostitute; that she ran away from Phrynion to Megara, and on her return to Athens was summoned before the Polemarch under surety. . . .

Each one of you must believe, therefore, that he is giving his vote in defence of his wife, or his daughter, or his mother, or on behalf of the State, the laws, and religion—to prevent respectable women from acquiring the same standing as the prostitute, and to protect those who have been reared by their families in every propriety and with every care, and given in marriage according to law, from having no better position than this woman, who with every sort of licentious behavior surrendered herself dozens of times a day to dozens of men, whenever anyone asked her. You must not think of me, the speaker, merely as Apollodorus, nor of those who will speak on the side of the defence as merely your fellow-citizens: you must regard this lawsuit as being fought by Neaera against the laws, over the actions done by her. So that while you are considering the case for the prosecution, you must listen to the laws themselves, by which this City-State is governed and in accordance with which you have sworn to give your verdict: you must ask what the laws ordain, and how my opponents have transgressed them. . . .

Kathleen Freeman, *The Murder of Herodes and Other Trials from the Athenian Law Courts* (London: Macdonald, 1946), 197–219.

We do not know if Neaera and Stephanus were found guilty of the charges. If convicted, Neaera and her children would have been sold into slavery, even though she was almost sixty years old. Stephanus would have lost his entire estate and his civic rights.

Suggested Further Readings

Mary R. Lefkowitz and Maureen B. Fant, *Women's Life in Greece and Rome* (Baltimore: Johns Hopkins University Press, 1982), is a collection of useful primary sources. It includes documents from several Greek city-states. Sarah B. Pomeroy, *Goddesses, Whores, Wives, and Slaves: Women in Classical Antiquity* (New York: Schocken Books, 1975), is the best introduction to both Greece and Rome. *Pandora's Daughters* (Baltimore: Johns Hopkins University Press, 1987 [1981]), by Eva Cantarella, translated by Maureen B. Fant, is a feminist history of Greece and Rome by a historian of Roman Law at the University of Parma. She surveys Greek laws, myths, ritual, and literature for evidence of men's attitudes toward women and tries to describe the reality of women's lives. A good bibliography can be found in *Women in the Ancient World* (New York: Oxford University Press, 1989) by Gillian Clark. It was published for the Classical Association of England. Mary R. Lefkowitz, *Women in Greek Myth* (Baltimore: Johns Hopkins University Press, 1982), is a series of separate essays. Economic Rights of Women in Ancient Greece (Edinburgh: Edinburgh University Press, 1979), by David M. Schaps, is very thorough.

–6–

CHINA

Imperial Women
of the Han Dynasty
(202 B.C.E.–220 C.E.)

The marriage of the Han dynasty Chinese poet Tsai Yen to her Tatar captor, an episode from her poem "Eighteen Verses Sung to a Tatar Reed Whistle." Detail from a later Chinese silk handscroll painting. (The Metropolitan Museum of Art, Gift of the Dillon Fund, 1973.)

The man who called himself Shi Huangdi (First Emperor) really was the first to rule a Chinese empire of diverse peoples. Between 221 B.C.E., when he named himself Shi Huangdi and founded the Qin dynasty (221–206 B.C.E.), and his death eleven years later, his government established the political institutions that subsequent Chinese administrations have followed. The older system of hereditary rulers of provincial units was abolished. Provincial boundaries were redrawn and governors were appointed by the central government, which could dismiss them for failure to carry out their duties properly. Shi Huangdi's government built roads and parts of the Great Wall, standardized weights and measures, and required official documents to be written in the newly regularized Chinese script. Little is known about the impact of this strong central government on women, except that its policies caused popular suffering.

After a short interlude of civil wars, a group of provinces led by Liu Bang (256–195 B.C.E.) triumphed. Liu Bang proclaimed a new dynasty, the Han, in 202 B.C.E. Liu Bang is usually known by his posthumous title of "Gaodi."

China had been undergoing fundamental changes since 221 B.C.E. It was not clear how much of the old, pre-Qin traditions would be reestablished. When Gaodi died, Empress Lu ruled the empire. She was able to do this in part because of the uncertainty of the times, in part because she was very competent, and in part because of the traditional power of women in the imperial family.

6.1 The Regency of Empress Lu

In China, men usually controlled property and political offices. However, women had much power and influence in the family. If the family was as politically powerful as that of the Han emperor, his female relatives could have a greater influence on events than all but a few powerful male officials.

Imperial women had various traditional functions, and a strong woman could sway important decisions. The emperor's grandmother was given the most respect. One of her traditional responsibilities was to choose the spouses of her grandchildren, including the potential heirs to the throne. Often she chose brides for the heirs from her own family. Because a bride who was a potential empress could extend her family's influence into unborn generations, her male relatives were often awarded key offices in the government.

Close female relatives of the emperor, such as aunts, sisters, and daughters (even concubine's daughters), were very desirable brides for men of other families. Such a female relative might be married to a foreign ruler as a public declaration of the friendly relations between the two countries. If relations threatened to turn hostile, she became, in effect, a hostage. In addition these wives maintained contact with the emperor's family. They were ideally placed to advise and interpret political events both to the Chinese government and to their husbands.

Traditionally, potential male heirs were sent to live in remote provinces. Their sisters remained in the palace, and many of them married husbands of influential Chinese families. Married female relatives of the emperor continued to have access to the palace, government officials, and the women's quarters. Using their influence with friends and allies, they could advance the fortunes of their husbands' families.

If a new emperor was a child, a regent temporarily ran the government with the powers of an emperor. Traditionally, Chinese regents were female, often the grandmother of the emperor. In Europe the regent might be the child's mother. Most female regents were efficient and so successful that they are omitted in surveys of the country's history. The regents who are mentioned are usually criticized.

Any female regent who took over the government in her own name or tried to replace the ruling family with another family is usually painted in dark tones. Empress Lu was cruel, and she tried to replace her husband's family with her natal family. She was the empress to the first emperor of the Han dynasty, Gaodi (202–195 B.C.E.)

Gaodi began his career as a village official. As the Qin dynasty was collapsing, central government faded and China was caught up in wars between local rulers. Banditry was widespread. Gaodi struggled to survive from 210 to 202 B.C.E. as a bandit and warlord. Eventually he either conquered all other significant leaders or made them his allies. He declared himself emperor and Lady Lu his empress in 202 B.C.E. and continued to place men he could trust in positions of power until his death in 195 B.C.E.

The new emperor, Hsiao-hsu, was a teenager, so his mother, Empress Dowager Lu, was made regent. She ruled until her death in 181 B.C.E. The historian Homer H. Dubs summarized her career as regent. (In this reading, the older spellings "Liu Pang" [for "Liu Bang"] and "Kao-tsu" [for "Gaodi"] are used.)

This period of fifteen years [195–181 B.C.E.] constituted a period of rest and recuperation after the fighting and destruction preceding the reign of Kao-tsu [Gaodi] and the civil war during it. The only serious conflict was an internal one, which did not come to a head until the very end of the period. Kao-tsu had eliminated all his important feudal kings except those of his own family, so that during this period there were no revolts, such as had plagued him. Peace was made with the only important external enemy, the Huns, and it was cemented by sending a girl of the imperial family to be a bride of the Hun emperor, the *Shan-yu*. There was only one war—with the state of Nan-yueh, located at the present Canton; but the mountains proved such a barrier that the war was confined to border forays, and the Chinese generals did not even try to cross the mountains. Thus the people secured a rest, the population could increase, and the country became prosperous.

The Chancellor of State, Hsiao Ho, who had administered Kao-tsu's empire, died in the second year of this period. He [had] nominated Kao-tsu's greatest fighter, Ts'ao Ts'an, as his successor, thus emphasizing the tradition that since the empire had been conquered by Kao-tsu's personal followers, it should be ruled by them. This tradition was followed as long as any capable followers of Kao-tsu remained alive and was the factor that prevented the overturn of the state.

Liu Ying, known as Emperor Hsiao-hui, proved a kindly but weak young man. He was only in his sixteenth year when he came to the throne, and the real power went to his mother, then entitled the Empress Dowager *nee* Lu. She had taken an active part in the conquest of the empire, had suffered severely in that contest, and had gathered around her a faction, chiefly composed of members of the Lu family (including two of her older brothers who had been generals of Kao-tsu and had been ennobled by him as marquises) and of her relatives by marriage, especially the valiant Fan K'uai, who had married her younger sister, the able and determined Lu Hsu. This faction enabled the Empress Dowager to enthrone her son, although he was not the oldest nor the favorite son of Kao-tsu. The oldest son was Liu Fei, who had been made King of Ch'i, the most important part of the empire next to Kuanchung. But Liu Fei was not the son of Kao-tsu's wife, and so could be passed over.

Since the Empress Dowager had only barely succeeded in enthroning her son, she felt driven to cultivate the interests of the people in order to bolster up her power. Hence, although she committed grave crimes, she proved a good ruler. She could not afford the unpopularity of misrule and was too intelligent to indulge in it. She lightened the taxes and removed some of the severe punishments that had been inherited from the Ch'in [Qin] dynasty, repealing, for example, the Ch'in law against the possession of proscribed books. She allowed the commutation of punishments, even of capital punishment, for money payment, which, in those days of severe and harsh punishments, was a lightening of penalties rather than an invitation to the wealthy to commit crime. The most serious crimes were not commuted.

But she came into conflict with her son the Emperor when she attempted to take vengeance upon her rival. She imprisoned closely in the Palace the favorites of her husband, especially the Lady *nee* Ch'i, who had almost succeeded in displacing her as Empress. The Empress Dowager wanted a keener revenge, but dared do nothing more as long as the Lady's son was alive. This ten-year-old boy, Liu Ju-yi, Kao-tsu's favorite child, had been made King of Chao with a capable and brave Chancellor to guard him. When this Chancellor would not send the boy to the capital, the Empress Dowager removed the Chancellor and had the boy brought. But he was a favorite of the Emperor too, so the sixteen year old Emperor met his half-brother at a village ten miles from the capital and carefully conducted him to his own apartments, where he guarded him by always keeping him by his side. After several months, one morning early the Emperor went out hunting, leaving Ju-yi sleeping. The Empress Dowager immediately had her step-son poisoned. The Emperor could do nothing to his own mother, not even for murder.

Then the Empress Dowager had the dead boy's mother, the Lady *nee* Ch'i, terribly mutilated and thrown out into the gully through which ran the sewer, naming her "the Human Swine." She took her son to see her mutilated rival; he did not recognize the poor lady; when an attendant informed him of her identity, the Emperor wept himself into a nervous breakdown. For a year he could not leave his bed. When he recovered, he sent this message to his mother: "Your deed was utterly inhuman. I am your son, so I cannot again govern the country." Then he gave himself over to drinking, to women, and to pleasure.

The next year Liu Fei came to court. At a family dinner the Emperor seated Fei above himself, as befitted the oldest brother. The Empress Dowager became angry and ordered two goblets of poisoned wine for Fei. Then she commanded him to drink a toast. But the Emperor took one of the goblets to drink; without a descendant on the throne the Empress Dowager would have been helpless; she hastily arose and upset her son's goblet. Then Fei took alarm and left. He feared for his life, but found that the Empress Dowager had merely acted in a fit of anger; so he made his peace with her by presenting her daughter, Kao-tsu's oldest child, the Princess Yuan of Lu, with a commandery and appointing this step-sister as his Queen Dowager.

Emperor Hui died in the seventh year of his rule. The Empress Dowager had married him to the daughter of Princess Yuan. Such a union was quite proper, since the girl had a surname different from that of her husband. But she had no child. The Emperor had however had a son by a lady of his harem; the Empress Dowager named this babe the son of the Empress and killed his mother. The babe was made Heir-apparent and was enthroned as Emperor. Since he was her grandson, and the Empress was her granddaughter, the Empress Dowager herself boldly took the Emperor's place in court and issued imperial decrees and edicts in her own name.

Then she strengthened her position by appointing four of her nephews from the Lu family as kings, and, to forestall trouble over the succession, if anything should happen to the babe, she took six babes of the Lu family and named them marquises, asserting that they were children of Emperor Hui.

This action brought her into conflict with one of the established practices of the dynasty, which was after her death to prove stronger than she. Kao-tsu had gathered his immediate followers and made them swear a solemn oath in a ceremony in which a white horse had been killed and the lips of each had been smeared with the blood. This oath was to the effect that no one except members of the imperial Liu family should be made king and no one should be made marquis except for deeds of valor. Kao-tsu had taken this step when he was plagued by the rebellions of those vassal kings not members of the imperial clan; but he had himself violated this oath in the appointment of his boyhood and close friend, Lu Wan, as King of Yen. The Empress Dowager's important officials had all been followers of Kao-tsu and had taken this oath; yet they respected her ability and recognized that she had materially assisted in winning the empire, so that she also was one of the followers of Kao-tsu; these facts and the power of the Lu faction kept the officials from making any overt move against her. The Senior Lieutenant Chancellor, Wang Ling, protested in private, but he was promoted to an advisory post which left him powerless. The Empress Dowager thus succeeded in establishing herself firmly in control. She had a committee of the high officials and nobles arrange the precedence of the nobles in the court, thus increasing the prestige of her faction.

In 184 B.C.E. the child emperor learned of his real mother. Boy-like he boasted, "The Empress could have killed my mother and pass[ed] me as her son. I am not yet grown up, but when I am grown up, I will change things." Such a threat to the Empress Dowager's power could not be tolerated; the child was pronounced insane, imprisoned to death in the palace prison, and the ministers were ordered to suggest his successor.

They knew that he was the only natural son of Emperor Hui; in seeming deference to the Empress Dowager but in real unwillingness to be a party to her action they replied merely that they accepted her orders. She then selected one of the six babes she had previously named as marquises and sons of Emperor Hui and appointed him Emperor. The ministers said nothing; this appointment was not their work; they consequently felt free to overturn it later.

In order to consolidate her power, the Empress Dowager had married some of Kao-tsu's sons to girls of her family, the Lu. One of them, Yu, did not love his wife and favored a concubine; he was slandered to the Empress Dowager as having said that after her death he would attack the Lu family. She summoned him to the capital and starved him to death in his lodgings. Another son, K'uei, was so oppressed by his wife, a Lu girl, who poisoned his beloved concubine, that he committed suicide. A third, Chien, died; the Empress Dowager sent to have his son killed and end his kingdom. There were left now only two out of the eight sons of Kao-tsu, only three of whom had died a natural death.

The Empress Dowager knew she could not live much longer; to perpetuate her clan's power she appointed her two nephews, Lu Ch'an and Lu Lu, the first as Chancellor of State, in charge of the civil government, and the second as First Ranking General, in charge of the military. To placate the Liu faction, she appointed its head, Liu Tse, a venerable cousin of Kao-tsu, as King of Lang-ya, and gave royal posthumous titles to Kao-tsu's mother, older brother, and older sister. Thus she prepared for the inevitable.

Pan Ku, *The History of the Former Han Dynasty*, vol. 2, trans. Homer H. Dubs (Baltimore: Waverly Press, 1938), 167–71.

Chinese rulers had many problems besides trying to prevent another family from taking over the government. The threat of military raids or invasions by the steppe horsemen of the north was often a serious concern. One frequent solution was to give expensive presents and a royal princess as a bride to the most powerful nomadic ruler. The Chinese bride gave the northern rulers an advantage in having access to someone who understood the Chinese imperial government. Gaodi (Kao-tsu) began the practice. Evidently the northerners valued the Chinese wives, as Empress Lu discovered when she received the following message from Mao-tun, the powerful leader of the Hsing-nu in 192 B.C.E.:

I am a lonely widowed ruler, born amidst the marshes and brought up on the wild steppes in the land of cattle and horses. I have often come to the border of China wishing to travel in China. Your majesty is also a widowed ruler living in a life of solitude. Both of us are without pleasures and lack any way to amuse ourselves. It is my hope that we can exchange that which we have for that which we are lacking.

Denis Twitchett and Michael Loewe, *The Cambridge History of China*, vol. 1, *The Ch'in and Han Empires, 221 B.C.–A.D. 220* (New York: Cambridge University Press, 1986), 387.

Empress Lu was furious. However, her advisors so impressed her with the danger of an invasion that her meek reply was a plea to spare her empire.

My age is advanced and my vitality is weakening. Both my hair and teeth are falling out, and I cannot even walk steadily. The *shan-yu* must have heard exaggerated reports. I am not worthy of his lowering himself. But my country has done nothing wrong, and I hope he will spare it.

Denis Twitchett and Michael Loewe, *The Cambridge History of China*, vol. 1, *The Ch'in and Han Empires, 221 B.C.–A.D. 220* (New York: Cambridge University Press, 1986), 387.

The Empress Dowager Lu died in 181 B.C.E. from a dog bite. Immediately, civil war broke out between Gaodi's Liu family and the Lu family. The whole Lu clan was massacred within six weeks.

6.2 Chinese Women as Pawns

The attractions of Chinese elite women were famous among China's northern foes. Their leaders kidnapped such women to be their concubines or wives. After the first great female Chinese poet, Tsai Yen, was kidnapped, she wrote a poem, "Eighteen Verses Sung to a Tatar Reed Whistle," that can still move us, even in translation.

I

I was born in a time of peace,
But later the mandate of Heaven
Was withdrawn from the Han Dynasty.

Heaven was pitiless.
It sent down confusion and separation.
Earth was pitiless.
It brought me to birth in such a time.
War was everywhere. Every road was dangerous.
Soldiers and civilians everywhere
Fleeing death and suffering.
Smoke and dust clouds obscured the land
Overrun by the ruthless Tatar bands.
Our people lost their will power and integrity.
I can never learn the ways of the barbarians.
I am daily subject to violence and insult.
I sing one stanza to my lute and a Tatar horn.
But no one knows my agony and grief.

II

A Tatar chief forced me to become his wife,
And took me far away to Heaven's edge.
Ten thousand clouds and mountains
Bar my road home,
And whirlwinds of dust and sand
Blow for a thousand miles.
Men here are as savage as giant vipers,
And strut about in armor, snapping their bows.
As I sing the second stanza I almost break the lutestrings.
Will broken, heart broken, I sing to myself.

VII

The sun sets. The wind moans.
The noise of the Tatar camp rises all around me.
The sorrow of my heart is beyond expression,
But who could I tell it to anyway?
Far across the desert plains,
The beacon fires of the Tatar garrisons
Gleam for ten thousand miles.
It is the custom here to kill the old and weak
And adore the young and vigorous.
They wander seeking new pasture,
And camp for a while behind earth walls.
Cattle and sheep cover the prairie,
Swarming like bees or ants.
When the grass and water are used up,
They mount their horses and drive on their cattle.
The seventh stanza sings of my wandering.
How I hate to live this way!

XI

I have no desire to live, but I am afraid of death.
I cannot kill my body, for my heart still has hope

That I can live long enough
To obtain one and only desire—
That someday I can see again
The mulberry and catalpa trees of home.
If I had consented to death,
My bones would have been buried long ago.
Days and months pile up in the Tatar camp.
My Tatar husband loved me. I bore him two sons.
I reared and nurtured them unashamed,
Sorry only that they grew up in a desert outpost.
The eleventh stanza—sorrow for my sons
At the first notes pierces my heart's core.

XIII

I never believed that in my broken life
The day would come when
Suddenly I could return home.
I embrace and caress my Tatar sons.
Tears wet our clothes.
An envoy from the Han Court
Has come to bring me back,
With four stallions that can run without stopping.
Who can measure the grief of my sons?
They thought I would live and die with them.
Now it is I who must depart.
Sorrow for my boys dims the sun for me.
If we had wings we could fly away together.
I cannot move my feet,
For each step is a step away from them.
My soul is overwhelmed.
As their figures vanish in the distance
Only my love remains.
The thirteenth stanza—
I pick the strings rapidly
But the melody is sad.
No one can know
The sorrow which tears my bowels.

XVII

The seventeenth stanza. My heart aches, my tears fall.
Mountain passes rise before us, the way is hard.
Before I missed my homeland
So much my heart was disordered.
Now I think again and again, over and over,
Of the sons I have lost.
The yellow sagebrush of the border,
The bare branches and dry leaves,
Desert battlefields, white bones
Scarred with swords and arrows,
Wind, frost, piercing cold,
Cold springs and summers
Men and horses hungry and exhausted, worn out—
I will never know them again
Once I have entered Chang An.
I try to strangle my sobs
But my tears stream down my face.

Kenneth Rexroth and Ling Chung, trans., *The Orchid Boat, Women Poets of China,*
4–7. © 1972 by Kenneth Rexroth and Ling Chung. Reprinted by permission of
New Directions Publishing Corp. World rights.

6.3 Princesses as Power Brokers

The marriage of a royal princess could be ordered for reasons of
foreign policy, but it could also be arranged to advance the
domestic policies of the government. Marriage to a royal princess
provided many benefits to powerful nondynastic families, especially if she had influence within the palace. A powerful emperor
could use a series of princess marriages to make alliances with
influential Chinese families, just as he might use princesses to
gain foreign allies.

Jennifer Holmgren describes some of the implications of these
domestic marriages, in which the princesses acted as power bro-
kers between the government and their husbands' families. She
explains that under the Chinese system princesses could receive

ranks and titles in their own right, rather than only through their
male relatives.

Ranks and titles conferred on a woman without reference to her
husband or son were to be treated as if granted to a man. In the case
of the princess, this condition was achieved by dispensing with the
general law that made married women liable for punishments meted
out to members of the husband's lineage. The princess's exemption
from this law meant that her status in no way depended on the position of her husband and his family. Rather, she retained her membership of the ruling line and was subject only to the throne. Because her
status was conferred without reference to her husband, it could pass
to her children. Thus, so long as they did not become wittingly involved in plots against the emperor, sororal cousins, nephews, and
nieces were, like their mothers, exempt from severe punishment.

The material wealth a princess brought into marriage symbolized
her condition. The lavish wedding gifts provided by the throne indicated the social and political superiority of her natal lineage over the
husband and his family; the fief and its accompanying stipend symbolized that marriage had not altered her status. If the marriage
lasted, most of the property eventually passed to the husband's family and out into the wider society through the woman's offspring, the
fief title going to her eldest son in accordance with the general law.
As befitting their elevated status as honorary members of the imperial line, the woman's sons received imperial patronage in selection
for high office. In this way, the sororal bond was transformed into an
arm of the ruling line, reaching out into the wider community and
establishing pockets of loyalty within other, potentially dangerous,
lineages without the threat of domination or usurpation.

Although the recipient lineage derived some comfort from the
knowledge that at least one of its branches was insulated from political disaster, the throne benefited more from the arrangement because
the princess could be counted on to put the imperial interest above
that of her husband's family. For the woman's part, her exemption
from severe punishment gave her a personal freedom denied to other
members of the society, including her brothers. Unlike male agnates,
who were perceived as a threat to the throne, the princess could
remain in the capital at the center of power. Moreover, being female,

she was not barred from the inner recesses of the palace as were the male officials of the outer court. Nor was she confined to the palace like an imperial mother or wife. In every respect, then, she was ideally placed to act as a power broker between the throne and families of the wider elite.

As a permanent member of the ruling line, the social status of the princess was higher than that of the imperial mother or wife. Indeed, her social position closely approximated that of the emperor himself. During the Southern Dynasties (A.D. 317–589), one woman used her exalted position to argue that, like her brother, the emperor, she too should have a harem. She was given thirty male "concubines." In short, although the princess never reached the political heights of an imperial mother or wife who acted as regent and de facto ruler of the state, and although her influence had no strong legal basis, her freedom of movement was considerable and her position solid. Because her status was not conditioned by ties beyond the throne, her influence depended on the accession of a strong ruler able to control his maternal relatives and to override any objections from the bureaucracy about her behavior. The tension between sisters and wives (princesses and empresses) at the imperial level was thus acute. Moreover, because all attention was directed toward a single male, competition among the princesses themselves was also intense—both among sisters and among different generations of female offspring. . . .

The political importance of the sororal bond for the throne meant that unmarried aunts, sisters, and daughters were always in short supply. Thus, those who were widowed (with or without children) usually remarried. If a recipient family fell from grace, the woman might well be summarily divorced and given to another lineage, young sons following her into the new alliance. Because a favorite sister was also well placed to obtain a divorce on grounds of incompatibility and because marital discord might itself bring political catastrophe to the lineage, it was not unusual for an imperial princess to become the de facto head of the husband's family, controlling its finances, organizing its marriages, and determining its political strategy. For this reason, some families tried to avoid a sororal relationship with the throne. The problem was not confined, however, to imperial relationships: any family interested in furthering its economic, political, or social condition through the upward marriage of a son chanced subordination to the wife and her kin.

Suggested Further Readings

An excellent collection of traditional stories that was frequently reprinted for the enlightenment of women is *The Position of Women in Early China, According to the Lieh Nu Chuan: "The Biographies of Eminent Chinese Women,"* translated by Albert Richard O'Hara (Washington: Catholic University of America Press, 1945). Different editors added comments that were appropriate for their readers, but this version is one of the earliest. A complement to the material in the last reading is Jennifer Holmgren, "The Harem in Northern Wei Politics—398–498 A.D.: A Study of T'o-pa Attitudes Towards the Institution of Empress, Empress-Dowager, and Regency Government in the Chinese Dynastic System During Early Northern Wei," *Journal of the Economic and Social History of The Orient* 26 (February 1983): 71–96. The following are also useful: Richard W. Guisso, "Thunder over the Lake: The Five Classics and the Perception of Women in Early China," *Historical Reflections/Reflexions Historiques* 8 (Fall 1981): 47–62; Donald Harper, "The Sexual Arts of Ancient China as Described in a Manuscript of the Second Century B.C.," *Harvard Journal of Asiatic Studies* 47, no. 2 (1987): 539–94.

–7–

WOMEN IN THE LATE ROMAN REPUBLIC

Independence, Divorce, and Serial Marriages

A woman playing a cithara in a Roman wall painting from the first century B.C.E. (The Metropolitan Museum of Art, Rogers Fund, 1903.)

As a republic, the city-state of Rome conquered adjacent territories on the Italian peninsula and then mastered its rival Carthage to gain control of the Mediterranean in 146 B.C.E. For the next 600 years Rome was the dominant power in the region, drawing wealth from all the Mediterranean borderlands into its treasury. The empire affected gender: as Roman soldiers fought in distant lands and generals conspired to control the state, their wives and daughters gained rights to control their own lives.

Politically the late republic period, 133–43 B.C.E., was focused on the transition of the Roman government from a republic to a monarchy. By this time, Rome's conquests had made its upper classes very wealthy, including wives and children. Marriage practices still remained more appropriate to the early period of the republic when every citizen farmed his own land. Then the women were completely dependent on the men, and a father could kill his children without fear of legal action. Roman women were almost as subordinate and dependent as those in classical Athens. They did not speak in public meetings. They could not buy and sell property without their male relatives' approval. Legally treated as minors, they were first the responsibility of their fathers, then of their husbands, and finally of appointed guardians.

But as the Romans became wealthy, their women were given property. Slowly customary practices changed, although the laws were little modified. Women in the late republic seemed to avoid the legal restraints that so confined their distant ancestors. Of course, marriages were not made for companionship but for personal advantage. Cicero's marriage (77–43 B.C.E.) to Terentia clearly was such a union. But as the advantageous marriages of his contemporary Pompey illustrate, divorce had become very easy. In Rome it was a time of shifting political alliances, with the losers often losing their wealth and lives. Cicero's career and its impact on his family is a tragic example.

7.1 Letters from Cicero to His Wife, Terentia

Illustrating Roman women's lives is difficult, because almost nothing written by a woman has survived, even though many were literate. Two well-known women were Cicero's wife, Terentia, and their daughter, Tullia. Terentia probably married Cicero in 77 B.C.E., and their daughter was born the next year.

Although not from the aristocracy, Terentia's family was wealthy, and her dowry was large enough to qualify her husband as a knight, the second rank of the aristocracy.

Initially Cicero won unusual political success as a consul and an acknowledged leader of the Senate, but in his lifetime Roman politics frequently degenerated into violent factional struggles. An enemy, Clodius, was elected as one of the tribunes, or magistrates, and used his position to attack Cicero by introducing bills to make him an outlaw, confiscate his property, and destroy his houses. Cicero fled Italy, leaving his family behind in Rome. The first letter from Cicero is dated April 29, 58 B.C.E. None of Terentia's letters have survived.

I set out from Brundisium on April 29th. I am making for Cyzicus through Macedonia. Ruined, alas, and prostrate as I am, why should I now ask you to come here, you, an invalid lady, exhausted in body and mind? Should I not ask you? Am I then to be without you? This, I think, is what I shall plead—if there is any hope of my return, encourage it and assist the matter; but if, as I fear, it is over and done with, make every effort to come here in any way you can. This one thing I would have you know—if I have you, I shall not think I am absolutely lost. But what will become of my dearest Tullia? It is now for you to see to that; I have no suggestions to make. But in any case, however matters turn out, we must do all we can for that poor damsel's matrimonial settlement and reputation. Again, what will my boy Cicero do? *He* I hope may always be in my bosom and between my arms. I cannot now write more; grief stays my pen. How you have fared I know not—whether you retain anything or have been, as I fear, utterly despoiled.

Piso [Tullia's husband] will, as you write, always, I hope, be our friend. As to the liberation of the slaves, there is nothing to upset you. In the first place yours have been promised that you will act as each of them severally deserves. Orpheus so far is doing his duty, nobody else in any marked degree. As regards the other slaves the arrangement is this: that if my estate passed out of my hands they were to be my freedmen, provided they could make good this claim; but if the estate still remains in my hands, that they should continue to be my slaves with the exception of an extremely small number.

Reprinted by permission of the publishers and the Loeb Classical Library from Cicero: *Cicero: The Letters to His Friends,* trans. W. Glynn Williams, Cambridge, MA: Harvard University Press, 1960, 197–9.

When Cicero wrote the above letter, he did not know what had happened to his family, but true to his character he feared the worst—poverty. Wallowing in self-pity, he nevertheless was able to order Terentia to gather political support for his return. Even though he feared the confiscation of his slaves and real property, he urged Terentia to try to pay Tullia's husband what was owed on her dowry. Finally, he authorized Terentia to manumit, if it became necessary, those of the family slaves who might be confiscated with his estate and sold. It is worth noting that at this time Roman women legally were not supposed to be able to conduct business without the approval of a male: father, husband, or a guardian.

Five months later, Cicero wrote the second surviving letter in this correspondence. He had learned that Clodius had been able to pass only an act for exile. His fashionable Roman house and two villas had been looted and torn down. Terentia took refuge with her half-sister, who was a vestal virgin, a state priestess. His October 5th letter includes the following:

I gather that you have hopes of the new tribunes of the plebs. On that we may rely, if we can rely on Pompey's friendliness; and yet I have my fears of Crassus. As for yourself, I see that you are acting in every respect most courageously and lovingly, nor does it surprise me; but what saddens me is the nature of a calamity in which my own miseries can only be alleviated at the cost of such miseries for you. For that most obliging of men, P. Valerius, had described in a letter to me (and I wept bitterly as I read it) how you were haled from the temple of Vesta to the Valerian Office. Alas, light of my life, for whom I yearn, to whom all used to look for help, to think that now, Terentia mine, you are thus harassed, thus laid low in tears and unseemly humiliation! And to think it is all my fault, who have saved others to perish myself!

As to what you write about our house, or rather its site, I assure you that I shall never feel myself fully restored until that has been restored to me. These things however are not in our hands. What distresses me is, that whatever expenditure has to be incurred, you, in your unhappy and impoverished circumstances, should be let in for part of it. Of course, if the business of my restoration is carried through, we shall get all we want; but if we are to be dogged by the same ill-fortune as heretofore, will you, my poor wife, throw away the little that is left to you? I implore you, my darling, as far as expense is concerned, let others, who can if they only will, bear the burden, and do not, as you love me, tax that indifferent health of yours. Day and night you are ever before my eyes. I see you taking upon yourself all our troubles, and I fear it is too much for you. But I also see that everything depends upon you: and for that reason, in order that we may succeed in what you are hoping and striving for, obey the dictates of health.

Reprinted by permission of the publishers and the Loeb Classical Library from Cicero: *Cicero: The Letters to His Friends,* trans. W. Glynn Williams, Cambridge, MA: Harvard University Press, 1960, 187–90.

The new tribunes were willing to recall Cicero, but Clodius's gangs were beating those who tried to help Cicero. Finally rival gangs were organized to control Clodius's thugs, and Cicero returned in August 57 B.C.E. Terentia had sold some of her own houses to raise money, without telling Cicero what she was going to do.

Cicero and Terentia then prospered for nine years before his good fortune again began to wane. In 49 B.C.E., when Caesar and Pompey began a civil war to control the empire, Caesar's armies threatened Rome. Cicero, an ally of Pompey, was concerned for Terentia's safety in a letter written to her on June 11th:

As for yourself, I would have you, first of all, take care of your health; in the next place, if it so please you, you will make use of those villas which are farthest away from men-in-arms.

Reprinted by permission of the publishers and the Loeb Classical Library from Cicero: *Cicero: The Letters to His Friends,* trans. W. Glynn Williams, Cambridge, MA: Harvard University Press, 1960, 205.

In 46 B.C.E. Cicero divorced Terentia, accusing her of dishonesty among other charges, all of which she denied. One year later his beloved daughter Tullia died in childbirth. His political downfall was imminent. The triumvirate formed after the assassination of Caesar was composed of Octavian; Lepidus; and Cicero's arch enemy, Antony, who was married to Clodius's widow Fulvia. In their proscription of 43 B.C.E., Cicero was declared an outlaw, killed, and his head given to Antony. Fulvia mutilated it, cutting the tongue, before Antony displayed the mutilated head to the Senate.

7.2 The Proscription of 43 B.C.E.

The proscription of 43 B.C.E. that led to Cicero's death listed many of Rome's aristocratic and wealthy families. Appian, in *The Civil Wars*, describes the awful events:

As soon as the triumvirs were by themselves they joined in making a list of those who were to be put to death. They put on the list those whom they suspected because of their power, and also their personal enemies. . . . For they made additions to the catalogue from time to time, in some cases on the ground of enmity, in others for a grudge merely, or because the victims were friends of their enemies or enemies of their friends, or on account of their wealth, for the triumvirs needed a great deal of money to carry on the war. . . . The triumvirs were short of money because Europe, and especially Italy, was exhausted by wars and exactions. . . . By now, too, some were proscribed because they had handsome villas or city residences. The number of senators who were sentenced to death and confiscated was about 300, and of the knights about 2000.

It was ordered that the heads of all the victims should be brought to the triumvirs at a fixed reward, which to a free person was payable in money and to a slave in both money and freedom.

Reprinted by permission of the publisher and the Loeb Classical Library from Appian: *Appian's Roman History*, trans. Horace White, Cambridge, MA: Harvard University Press, 1961, 147–9, 151–3.

Some of the proscribed were betrayed by their wives, sons, daughters, brothers, slaves, or others. Some of the proscribed were protected by their relatives, slaves, or friends. Appian includes more stories of faithful wives than of unfaithful ones:

Acilius fled from the city secretly. His hiding-place was disclosed by a slave to the soldiers, but he prevailed upon them, by the hope of a larger reward, to send some of their number to his wife with a private token that he gave them. When they came she gave them all of her jewelery, saying that she gave it in return for what they had promised, although she did not know whether they would keep their agreement. But her fidelity to her husband was not disappointed, for the soldiers hired a ship for Acilius and saw him off to Sicily. . . .

The wife of Apuleius threatened that if he should fly without her, she would give information against him. So he took her with him unwillingly, and he succeeded in avoiding suspicion in his flight by travelling with his wife and his male and female slaves in a public manner. . . . The wife of Rheginus concealed him by night in a sewer, into which the soldiers were not willing to enter in the daytime, on account of the foul odour. The next night she disguised him as a charcoal dealer, and furnished him an ass to drive, carrying coals. She led the way at a short distance, borne in a litter. One of the soldiers at the city gates suspected the litter and searched it. Rheginus was alarmed and hastened his steps, and as if he were a passer-by admonished the soldier not to give trouble to women. The latter, who took him for a charcoal dealer, answered him angrily, but suddenly recognizing him (for he had served under him in Syria), said, "Go on your way rejoicing, general for such I ought still to call you."

. . . Other women betrayed their husbands infamously. Among these was the wife of Septimius who had an amour with a certain friend of Antony. Being impatient to exchange this illicit connection for matrimony, she besought Antony through her paramour to rid her of her husband. Septimius was at once put on the list of the proscribed. When he learned this, in ignorance of this domestic treachery he fled to his wife's house. She, as though with loving anxiety, closed the doors, and kept him until the murderers came. The same day that her husband was killed she celebrated her new nuptials.

Reprinted by permission of the publisher and the Loeb Classical Library from Appian: *Appian's Roman History,* trans. Horace White, Cambridge, MA: Harvard University Press, 1961, 205–9, 179.

7.3 Hortensia's Speech

After they sold the property and goods of the proscribed, the triumvirs were still short of the cash they needed for their armies. So they proposed an extraordinary tax on wealthy women. The women's response was a famous speech by Hortensia in which she describes women's wealth and indirect political power. Note for later reference the types of property that women owned. Continuing Appian's narrative:

The triumvirs addressed the people on this subject and published an edict requiring 1,400 of the richest women to make a valuation of their property, and to furnish for the service of the war such portion as the triumvirs should require of each. It was provided further that if any should conceal their property or make a false valuation they should be fined, and that rewards should be given to informers, whether free persons or slaves. The women resolved to beseech the womenfolk of the triumvirs. With the sister of Octavian and the mother of Antony they did not fail, but they were repulsed from the doors of Fulvia, the wife of Antony, whose rudeness they could scarce endure. They then forced their way to the tribunal of the triumvirs in the forum, the people and the guards dividing to let them pass. There, through the mouth of Hortensia, whom they had selected to speak, they spoke as follows:

"As befitted women of our rank addressing a petition to you, we had recourse to the ladies of your households; but having been treated as did not befit us, at the hands of Fulvia, we have been driven by her to the forum. You have already deprived us of our fathers, our sons, our husbands, and our brothers, whom you accused of having wronged you; if you take away our property also, you reduce us to a condition unbecoming our birth, our manners, our sex. If we have done you wrong, as you say our husbands have, proscribe us as you do them. But if we women have not voted any of you public enemies, have not torn down your houses, destroyed your army, or led another one against you; if we have not hindered you in obtaining offices and honours,—why do we share the penalty when we did not share the guilt?

"Why should we pay taxes when we have no part in the honours, the commands, the state-craft, for which you contend against each other with such harmful results? 'Because this is a time of war,' do you say? When have there not been wars, and when have taxes ever been imposed on women, who are exempted by their sex among all mankind? Our mothers did once rise superior to their sex and made contributions when you were in danger of losing the whole empire and the city itself through the conflict with the Carthaginians. But then they contributed voluntarily, not from their landed property, their fields, their dowries, or their houses, without which life is not possible to free women, but only from their own jewelery, and even then not according to fixed valuation, not under fear of informers or accusers, not by force and violence, but what they themselves were willing to give. What alarm is there now for the empire or the country? Let war with the Gauls or the Parthians come, and we shall not be inferior to our mothers in zeal for the common safety; but for civil wars may we never contribute, nor ever assist you against each other! We did not contribute to Caesar or to Pompey. Neither Marius nor Cinna imposed taxes upon us. Nor did Sulla, who held despotic power in the state, do so, whereas you say that you are re-establishing the commonwealth."

While Hortensia thus spoke the triumvirs were angry that women should dare to hold a public meeting when the men were silent; that they should demand from magistrates the reasons for their acts, and themselves not so much as furnish money while the men were serving in the army. They ordered the lictors to drive them away from the tribunal, which they proceeded to do until cries were raised by the multitude outside, when the lictors desisted and the triumvirs said they would postpone till the next day the consideration of the matter. On the following day they reduced the number of women who were to present a valuation of the their property from 1,400 to 400, and decreed that all men who possessed more than 100,000 drachmas, both citizens and strangers, freedmen and priests, and men of all nationalities without a single exception, should (under the same dread of penalty and also of informers) lend them at interest a fiftieth part of their property and contribute one year's income to the war expenses.

Reprinted by permission of the publisher and the Loeb Classical Library from Appian: *Appian's Roman History,* trans. Horace White, Cambridge, MA: Harvard University Press, 1961, 195–9.

Hortensia's speech is a valuable statement, in which she argues that women did not publicly participate in politics and hence were personally immune to political attacks. That helps explain why Terentia did not accompany Cicero on his first exile. She may have been in poor health as he suggests, but she was not in physical danger and her property was safe, according to Hortensia. Since she was immune from political attack, she could lead the political campaign to restore Cicero's property and reputation. However, the most important reason for her leadership was that she had the political knowledge, ability, and contacts to carry the campaign to its successful end. Nevertheless, Cicero could abandon her when it was convenient.

7.4 The Roman Family

Hortensia listed considerable property owned by the proscribed women. It included farms, houses, slaves, cash, and jewelry. Legally Roman women could not buy and sell, and yet Terentia sold some of her houses without Cicero's approval or knowledge. Recent research indicates that patriarchal control was not as universal as once thought and that, by Cicero's lifetime, adult Roman women were often independent of male control. The argument depends on the demographic fact of the short life-spans of men and women in the ancient world. Susan Treggiari explains how married women were affected:

Originally it seems to have been the norm for a bride to enter into the control of her husband. This control, *manus*, was theoretically separate from marriage, but normally synchronous with it. It must be viewed together with the father's power, *patria potestas*, which later jurists saw as characteristic of Romans. Paternal power was held by the oldest male ascendent in a family, the *paterfamilias*. It gave him power of life and death over his legitimate children, his *filiifamilias*, and full rights over property, including anything they might acquire. Daughters were removed from the father's power when he gave them in marriage into the control of a husband. If sons in power [of the *paterfamilias*] married and had children, these grandchildren were also in the grandfather's power. So were the son's wives if they came in *manum*. . . . When the *paterfamilias* died, both sons and daughters in power became independent. Each son became a *paterfamilias*, whatever his age, with power over his own children if he had any. Daughters were not controlled by their brothers or mothers. [Surviving] women throughout their lives and children below puberty had to have a guardian [for certain legal actions] if they were independent.

During a transitional period of Roman law which is hardly documented in our sources, there was a trend away from the custom that the bride entered *manus* on marriage to the norm that she did not. This left married women usually in the power of their fathers as long as the latter lived. But, given ancient expectation of life, it is probable that many women were fatherless for a relatively long period of their married lives. The pattern . . . for the middle ranks of Roman society is that girls married in their late teens and men in their mid- to late twenties. If expectation of life at birth is put between twenty and thirty, then 46 per cent of fifteen-year-olds had no father left alive. The percentage grows to 59 per cent of twenty-year-olds and 70 per cent of twenty-five-year-olds. So there is about a 50-per-cent chance that a woman was already fatherless at the time of her first marriage.

Susan Treggiari, "Divorce Roman Style: How Easy and How Frequent Was It?" © The Australian National University 1991. Reprinted from *Marriage, Divorce, and Children in Ancient Rome*, 31–2, edited by Beryl Rawson (1991), by permission of Oxford University Press.

Marriage and divorce were free, that is, they depended mainly on the voluntary choice of husband and wife. As Susan Treggiari continues:

The essential characteristic of Roman marriage was the consent of each partner. (If there was a *paterfamilias*, his consent at the initiation of the marriage was also required: for a daughter his consent might be assumed unless he evidently dissented.) Consent was signified at the beginning of a marriage. There was no prescribed form of words or action or written contract which had to be used at all weddings. Nor did any priest or public official act as president or witness of a ceremony. . . . Various ritual phrases may have been used and there was often a celebration and written documents which accompanied the dowry and which provided circumstantial evidence that a marriage was intended. But the point is that all depended on the couple (and any *paterfamilias,* but in the classical period he could not act alone). The continuance of the marriage, once they had entered upon it, depended upon their continued will to be married. . . .

If the initiation and continuance of a marriage depended on the consent, explicit or implied, of both spouses (and of any extant *paterfamilias* of either of them), then it follows logically that divorce may be produced by the withdrawal of that consent by one of the parties, or perhaps we should say, more positively, by the decision of one party not to retain the relation.

Susan Treggiari, "Divorce Roman Style: How Easy and How Frequent Was It?" © The Australian National University 1991. Reprinted from *Marriage, Divorce, and Children in Ancient Rome,* 32–4, edited by Beryl Rawson (1991), by permission of Oxford University Press.

Normally a husband or wife would use a verbal formula such as "take your things for yourself" to end the marriage. In one case a divorce was declared by the court when a man married a second wife without notifying the first. The court argued he had withdrawn his consent when he married the second woman. Of course a woman could also withdraw her consent, although men divorced women much more frequently than women divorced men.

When a couple divorced, the husband had to return the wife's dowry, which in the case of Terentia was large and which Cicero had used for thirty years. If the wife was divorced for adultery or other serious misbehavior, she might forfeit one-sixth of her dowry. If the wife had not become pregnant in a reasonable time, she could be divorced by her husband. If a husband was divorced for "matrimonial offenses," he had to repay the dowry at once or within six months. However, he was almost always awarded custody of the children.

As they considered possible marriage partners, most Romans did not expect to be in love at the time of their marriage. Though some married couples fell in love after the ceremony, still, romantic love was not expected in a marriage partner.

Since marriage was not a romantic commitment but had a familial, business, or political aspect, ambitious Romans, such as Cicero's ally Pompey, could marry and divorce several times as their careers progressed. Cicero's daughter was very eligible for marriage with ambitious men, since her father was politically influential, and she was married three times. Among Romans who had serial marriages, families became complex, especially from the wife's perspective. The children of a divorced woman lived with their father; furthermore, if she married again, her new husband might bring stepchildren into the marriage. K.R. Bradley described relationships resulting from Pompey's marriages.

Pompey's first wife, Antistia, was the daughter of the Antistius who presided in 86 [B.C.E.] at Pompey's trial for *perculatus* (embezzlement). During the trial Antistius is said to have been so impressed by the defendant that he offered Pompey his daughter in marriage. A betrothal was arranged, and a few days after Pompey's acquittal the marriage was celebrated. Antistia, it can be supposed, was several years younger than her husband, who was just about nineteen and marrying for the first time. But as far as is known there was no issue from the marriage, which after only four years came to an end. The reason was that in 82 Sulla, in a deliberate act of political calculation, pressured Pompey into an alliance with him by encouraging the young man to divorce Antistia and to marry instead Sulla's stepdaughter, Aemilia. Pompey obliged. But the situation was hampered by the fact that Aemilia already had a husband, M'. Acilius Glabrio, consul in 67, and indeed was in the late stages of a pregnancy. Yet her divorce too was quickly arranged, the marriage to Pompey effected, and Aemilia's presence in a new household established. It happened that the new marriage was very brief, for Aemilia died giving birth to her child (M'. Acilius Glabrio) so again Pompey was still without a child of his own. Technically, however, he did become a stepfather in 82, though contact between Pompey and the infant Glabrio was probably negligible: although born in Pompey's house the child was presumably transferred to his father's house to be reared.

From c. 80 until the end of 62 Pompey was married to Mucia, the daughter of a Metella and the half-sister of the Metelli [brothers] who were consuls in 69 and 68. There is no explicit testimony to prove that the match was politically contrived, but in view of Mucia's Metellan connections it can hardly have been otherwise. The marriage produced three children, Cn. Pompeius, Pompeia and Sex. Pompeius, all of whom were probably born in the early years of the union. In 77 Pompey was away on campaign and wintered with his army in Cisalpina before moving in 76 to Spain, where he remained occupied with the war against Q. Sertorius until 71. The amount of time he spent with his young children cannot therefore have been great. Whether the children had any association with their step-brother Glabrio is unknown, but the point of the indirect familial relationship is to be noted.

Returning to Rome in 62 from his great eastern expeditions, Pompey promptly divorced Mucia, allegedly for her infidelities during his absence. The marriage lasted for eighteen years or so and in Roman terms had been successful: children had been produced. But for most of the time the principals had been separated by the demands of Pompey's career. In due course Mucia became the wife of M. Aemilius Scarus (once briefly Pompey's brother-in-law) and bore him a son. Pompey thus acquired a second stepson, his children a half-brother considerably younger than themselves and one who belonged, though related to them, to a different household.

In yet another politically motivated move, Pompey in 59 next married Julia, Caesar's daughter, the marriage at once requiring cancellation of Julia's impending union with Q. Seruilius Caepio and making her stepmother of Pompey's children. Yet it happened that she was of their generation, being practically coeval with Sex. Pompeius and so about sixteen when she married a husband thirty years her senior. Despite the difference in age, the marriage is said to have been passionate on both sides, and in the five years it lasted Julia became pregnant twice. The first pregnancy terminated in a miscarriage due to Julia's belief that Pompey had been killed in a bout of urban violence; and the second concluded with Julia dying in childbirth, her daughter surviving only a few days. Had she lived the child would have been much of an age with Pompey's grandchildren. . . .

Like Julia, Pompey's last wife, Cornelia, daughter of Pompey's colleague in the consulship of 52, was much younger than her husband and the criticism was made when they married, in 52, that she would have been a more suitable bride for one of Pompey's sons. As it was she became a second coeval stepmother to Pompey's children. The marriage lasted until 48 when Cornelia became a widow for the second time . . . but as far as is known it did not produce any new children for Pompey, who at the time of his death was almost fifty-nine.

K.R. Bradley, "Remarriage and the Structure of the Upper-Class Roman Family." © The Australian National University 1991. Reprinted from *Marriage, Divorce, and Children in Ancient Rome*, 91–3, edited by Beryl Rawson (1991) by permission of Oxford University Press.

Why did Roman women agree to these often hasty marriages planned by their fathers or brothers? Though men made the arrangements, brides agreed to cooperate. Many Roman women accepted a daughter's obligation to promote her family's political fortunes. Others were personally ambitious and, without prospects of their own careers, sought prominence in marrying famous men.

Suggested Further Readings

The original documents in Mary R. Lefkowitz and Maureen B. Fant, *Women's Life in Greece and Rome* (Baltimore: Johns Hopkins University Press, 1982) illustrate most of the important points of the known history of women in Rome. The basic book for an introduction to the topic is Sarah B. Pomeroy, *Goddesses, Whores, Wives, and Slaves: Women in Classical Antiquity* (New York: Schocken Books, 1975). Pomeroy's book was the first to introduce Roman women to the modern reader. Another excellent source is *Pandora's Daughters* (Baltimore: Johns Hopkins University Press, 1987) by Eva Cantarella. *Women in Roman Law & Society* (Bloomington: Indiana University Press, 1986), by Jane F. Gardner, thoroughly discusses the evolution of the application of the laws affecting women. Beryl Rawson has edited two comprehensive collections of essays on various topics: *The Family in Ancient Rome* (Ithaca, NY: Cornell University Press, 1986) and *Marriage, Divorce and Children in Ancient Rome* (New York: Oxford University Press, 1991). Under the Republic only landowners could be soldiers, and, since the wars were long and frequent, the impact on women and children was great. John K. Evans, in *War, Women and Children in Ancient Rome* (New York: Routledge, 1991), examines this interesting topic. *Fathers and Daughters in Roman Society, Women and the Elite Family*

(Princeton: Princeton University Press, 1984), by Judith P. Hallett, examines paternalism's impact on women's lives. For those interested in Byzantine elite society, Kenneth G. Holum's *Theodosian Empresses: Women and Imperial Dominion in Late Antiquity* (Berkeley: University of California Press, 1982) explores the political role played by Christian empresses in the eastern part of the Roman empire.

–8–

WESTERN EUROPE
Christian Women on Manors, in Convents, and in Towns

The writer Christine de Pisan (ca. 1365–1430). Widowed when young, she decided to support herself by writing. (The Bettmann Archive.)

As Rome's imperial center moved eastward to Constantinople in the fourth century C.E. and the Roman grasp on western Europe weakened, then collapsed in the wake of Germanic invasions of the fifth century, a new civilization gradually arose.

Western European cultural unity developed from diverse sources, often forcibly blended by conquest: the legacy of the Mediterranean, the new Germanic peoples invading from the East, older indigenous peoples such as the Celts and Vikings, and the developing Christian religion. Each of these traditions had a distinctive view of women. Tracing the impact of cultural transformation on free and bonded women that took place between 400 and 1500 C.E., a period of over 1,000 years, has generated a voluminous literature. The women of this chapter are representative of their times within the long medieval era.

8.1 Christianity's Dual Vision of Women

Christianity was a dominant force in the lives of most of these women. Jesus was surrounded by women as well as male disciples when he taught in the Roman province of Palestine, and it was to his female followers that the angel announced, "He has risen!" As the early Christian religion spread along the shores of the Mediterranean, women became teachers, prophetesses, missionaries, and martyrs. A rare fragment dictated from prison in North Africa by Vibia Perpetua imparts the emotional power of being a Christian under Roman persecution. The twenty-two-year-old recent mother refused her father's urging to renounce her faith and save her life. Perpetua describes the horror of the crowded Carthage dungeon, her fears for the health and future of her nursing baby, and finally her visions of her struggle toward redemption. In her last vision, she became a gladiator fighting in the arena of a vast amphitheater:

I was undressed and . . . my supporters began rubbing me with oil. . . . I saw the Egyptian rolling in the sand in front of me. . . .

The adversaries approached one another and began to exchange blows. The Egyptian tried to grab my feet. I kicked at his face with my heels. All at once I was lifted up into the air, and I could land my blows without touching the ground. Finally, to hasten the end, I knitted together the fingers of both hands, grabbed the Egyptian's head, fell upon his face, and with a kick of the heel smashed his head. The crowd cheered. . . . I approached the master gladiator and accepted the branch [of victory]. He kissed me and said, "My daughter, peace be with you." Triumphant, I headed for the Gate of the Living.

Pauline Schmitt Pantel, ed., *A History of Women in the West,* vol. 1, *From Ancient Goddesses to Christian Saints* (Cambridge: Harvard University Press, 1992), 476–7.

In reality, Perpetua did not survive the arena; she, a slave woman named Felicity, and a number of male Christians were executed in 203 C.E. As a martyr, Saint Perpetua was honored by the church. For women, scores of female saints and the Virgin Mary offered a feminine vision of Christianity in religious institutions dominated by the church fathers.

When persecution of Christians ended in the Roman empire in 312 C.E., Christianity's institutional hierarchy was firmly in the hands of men, who were pope and patriarchs, bishops and priests. Yet, like Buddhism, Christianity promised spiritual equality to women and men. In the letters of Paul, amplifying the teachings of the Gospels for early Christians, this is stated:

For in Christ Jesus you are all sons of God, through faith. . . . There is neither Jew nor Greek, there is neither slave nor free, there is neither male nor female; for you are all one in Christ Jesus.

Galatians 3:26–8, Holy Bible, Revised Standard Version.

As Paul corresponded with scattered congregations, answering their queries about how Christians should live, his statements of spiritual equality appear less frequently than those about submission to the social order of the world. Verses in several New Testament epistles rephrase the same prescription:

Wives, be subject to your husbands, as is fitting in the Lord. Husbands, love your wives, and do not be harsh with them. Children, obey your parents in everything, for this pleases the Lord. Fathers, do not provoke your children, lest they become discouraged. Slaves,

obey in everything those who are your earthly masters, not with
eyeservice, as men-pleasers, but in singleness of heart, fearing the
Lord.

Colossians 3:18–22, Holy Bible, Revised Standard Version. Also see Ephesians
5:21–31 or Titus 2:2–7.

Despite his naming outstanding Christian women—Phoebe, Pris-
cilla, Apphia, Lydia, Damaris, Persis—who were his "helpers,"
Paul denied them a public role in worship.

As in all the churches of the saints, the women should keep silence in
the churches. For they are not permitted to speak, but should be
subordinate, as even the law says. If there is anything they desire to
know, let them ask their husbands at home. For it is shameful for a
woman to speak in church.

1 Corinthians 4:33–5, Holy Bible, Revised Standard Version.

I desire then that in every place the men should pray, lifting holy
hands without anger or quarreling; also that women should adorn
themselves modestly and sensibly in seemly apparel, not with braided
hair or gold or pearls or costly attire but by good deeds, as befits
women who profess religion. Let a woman learn in silence with all
submissiveness. I permit no woman to teach or to have authority over
men; she is to keep silent. For Adam was formed first, then Eve; and
Adam was not deceived, but the woman was deceived and became a
transgressor. Yet woman will be saved through bearing children, if
she continues in faith and love and holiness, with modesty.

1 Timothy 2:8–15, Holy Bible, Revised Standard Version.

The issues raised by women within the first-generation Christian
communities would recur in medieval Europe, as they do still in
the twentieth century.

8.2 Conversion of the Franks

Clovis, king of the Franks, was converted to Christianity in 496 C.E., in part through the influence of his Christian wife, Clotild. At that time all the Franks were baptized, but the church had few priests or local churches within the nation. Ever since the Emperor Constantine in the fourth century C.E. had legitimized Christianity in the Roman Empire, missionaries had sought to establish the church in pagan territories by decree of the converted ruler, rather than by the tedious process of convincing the mass of subject peoples. And just as Helena, Constantine's mother, had introduced Christianity to the Roman Court, aristocratic women were often the first Frankish Christians. Clotild and her noblewomen were relied on for more than their influence on their families. Their patronage was essential to extending the church and to actually spreading Christian doctrines among the people.

The appeal of Christianity to women caught in the warfare endemic to Germanic expansion in northern Europe is evident in the story of Radegund, born in the second generation of Frankish Christians. It was a violent period, in which life-spans were shortened by disease, war, assassination, and poisoning. The impact of violence on women is illustrated by the experiences of Radegund (ca. 525–587 C.E.) and Clothar, a son of Clovis and Clotild. Radegund was a Thuringian princess, whose father was murdered by her uncle. When Radegund's uncle viciously murdered a number of Frankish women and children, war broke out. The Thuringians were almost destroyed by the Franks. The child princess was a prize the Frankish victors gambled for, and Clothar won her. The Franks often married captured aristocratic women, probably in the hope of gaining the loyalty of their defeated foes.

Clothar had Radegund educated at his court. After about ten years, when he was king of the Franks, he married her. Then he was in his forties, a polygamous man with at least five wives. Radegund bore no children, an ancient reason for divorce. When she was in her late twenties, Radegund left her husband to live on her own property. She took religious vows when she learned that her husband had executed her brother in 550 C.E. Nevertheless, Clothar's wealth enabled her to found a convent at Poitiers that became one of the largest in the

Frankish kingdom. After her death she became a saint. At Poitiers she wrote a poem about the brutal events of her childhood.

Oh, sad state of war, malevolent destiny
That fells proud kingdoms in a sudden slide!
The rooves that stood so long in happiness are broken
To lie fallen beneath the vast charred ruin.
The palace courts, where art once flourished
Are vaulted now with sad, glowing ashes.
Towers artfully gilded, then shone golden-red,
Now drifting ashes blur the glitter to pallor.
The captive maid given to a hostile lord, her power fell
From the heights of glory to the lowest depths.
The entourage of servants, standing resplendent, her
      youthful peers
Were dead in a day, besmirched with funeral ashes.
The bright attendant halo of powerful ministers
Now lie still without tomb or funeral service.
The conquering flame belching, reddens the golden hair of
      her beloved
While the milk-white woman lies on the ground.
Alas the corpses lie shamefully unburied on the field,
An entire people, strewn in a common grave.
Not Troy alone must mourn her ruins:
The Thuringian land suffered equal slaughter.
The matron was rapt away, with streaming hair, bound fast
Without even a sad farewell to the household gods.
Nor could the captive press a kiss on the threshold
Nor cast one backward glance toward what was lost.
A wife's naked feet trod in her husband's blood
And the tender sister stepped over the fallen brother.
The boy torn from his mother's embrace, his funeral plaint
Hung on her lips, with all her tears unshed.
So to lose the life of a child is not the heaviest lot,
Gasping, the mother lost even her pious tears.
I, the barbarian woman, seek not to count these tears,
Nor to keep afloat in the melancholy lake of all those drops.
Each one had her own tears; I alone have them all,

Anguish is private and public both to me.

Fate was kind to those whom the enemy struck down.

I, the sole survivor, must weep for them all.

Jo Ann McNamara, John E. Halborg, and E. Gordon Whatley, eds., *Sainted Women of the Dark Ages* (Durham, NC: Duke University Press, 1992), 65–6.

Noble women like Radegund gave their own land to the church, sometimes for local benefit and occasionally for a nunnery. Normally such gifts included farms, whose rents went to the convent or parish church. Often the woman making the donation for a nunnery joined the community as a nun and became the abbess. Widows joined for the companionship of women their own age or to avoid a marriage urged by their families. Younger women also joined the community to avoid arranged marriages, although abduction by their families remained a hazard. Escaping worldly woes undoubtedly motivated some wealthy women who entered convents, but a spiritual vocation for a life of contemplation and prayer was common to many who remained in the convents. Convents offered religious havens only to wealthy women. They did not accept as sisters the serf and slave women who worked on the land.

A convent normally functioned as a local church, with the nuns assisting the priests in the service. Abbesses heard confessions from the monks and nuns attached to the communities. These nunneries were important to the development of the Roman Catholic church in the Merovingian dynasty; they provided shelter for missionaries, their support was often given to nearby church organizations, and they conducted schools for boys and girls. Some schools became so famous that they attracted students from as far away as England. Male students became clerks and priests, while females married or entered convents.

By the time Charlemagne was declared emperor in 800 C.E. a reform movement in the Catholic church had reduced the independence of religious women and cloistered (secluded) the nuns. The emperor took away farm lands and other income properties from many of the nunneries, and their autonomy was rescinded and replaced with control by their bishops. No longer could nuns assist in the mass; they were restricted to lighting candles and ringing bells because bishops thought the sacraments were polluted by their touch. Nuns could not leave on a journey without their bishops' approval, although monks only needed their superior's permission. Only girls were now allowed to attend convent schools.

Married women did gain from the reform movement's demand for strict monogamy. No doubt a desire for the improvement of wives' treatment in marriage was one of the reasons for aristocratic women's support of Christian missionaries earlier in the fourth and fifth centuries. At that time the church's teachings were in conflict with Germanic polygamous marriages, frequent divorces, and adultery. The church sought to impose its doctrines, but its leaders proceeded slowly and carefully.

Monogamy without the possibility of divorce as the sole form of legitimate marriage was a principle that differentiated Christians from most other peoples of the ancient and medieval worlds. Christianity promised a wife more security from rivals, enhanced social status, and gave a superior chance for her children to inherit their father's wealth. Even as Catholics gained European adherents, the church was unable to impress its beliefs on the male Frankish aristocracy for some three centuries. The Franks were not only polygamous, the men also had concubines. Among the aristocracy marriages were easily broken by either party—mostly by the men.

During Charlemagne's reign a serious effort was begun to make marriage indissoluble. Charlemagne prohibited the remarriage of a divorced man or woman as long as either partner was still living. Although he had five wives, he followed his own prohibition after it was made and did not remarry until each of his wives died, though even in his old age he had children by four concubines.

It was his son Louis, appropriately called the Pious, who attacked concubinage and tightened the laws on divorce. To reduce concubinage, he excluded children born outside of marriage from inheriting from their fathers. Louis condemned anyone who repudiated a divorced living mate for any reason and urged reconciliation even in cases of adultery. He forced public penance by men who killed or repudiated their wives. The change in social attitudes can be illustrated by the experiences of Louis and his second wife, Judith of Bavaria.

Louis was forty years old when his first wife, Ermengard, died.

His counselors feared he would become a monk and urged him to remarry. They were probably surprised with his choice of Judith, a young woman, reportedly beautiful, cultivated, and musically gifted.

When their son Charles was born, Judith began trying to obtain an inheritance of a kingdom for him. Louis had already divided the empire among Ermengfard's sons, so Charles's portion would reduce their shares. Ermengfard's sons organized a publicity campaign accusing Judith of debauchery, witchcraft, and adultery with Count Bernard, the court chamberlain. The proclamation on the reconciliation of divorced couples had just been published, and they realized that having Judith condemned for adultery might not alienate her from Louis; they had to physically separate the couple.

The older sons organized a revolt in 830 C.E. At first successful, they were able to persuade Louis to convict Judith of adultery and have her imprisoned in Saint Radegund's nunnery at Poitiers. But soon Louis allowed Judith to purge herself with an oath, as Frankish tradition allowed, and reclaimed her as empress. The sons of Ermengfard tried again, with a second revolt. This time they sent Judith to Italy and forced Louis to become a monk. All to no avail. Louis's troops won; he left the monastery and brought Judith back as empress. Judith's victory on behalf of her son became evident twenty-five years after the death of Louis, when Charles the Bald gained the throne of the western portion of the empire, which encompassed much of modern France.

Charlemagne and Louis lived in a period when education was patronized by the court. Hence the initial attack on Judith was made through written tracts; one was entitled *Two Books in Favor of the Sons and against Judith the Wife of Louis*. Only after the written attacks failed did the sons turn to the civil wars that destroyed much of Carolingian learning.

8.3 Nuns as Popular Authors: Hildegard of Bingen

Medieval western Europe has the distinction of retaining literature that was written by women. Although women in the ancient world may have written much, very little that has survived can be identified with a female author. Most medieval female literature is on religious subjects—doctrinal debates, prayers, or hymns—but often in forms difficult for the modern reader to comprehend.

In the early medieval years, when feudal manors dominated the European landscape, all formal education for women and men was religious. In this era, sainthood remained a route to fame for women. This was the path of St. Clothild, St. Radegund, and St. Hildegard.

Hildegard of Bingen is an author whose fame has been recovered by feminist scholars. She was a mystic who wrote on scientific subjects. She was also one of the international celebrities of her day. She corresponded with people in all walks of life, including popes, emperors, kings, and other nobility, as well as monks and nuns.

She was born in 1098 C.E. to a noble family. Because she was the tenth child, her parents dedicated her to the church as a tithe. When she was eight years old, she went to live with the highborn female hermit Jutta of Sponheim, who began educating her. The hermit's fame attracted others who began living at the hermitage. It became a monastery with Jutta as abbess. When Jutta died in 1136, Hildegard was named as her successor. Patricia Labalme picks up her life's history at that point:

In 1147 she founded a new convent at Rupertsberg near Bingen, where she remained until her death in 1179. She knew Latin, Scripture, the liturgy, some biblical exegesis, music—a number of songs are attributed to her—and something of natural science and the more philosophic study of the cosmos. Her visions were read and praised by popes; a papal commission to investigate her miracles and visions gave them a favorable report in 1147. . . . Her science was respected enough to be studied by Paracelsus' teacher in the sixteenth century; and a twentieth-century historian of science treats her as one of the more original medical writers of the Latin West in the twelfth century.

In her works, Hildegard discusses the spheres of the heavens in terms of the elements, the universe as a series of concentric spheres; the zones of the atmosphere; the seasons as caused by the winds; the movement of heavenly bodies; the structure and inner workings of the human body; the nature of metals, stones, plants, trees, and animals. As a mystic, she claimed that she had no human sources for her material, that a voice from heaven told her to speak and write what she had seen, but there are suggestions in her works of the influence of current Neoplatonic thought, particularly of the Chartrians. . . . In two of her three major visions, *Scivias,* begun in 1141, and the *Liber divinorum operum simplicis hominis,* begun in 1163, Hildegard describes her visions pictorially and then interprets them. The visions are either symbolic—mountains with windows in them, winged figures of great light, the firmament as a huge egg—or narrative—the rebellion of the angels and the fall of man. The interpretations are either religious—the mountain represents the strength and stability of the kingdom of God; the universe declares the omnipotent God, incomprehensible in his majesty, inestimable in his mysteries—or scientific—telling how the body is formed in the uterus, how the rings of the firmament are shaped—or philosophical, the cause of man's actions. In the *Scivias,* Hildegard presents the universe with the earth as a sphere at the center of concentric zones whose outermost zones are spherical, ultimately egg shaped; in the *Liber* she shifts to the more conventional view of concentric spheres. . . . The *Liber* also contains a long section on the creation, using the Genesis text but interpreting it to include current scientific views of the cosmos. . . .

Hildegard's visions were something of a "best seller"; everyone who was anyone wanted a copy, and people talked about them without having read them. Her prophetic gifts were admired by popes and emperors. . . . When Pope Anastasius writes to her saying how much he has heard about her, how highly his predecessor thought of her, and asking her to send him her writings, she answers with a stirring attack and exhortation that must have surprised him: "O man, who has wearied of restraining the magniloquence of pride among the men placed in your bosom. . . . Why do you not recall those who are shipwrecked, who cannot rise from their troubles without help? Why do you not cut the root of evil which suffocates the good and useful plants? You neglect Justice, the daughter of the king . . . who was committed to your care. You permit her to lie prostrate on the earth, her diadem smashed, her tunic torn." Hildegard's treatment of the emperor Frederic Barbarossa is similar. . . .

The bulk of the correspondence is with less important figures, though the list includes archbishops and abbots, many of whom address Hildegard as *magistra.* Apparently her visions and prophecies gave her a reputation for extraordinary wisdom; she was the "Dear Abby" of the twelfth century, to whom everyone came or wrote for advice or comfort. . . . An abbess writes that she wants to renounce her position and wall herself up in the solitude of a cell. Hildegard tells her that her mind is clouded by the evil around her, that the peace and rest she seeks is not what God intended, that she must continue to use the light she has been given to lead others to pasture.

Elizabeth of Schonau, a visionary herself who later became a saint, writes with a distressing problem: rumors are circulating about her, and prophetic writings are appearing under her name which she claims to have nothing to do with. She has been having visions, but she has kept them hidden because she did not want to appear arrogant or as the author of novelties . . . until the angel who brings them angrily accused her of hiding the gold, God's word, which she was given to pass on to others; then the angel angrily beat her with a whip. That convinced her to reveal them to her abbot, who made them public, but when the predictions did not come true, she was ridiculed. The next time she saw the angel, she asked for an explanation, and he told her that her prophecies of disaster had moved people to amend their ways, so that God had spared them. Unfortunately, people continued to make fun of her so she turned to Hildegard for consolation. Hildegard told her that man is a small, earthen vessel, made by God to do his work; all creatures but man follow God's commands. Those who sing God's mysteries are like a trumpet, which can give forth a sound only if someone blows into it. She ended with a confession and a prayer: "I too lie in the cowardice of fear, sometimes making a small sound on the trumpet by means of the living light; whence God help me, that I may remain in his service.". . .

Hildegard had problems of her own in her administration, some of which are described in the letters. Toward the end of her life, a young man who had been excommunicated was buried in the cemetery adjoining her convent, and the ecclesiastical authorities of the region demanded that the body be removed. She refused to comply on the ground that he had received the last rites. Even when her convent was placed under interdict [excommunicated], she held firm, and after considerable correspondence and negotiation, the ban was lifted. She was, in other words, capable of practical action, as well as of theoretic advice.

Patricia H. Labalme, ed., *Beyond Their Sex: Learned Women of the European Past* (New York: New York University Press, 1980), 22–7.

8.4 A Nun's Poetry

Christians, accepting the Jewish account in Genesis of Eve's role in tempting Adam, agreed that women's redemption depended on their assuming the burden of motherhood. Religious women like Hildegard, married as virgins in celibacy to Christ, never became mothers and, along with many of their male contemporaries, elevated the miraculous virginity of Mary, whose son's birth did not impair her chastity, to a central place in worship. Hildegard wrote many lyric verses contrasting Eve's fall with Mary's redemption.

Eve

Pierced by the light of God,
O shining maid Mary,
flooded with the Word of God,
your body blossomed
from the entering Spirit of God,
who breathed on you and purged you
of the poison that Eve took
in the breach of purity—
when she caught the infection
from the devil's suggestion.

The Virgin Mary

Because a woman built the house of death
a shining maid tore it down:
so the sublimest blessing
comes in the form of a woman
surpassing all creation,
for God became a man in a maid
most tender and blessed.

Barbara Newman, *Sister of Wisdom: St. Hildegard's Theology of the Feminine* (Berkeley: University of California Press, 1987), 174, 185.

8.5 Christine de Pisan, Professional Writer

Hildegard was a mystic and an abbess. Another woman writer, Christine de Pisan (ca. 1365–1430), was unique—a professional who managed to support her family largely through the sale of her writings. Patricia Labalme interprets her life:

She was brought from Bologna to the French court by her father, who was physician, astrologer, and important councillor to Charles V. Though her mother thought girls should spin, her father thought them none the worse for letters and gave her a good vernacular education in Italian and French and the rudiments of Latin learning. Widowed young from her marriage to a royal secretary, Christine decided not to remarry, as most women would have done in her day, but instead to find a way to support her children and her widowed mother by herself. To console herself from the lawsuits that assailed her inheritance she began to study [history]. . . . She went on to read philosophy and poetry, and finally to write herself.

The corpus she produced was astonishing in size and range: lyric poetry, courtly romance, moral tales, literary criticism, instruction for knights, instruction for women, and then a set of tracts on important public matters—pleas for the end of schism in the church, and for the end of immorality at the court, and especially for peace among the warring factions in France. And she was listened to. Her manuscripts, dedicated to important personages, male and female, brought fat purses in return, and they were quickly copied for aristocratic libraries in France, Burgundy, and Italy. This was partly because of the importance her late father had once held at court and partly because she wrote with imagination and intelligence. But she also was introducing successfully into France certain of the literary roles developed by her Italian countrymen, Dante, Petrarch, and Boccaccio, and adapting them to the style of her sex. . . . If she sometimes referred to herself as "a woman in the shadow of ignorance," she hastened to add, "but endowed by God's gift and nature's . . . in the love of study." If she sometimes referred to herself as "a poor creature, a little ignorant woman," she also announced, "now, I am truly a man."

Patricia H. Labalme, ed., *Beyond Their Sex: Learned Women of the European Past* (New York: New York University Press, 1980), 157–8.

When de Pisan identified herself as a man, she meant that in dealing with the lawsuits over her inheritance and developing a writing career, she was aggressive and independent. She did not hesitate to attack misogyny. In this document de Pisan criticizes the mockery of women in Jean de Meung's popular *Roman de la Rose:*

How can it be good and useful that he [de Meung] accuses so excessively, impetuously, and falsely, blames and defames women for several serious vices, claiming that their morals are full of perversity, and throughout so many rejoinders and by means of all of his characters he cannot seem to repeat his accusations often enough? . . .

He is so insistent about not telling a secret to a woman, who is so bereft of discretion, as he recalls, and I can't imagine where in the devil he found so much nonsense and so many futile words as are hurled at them throughout that long trial, but I beg all those who consider this quite authentic and put so much faith in it to tell me how many men they have known to be accused, killed, hanged, or even reproached in the street because of the denunciation of their wives; I think they will find them very thinly scattered. Although it would certainly make good sense, and also be praiseworthy, for everyone to keep a secret to himself for greater security, as there are always a certain number of evil people, and recently, as I have heard, someone was accused and even hanged for having confided in a companion he trusted. . . .

Moreover, the poet speaks so unnecessarily and in such an ugly way of married women who deceive their husbands, a matter of which he can scarcely know from experience and of which he speaks very categorically. . . . Heavens, what an exhortation, and to what good purpose? Indeed, as he blames women in general, I am led to believe it is because he has never known or frequented any virtuous women, but through knowing a few who are dissolute and evil, as the lecherous are in the habit of doing, he believed or pretended to know what all are like, just because he never had any experience of others. If only he had blamed the dishonest ones and suggested that this sort should be shunned it would have been good and just advice. But no! instead he accused all women without exception.

Charity Cannon Willard, "The Franco-Italian Professional Writer: Christine de Pizan," in Katharina M. Wilson, ed., *Medieval Women Writers* (Athens: University of Georgia Press, 1984), 342–3. © 1984 by the University of Georgia Press.

Christine de Pisan wrote a series of popular self-help books. Her advice to the wife of a knight on how to manage the estate while her husband was at war is interesting for two reasons. It shows what varied information the wife needed and how much research de Pisan had to do to write it. Remember that local knights had a yearly obligation to fight for their lords, which few were able to avoid when France was fighting England during the Hundred Years' War.

A style of life somewhat different from that of baronesses is suitable for the simple ladies who live in fortified places or on their estates outside of town, but as most often knights, squires, and other gentlemen must travel to follow the wars, it befits their wives to be wise and able to manage their affairs capably, because they must spend much of their lives in their households without their husbands, who are often at court or even in distant countries. Thus it turns out that they may have the responsibility of managing their property and be placed in charge of their revenue and their lands, so it is important for any woman in such a situation, if she wants to act with good judgment, to know the yearly income of her estate. She should manage to the best of her abilities, by gentle word and good counsel addressed to her husband, to see to it that they confer together and agree to follow the course of action best suited to their revenues, so that at the year's end they do not find themselves in debt to their retainers or other creditors, for certainly there is no disgrace in leading one's life according to one's income, however small it may be, but it is rather shameful to live so extravagantly that every day creditors come to shout and to bellow at the door, sometimes even raising a club in menace, or that it becomes necessary to offend one's men or tenants to the point where some sort of extortion results. It is important for such a lady to be informed about the rights of domain or fiefs, of secondary fiefs, contributions, the lord's right of harvest, shared crops, and all such things as constitute the rights of possession according to the customs of various countries, so that she won't be misled. Because the world is full of governors of lands and of lord's jurisdictions, who are intentionally dishonest, she must also be aware of all this and be able to protect herself so that it won't turn to her disadvantage. If she is knowledgeable in accounts and often gives attention to them, she will also inform herself as to how her agents deal with her tenants or men, so that these will not be deceived or annoyed beyond reasonable bounds, for this would be against both her and her husband. In the matter of penalties against poor folk, she should be, for the love of God, more compassionate than rigorous.

With all these things, she should be a good manager, knowledgeable about farming, knowing in what weather and in what season the fields should be worked, the best way to have the furrows run according to the lay of the land, and whether it is dry or moist land, the depth of the furrows, and that they should be straight and evenly laid out and properly sown with seed suitable for the land. Likewise, she should know about the work in the vineyards, if the land should lie in a country where there are grapes, and she should see to it that she has good workers and supervisors in all such undertakings, and not hire people who change masters from season to season, for that is a bad sign, or workers who are too old, for they will be lazy and feeble, or too young, for they will be frivolous. She should also insist that they get up early, and if she is a good manager she will not depend on anyone else to see to this, but will herself arise, put on a cloak, go the window, and watch to see them go out, for they are usually inclined to be lazy in this matter. She should often take her recreation in the fields in order to see how the work is progressing, for there are many who would willingly stop raking the ground beyond the surface if they thought nobody would notice, and there are those who are capable of sleeping in the shade of a willow tree in the field, leaving the workhorse or oxen to graze meanwhile in a field, caring only to be able to say in the evening that they have put in their day. The good manager will keep her eye on all this. Furthermore, when the grain is ripening, even as early as the month of May, she will not wait for the season when labor is in short supply, but will engage her workers for August, taking good, strong and diligent fellows, and she will arrange to pay them either with money or in grain.

Charity Cannon Willard, "The Franco-Italian Professional Writer: Christine de Pizan," in Katharina M. Wilson, ed., *Medieval Women Writers* (Athens: University of Georgia Press, 1984), 343–4. © 1984 by the University of Georgia Press.

This was only the first half of her instructions. The remainder dealt with the care of animals (sheep, cattle, oxen, and horses); winter work (cutting walnut posts for grapevines); work for her maids (milking, weeding, hunting for herbs); and the preparation of cloth, both woolen and linen.

8.6 Parisian Women's Occupations in 1292 and 1313 C.E.

Elite women have dominated this chapter as their class dominated medieval European literate culture. By the late medieval years, more women lived in the growing towns. Some were literate, but few of their own writings are preserved. Many townswomen were workers. Scholars trace their occupations, incomes, and the conditions of their labor through tax lists and inventories of estates. The following reading is David Herlihy's summary of two tax lists for Paris. Notice the variety of occupations in which women are employed.

In the large survey of 1292, nearly 48 percent of the male heads of households show an occupation, as do more than 39 percent of the female heads. In the smaller survey of 1313, the percentages show an occupation increase to 74 [percent] for the men and 47 [percent] for the women. The reason for the increased percentages seems again to be the omission of many poor persons and presumably the unemployed in the later survey. . . .

What was the contribution of women in the large and complex economy of Paris? . . .

In 1292, women appear in 172 occupations; in 1313, they are seen in 130 occupations. (The comparable figures for men are 325 occupations in the earlier year and 276 in the later.) Women are thus represented in a large number of trades and in all the principal economic sectors. As drapers, money changers, jewelers, and mercers, they appear among the richest professions. There are even women moneyers, or mint workers. They are copyist and artist. There are women tavern keepers, firewood dealers, and even masons, shoemakers, girdle makers, millers, smiths, shield makers and archers. . . .
A lady juggler and dancer are present among the taxpayers of

1292. Very few occupations seem to have been composed exclusively of males. Those which involved either distant travel or heavy hauling—such as the occupations of sailors and porters—appear without women. Women were also excluded from some licensed professions such as those of notary and lawyer. . . . Although women show a wide distribution across the occupations, they also show a marked tendency to specialize in particular trades. . . .

Not surprisingly, the vast majority of household servants [197] were female. . . . Most household servants were probably young girls newly immigrated from the countryside.

Women were important in the preparation and sale of food. There are five women "friers," five millers, five sellers of milk, four soup makers, four sellers of oil, three brewers, three sellers of cheese, two wine dealers, and several types of bakers . . . in the taille [list] of 1292. Somewhat surprisingly, professional cooks were usually men—11 out of 12 in 1313.

Women were prominent as *regratieres,* peddlers who sold foodstuffs and salt. They were also numerous among the peddlers of rags and old clothes. Women washed the clothes, although eight male *lavandiers* also appear in the taille of 1292.

Women were also very prominent in the care of the sick and the prescription of medicine. There are eight lady doctors and two *ventrieres,* or midwives, at Paris in 1292. Three other women with the title of *mestresse* (mistress) may have been doctors. . . . Barbers too performed medical services, such as bloodletting or the setting of bones; thirteen were women in both 1292 and 1313. The many nurses (twelve *nourrices* in 1292) in the tax lists were all female. Spice dealers were also pharmacists; two were women in 1292 and two again in 1313. Finally, women administered the women's bathhouses at Paris (there were three *estuveresses* [keepers of hot baths] in 1313), which adult males were not supposed to enter.

Notable among the industries that employed women in significant numbers were the sale of wax and candlemaking. . . .

An industry that women dominated was the making of silk cloth. The raw silk had to be imported, chiefly by Lombard and Jewish merchants, from southern Europe, but women almost excusively were engaged in producing the silk fabric. . . .

As the chief spinners and weavers of silk, women were very visible in the making of luxury fabrics and clothes. They embroidered cloths ... and made lace ... , purses ... , pillow cases and altar cloths ... , and ribbons, coifs, and hats. ...

Gold thread was often used in embroidery, and this probably explains the appearance of women goldsmiths. ...

Women were visible too in the production of another fabric: linen. ... There were eight female *linieres* registered at Paris in 1292 (as compared with eleven males) and four linen weavers. ...

Patterns of employment are different in regard to woolens, by far the largest of the fabric industries. There were seventy-three male weavers at Paris in 1292 but only nine female, and these latter may have been working in silk or linen. ... Women doubtless spun wool into yarn, but there are only six spinners identified at Paris in 1292, and we cannot be certain that they were spinning wool rather than flax or silk. It almost appears as if the spinning of wool, though widely done by Parisian women, was not considered a primary profession worth naming in the surveys.

David Herlihy, *Opera Muliebria: Women and Work in Medieval Europe* (Philadelphia: Temple University Press, 1990), 142–8. © 1990 by McGraw-Hill, Inc. Reproduced by permission of McGraw-Hill, Inc.

Suggested Further Readings

Books on medieval European women are plentiful. What follows are suggestions to illustrate the depth of what might be found in the average college library. For those interested in France, Suzanne Fonay Wemple, *Women in Frankish Society: Marriage and the Cloister, 500 to 900* (Philadelphia: University of Pennsylvania Press, 1981) is a good introduction. The latest study of Hildegard of Bingen is Barbara Newman, *Sister of Wisdom: St. Hildegard's Theology of the Feminine* (Berkeley: University of California Press, 1987). Newman concentrates on textual analysis, but she includes biographical details. Judith C. Brown, *Immodest Acts: The Life of a Lesbian Nun in Renaissance Italy* (New York: Oxford University Press, 1986) is about a seventeenth-century religious woman whose story is told mostly from the Catholic church's investigation of her life. Several published studies focus on women's work. An excellent introduction is a collection of articles edited by Barbara A. Hanawalt, *Women and Work in Preindustrial Europe* (Bloomington: Indiana University Press, 1986), in which peasants, slaves, wet nurses, midwives, and urban women are discussed. Two volumes of *A History of Women in the West,* George Duby and Michelle Perrot, eds. (Cambridge, MA: Harvard University Press, 1992) include articles on topics discussed in this chapter. Volume 1, *From Ancient Goddesses to Christian Saints,* considers early Christian women. Volume 2, *Silences of the Middle Ages,* is entirely on women in medieval Europe. Articles written by different authors are grouped into themes: norms of control, family and social strategies, vestiges and images of women, and women's words. An excellent sample of documents can be found in Julia O'Faolain and Lauro Martines, eds., *Not in God's Image: Women in History from the Greeks to the Victorians* (New York: Harper and Row, 1973).

–9–

THE MIDDLE EAST
Islam, the Family, and the Seclusion of Women

A garden scene from early fifteenth-century Iran. (The Metropolitan Museum of Art, the Cora Timken Burnett Collection of Persian Miniatures and Other Persian Art Objects, bequest of Cora Timken Burnett, 1957.)

The customary date for the beginning of the civilization and religion of Islam is 622 C.E. In that year Muhammad left Mecca and became the governor of Medina, another town on the west side of the Arabian peninsula. The new religion exploded out from Medina—in 40 years Muslims, converts to Islam, had conquered an area that included the rest of the Arabian peninsula and modern Egypt, Syria, Iraq, and Iran. Muhammad and those converted to Islam during his lifetime shared the values of the Bedouins, nomadic herders of camels and goats. Muhammad received revelations from Allah, or God, that were appropriate for his pastoral followers. These revelations have been collected and published under the title of the Quran. As Muslims conquered large commercial urban cities, they faced different cultures and social problems. Over the centuries Muslim scholars interpreted the revelations found in the Quran.

The last reading in this chapter discusses some of the conflicts pertaining to women that arose in the Islamic cultures. It describes Muslim women in Cairo, Egypt, in the middle of the fourteenth century. By then Egypt had been ruled by Muslims for seven centuries. Historians have often portrayed Muslim women as oppressed by unusually severe forms of patriarchy. In describing tenth-century Baghdad the statement is unquestionably accurate. Overall, however, it is inaccurate, because Muslim women's rights have varied significantly with time, by region, and by class. There is far too much diversity to be adequately described in a few pages, but a few instances can suggest the complexity of the topic.

9.1 The Quran

Verses in the Quran are seldom quoted by authors writing for a general audience because the exact meanings of words employed in the translations may not be clear on a first reading. As a result, explanatory notes on a critical verse may be longer than the original quotation. The following verse is relatively understandable and is specifically mentioned in the subsequent reading.

And say to the believing women
That they should lower
Their gaze and guard
Their modesty: that they

ticide, and another was payment of the male dower to the bride, not to her guardian. Possible improvements for some were regulations about female inheritance—half that of a male heir—and of women's control over their property; these had been known, however, among pre-Islamic Arabs, as evidenced by Muhammad's first wife, the wealthy widowed merchant Khadija. Much less favorable *Quranic* prescriptions were free divorce for men, while for women divorce became very difficult, and polygamy for men. Predominantly, pre-Islamic Arab women had equality in divorce. Polygamy is presented by the *Quran* as helping the condition of unprotected widows and orphans, who were numerous in those warlike times. Men are first admonished not to take additional wives unless they can treat them all equally, and they are then told that no matter how hard they try, they will not be able to treat all equally. This contradiction is taken by modernist Muslims to show that the *Quran* meant to discourage or forbid polygamy, but this is unlikely, as polygamy is encouraged in specific circumstances. Veiling and seclusion are not enjoined in the *Quran,* although later Muslim interpretation says that they are. One verse of the *Quran* tells women to veil their bosoms and hide their ornaments, and the term "ornaments" was later taken to mean everything except hands, feet, and perhaps the face, though this interpretation makes no logical or linguistic sense. If everything was to be veiled, there would be no point in ordering bosoms veiled separately. Another verse tells women to draw their cloaks tightly around them so that they may be recognized and not annoyed. These are the only words taken to refer to veiling.

Other verses, however, indicate that after Muhammad had taken several wives and had some problems with men talking to these wives, there was a revelation saying that men should talk to the Prophet's wives only from behind a curtain and that his wives should be limited in other ways as well. The Prophet's wives apparently came to be subject to types of veiling and seclusion that resembled those later followed by the urban upper and middle classes. It would be simplistic to say, however, that later veiling was simply an emulation of the practices of the Prophet's wives. In her book on Muhammad's favorite wife, Aisha, Nabia Abbott notes that this turn toward veiling the wives was itself a reflection of greater prosperity among the Muslim ruling group, which enabled them to hire servants, and to keep women from duties outside the home, and also of the Muslims' greater contact with surrounding societies where women were veiled.* Hence as the society of the Muslims came increasingly to resemble that of surrounding and conquered peoples, it is not surprising that many of those peoples' customs and practices regarding women, which were found appropriate to their stratified social structures and their reliance on family regulation to maintain general social control, were also found appropriate by the Muslims and were adopted or adapted by them.

In addition to the *Quranic* points on female behavior already mentioned, men are given control of their wives, extending in some cases to beating, and adulterers of both sexes are punished, when there is confession or *four* eyewitnesses to the act, by lashing.

It is often said that Islamic practices regarding women are so resistant to change because they have the sanction of the *Quran,* which believing Muslims take to be the literal word of God. Although this has some truth, we should be aware of how much breaking and bending of *Quaranic* admonitions there have been throughout Muslim history. . . . Adultery or fornication have rarely been punished in accordance with the *Quran's* teachings: the *Quranic* four eyewitnesses are rarely demanded and very often the girl or woman is killed by a member of her own family—frequently her brother. Stoning to death, a custom practiced by Jews and some Christians, was sometimes adopted and is often considered Islamic, even though the *Quran* says otherwise.

In general, the *Quran* was followed on sexual and other matters when it was not too inconvenient or repugnant to men or the patriarchal family to do so, and not followed when it was. The divergences went mostly in the direction of reviving and reinforcing patriarchal tribal customs as in rules of inheritance, or else in adopting customs from the Byzantines and Persians, such as veiling and seclusion, and reading those customs back into the *Quran*. In some cases, however, practice might be less male-dominated than a mere reading of the *Quran* might suggest, notably with regard to divorce. Since marriages were carefully arranged and the groom's parents paid a signifi-

---

*Nabia Abbott, *Aishah the Beloved of Mohammed* (Chicago: The University of Chicago Press, 1942).

cant bride-price, the groom could be in trouble with his family if he divorced quickly or lightly. Polygamy was often favored over divorce.

Nikki R. Keddie, "The Past and Present of Women in the Muslim World," *Journal of World History* 1 (1990): 77–108.

9.2 Aisha, Muhammad's Beloved Wife

As Keddie mentioned, Muhammad's experiences with his wives are still cited as sanctions for Muslim family practices. Since Aisha was his favorite, following the death of Khadija, she was an actor or observer in many significant events in the Prophet's life. She was also the youngest of the wives and lived more than four decades beyond his death. Thus she is one of the most important of the *traditionalists,* those who heard and transmitted events and words from the Prophet's life. She is credited with 2,210 traditions in the *hadith.* Few women have been as notable in the history of a major world religion. Aisha's father, Abu Bakr, was Muhammad's first convert outside his family and was the second most influential friend (after Khadija) in his career. Aisha was born about 614 C.E. Nabia Abbott wrote her biography:

She herself could not remember the time when both her parents were not Muslims and when Muhammad himself did not visit at her father's house morning and evening. Doubtless Muhammad had taken some notice of this lively girl-child of his "brother" in the faith. . . .

Though the advantages of a marriage between Muhammad and the family of Abu Bakr may have been early and readily evident to both parties, yet it seems that neither of them was the first to conceive the idea of a marriage. . . . Tradition generally credits a maternal aunt of Muhammad, Khawlah bint Hakim, with putting the idea into Muhammad's head. . . . Tradition reports that Khawlah served the prophet, which may mean that she sometimes took care of his simple household after Khadija's death. She was close enough to him to feel free to suggest that he marry again.

"Whom shall I marry, O Khawlah? You women are best knowing in these matters," answered Muhammad.

"If you wish a virgin, there is the daughter of him who you love best, Aisha bint Abu Bakr; but if you wish a nonvirgin, there is the widow Sawdah bint Zamah who believed in you and followed you."

"Go," said Muhammad, "bespeak them both for me."

. . . Muhammad, within a few months of Khadija's death in A.D. 619, married in quick succession the widow Sawdah and the six-year-old Aisha. The marriage of the latter, however, was not consummated until three years later in Medina.

Nabia Abbott, *Aishah the Beloved of Mohammed* (Chicago: University of Chicago Press, 1942), 1–4. © 1942 by the University of Chicago. In this and in subsequent extracts from this book, the spellings of Aisha and Muhammad have been modernized.

Muhammad's consummation of his marriage to Aisha when she was nine years old is the basis of the belief of orthodox Muslims that marriage to a woman as young as nine is permitted. His polygamous marriages and acquisition of a concubine are the basis for later Muslim family law.

Muhammad built a mosque, and for members of his family a number of small private apartments were built in the court of the mosque. Aisha lived in one.

But, wife or no wife, she was at heart still a child, not yet ready to put away childish things. The elderly Muhammad understood and let nature take its course. Coming home, he would see his child-wife busy with her toys.

"What are these, O Aisha?" he would ask.

"Solomon's horses," or "My girl-dolls," would come her unconcerned answer. Muhammad smiling watched her at play. On other occasions he would find her surrounded by her playmates, who seeing him approach would disperse or go into hiding, thus spoiling the play business of the day. But Muhammad, so Aisha herself tells us, would call these children together again and himself join in their games.

Nabia Abbott, *Aishah the Beloved of Mohammed* (Chicago: University of Chicago Press, 1942), 7–8. © 1942 by the University of Chicago.

Muhammad continued to marry women, usually widows. The next wife was Hafsah, the daughter of Umar ibn al-Khattab, another supporter and an ally of Abu Bakr. Wives in a harem are traditionally jealous of each other. However, Aisha and Hafsah were friends. As the number of wives increased it was natural for them to divide into factions. The factions within the harem were allied with factions outside the harem. As Nabia Abbott explains, with Muhammad's marriage in 626 C.E. to Umm Salamah of the Makhzumite clan, a family rift occurred that reflected outside rivalries:

Aisha and Hafsah, acting as one in the interest of their fathers, represented the party in power. Umm Salamah leaned toward Fatima and Ali [Muhammad's daughter and her husband] and, as Muhammad's harem increased, drew into her circle Ramlah bint Abi Sufyan, . . . and Maimunah bint al-Harith, both of whom Muhammad married, primarily for political reasons. . . . Here, then, were reflected the earliest political parties in Islam. Aisha and Hafsah represented the plebeian but powerful Abu Bakr and Umar, who, having wholeheartedly launched and started Muhammad on a successful prophetic career, were ambitious to reap their rewards as heirs to his power. There was the aristocracy of Mecca represented by the Makhzumite Umm Salamah and the Umayyad Umm Habibah. There was finally the *ahl al-bait,* or legitimist party, with the timid Fatima for its main hope. . . . With Aisha's party in power the other two, each opposed to or envious of it, found it convenient sometimes to unite their forces; though at other times their own specific ambitions and jealousies led them to go their separate way[s], as groups and even as individuals. The rest of Muhammad's wives, with no particular axes of their own to grind, allowed their emotions or the demands of the hour to sway them now toward Aisha, now toward Umm Salamah.

Nabia Abbott, *Aishah the Beloved of Mohammed* (Chicago: University of Chicago Press, 1942), 15–16. © 1942 by the University of Chicago.

Not only were the followers of Muhammad divided into factions, but there were others in Medina, called "hypocrites," who did not support him, and some of these were ready to spread unfavorable gossip. Aisha, in the "affair of the slander," provided them with a unusual opportunity to attack the prophet's family. The incident occurred on the return from a battle. In battle women cared for the wounded, carried water, and exhorted the warriors to greater efforts. Muhammad's wives frequently went into battles with him. Aisha had accompanied Muhammad on this expedition.

On the last day of the return journey orders were given to break camp in the dark and early hours of the morning. Aisha left the crowd and walked out some distance to satisfy a natural need. On her return she missed a necklace of Yamanite agates that she had been wearing. She retraced her steps in search of it and eventually found it. Returning to the camp, she found the grounds deserted. To her cry for help there came no answer. For the men, assuming Aisha to be in her litter, had placed it on her camel and led it away. They thought nothing of the lightness of the load, for Aisha was a light and slender girl. There was nothing for her now to do but sit and wait in the hopes that her absence would be soon discovered and a search party sent back for her. Waiting there alone in the still hours of the morning she soon fell asleep. She awoke to find an embarrassed young man, Safwan ibn al-Muattal, and his lone camel by her side. Gallantly the young man helped her to mount his camel and silently he led her on the way to Medina. Her absence was not discovered until Muhammad and his party had reached Medina late in the afternoon. But presently Safwan arrived leading his camel bearing the missing Aisha.

Muhammad seems to have dismissed the matter there, but not so some of the "faithful" and certainly not the "hypocrites." . . .

As the days ran into weeks the scandal assumed alarming proportions, yet none dared mention it to Aisha. She, however, had sensed a definite coolness toward her on the part of Muhammad. Something like a month passed before one of the women told her of the scandal that had become the talk of the town.

Nabia Abbott, *Aishah the Beloved of Mohammed* (Chicago: University of Chicago Press, 1942), 30–2. © 1942 by the University of Chicago.

Aisha sought her parents' advice, but they could think of nothing. "By this time Muhammad himself was no doubt thoroughly

alarmed at the magnitude of the scandal and the political significance it could assume" (Abbott, 33). He was probably torn between his love for Aisha and doubts of her virtue. He talked to
Ali, his son-in-law, who was critical of Aisha; Ali said, "O Mes-
senger of Allah, Allah has placed no narrow limits on you. Many
are the women like her. Examine her maid for the truth of the
matter" (Abbott, 33). The maid supported Aisha, as did most of
the others to whom Muhammad turned. Then he brought up the
matter from the pulpit of the mosque, causing accusations and
counteraccusations to fly, until he quieted the crowd. The next
morning Aisha's parents were with her when Muhammad entered her house for the first time in about a month. He pleaded,
"O Aisha if you are innocent Allah will absolve you. But if you
are guilty, ask forgiveness of Allah and repent, for Allah pardons
those of his servants who confess and repent" (Abbott, 35).

She expected her parents would defend her. When they didn't,
she proclaimed her innocence, called on Allah's help, and retired to her bed. Soon after Muhammad "began to show some of
the physical symptoms generally accompanying his revelations"
(Abbott, 35–6). The Prophet said,

"Good tidings, O Aisha," he called out to her. "Allah most high has
exonerated you."

"Rise and come to Muhammad," urged her parents.

"I shall neither come to him nor thank him. Nor will I thank both
of you who listened to the slander and did not deny it. I shall rise,"
she concluded, "to give thanks to Allah alone."

Muhammad went out to the people and gave utterance to his revelations which are to be found in Surah 24 of the *Quran* and which
still form the Islamic law of adultery.

Nabia Abbott, *Aishah the Beloved of Mohammed* (Chicago: University of Chicago
Press, 1942), 36–7. © 1942 by the University of Chicago.

This Surah requires four witnesses for the conviction of adultery.
Muhammad died in 632 C.E., when he was sixty-two and Aisha
was eighteen. She was too young to have had much influence on
Muhammad, although she remained his favorite until the last.
Aisha lived 46 years after his death, and in her maturity she made
important contributions to Islam.

Her father, Abu Bakr, was named the first caliph, and his ally Umar was the second. Practically nothing is recorded of Aisha's activities during these years, when her faction controlled Islam. Muhammad's wives were called the Mothers of the Believers. People came to Aisha and the others for guidance based on the Prophet's practices and words.

With the assassination of Umar, the leadership of Islam shifted out of the control of Aisha's allies. She gradually became more public in her opposition to the new caliph. Umar's successor Uthman created opposition with his nepotism. Aisha made inflammatory speeches against him at the mosque in Medina. As the opposition began to call for his blood, she backed off and went on a pilgrimage to Mecca. When Uthman was assassinated and her enemy Ali, Muhammad's son-in-law, was made caliph, she helped organize an opposition from Mecca. Eventually civil war broke out, and Aisha played an active role in the first and only battle, the Battle of the Camel.

Aisha's coleaders, Talhah and Zubair, had overthrown Ali's governor in Basra. Ali led an army against them. They met in battle December 4, 656 C.E. Aisha rode in an armored enclosure (pavilion) on her well-known camel Askar.

Kab ibn Sur led Aisha to the scene of the attack in the hope that her presence and influence might yet avert a major clash. Seated in a mail-covered pavilion mounted on her own camel, Askar, Aisha went into the midst of the fray. But it was of no use. The fight was on in earnest, and the Basrans were getting so much the worst of it that they began to take flight. It was then that Aisha, herself no coward, rose to the emergency of the situation. She ordered Kab to leave her and approach the front ranks with cries for peace and the judgment of the *Quran,* giving him, according to some versions, her own copy of the sacred text to raise aloft and secure the attention and hoped-for compliance of the fighters. But Kab was immediately shot down by an arrow. Aisha herself strove valiantly to halt the fight and rally her forces with loud and repeated cries of "O my sons, endurance! Remember Allah Most High and the Reckoning." When this failed to stop the fight, she tried once again, this time with a curse on the murderers of Uthman and their followers. The fighters picked up the curse for a battle cry as it were and returned to the attack. Like a general ordering his forces, she sent word to her commanders to hold fast their positions. Her party's forces were in desperate need of an able commander-in-general. . . .

It is not surprising, then, that the severest fighting now centered around Aisha and her camel. Fearless herself, this Mother of the Believers roundly denounced strife and cowardice, on the one hand, while on the other, she continued to incite her warriors to heroic action with battle cries and martial poetry much after the fashion of the pagan "lady of victory" of pre-Islamic days, whose capture in battle meant certain defeat. Thick and fast flew the arrows around her red pavilion. Several groups of her warriors outdid others in their courageous defense of her. . . . Many were the sons [warriors] (seventy is the usual number given) who thus won a hero's death at this Battle of the Camel, as it came to be called. . . . Ali, realizing the role of Aisha on her camel, gave orders to hamstring the animal. The disabled creature fell and with it fell all of Aisha's hopes. Her personal courage had availed little. The battle was lost and with it was lost also her cause.

Nabia Abbott, *Aishah the Beloved of Mohammed* (Chicago: University of Chicago Press, 1942), 158–61. © 1942 by the University of Chicago.

Aisha escaped capture. Eventually she made her peace with Ali and never again took a public stand. Later, Ali was assassinated. Shiite Muslims consider him the first imam, or holy leader.

In the centuries after Muhammad's death Islamic scholars struggled to interpret Islamic law (*shar'ia*), including the proper relations between men and women. Finally, in the tenth century, a consensus was reached, and thereafter conformity was expected. The laws were considered to be infallible and divine. Muslim law required women to remain in seclusion and to be veiled in those exceptional circumstances when they must be seen in public. In practice women found ways to gain considerable control over their lives in spite of these restrictions.

9.3 Muslim Women in Medieval Cairo

Rural women living in villages that were seldom entered by non-relatives frequently moved openly outside their homes without

veils. Evidence of urban women's resistance to seclusion is recorded in the attacks by Islamic scholars on the errors of their
contemporaries. Huda Lutfi used this literature when she examined *al-Madkhal,* a four-volume religious analysis of the social
life of residents of the Egyptian cities of Cairo and Misr. Writing
in the mid-fourteenth century, the author Ibn al-Hajj blamed
religious scholars (ulama) in Egypt for the improper religious
practices in the two cities. His approach was to identify and
describe a practice—for example, the clothes women wore—that
was improper under Islamic law. Then he prescribed the proper
corrective measures. Huda Lutfi was able to find many instances
where women disobeyed the *shar'ia* (legal rules).

Ibn al-Hajj shared with many in the ancient world a concept
of separate spheres for men and women. Neither should invade
the space of the other. Men had the public domain and women
the private area of their homes. Ibn al-Hajj was unusually strict—
ideally, a woman could exit her secluded area only three times
in her entire life: when she went to her husband's house after the
marriage, when her parents died, and when she died. When a
woman entered the world outside her home, he warned, the
mere presence of her female body endangered the order of the
male domain. Such acts threatened anarchy or chaos. Women,
to him, were causes of social anarchy because they were ignorant of religious knowledge, they followed "vile" folk traditions,
and they were inherently mentally and physically inferior to
men. Hence the frequent mingling of Egyptian men and women
on religious and social occasions was particularly horrifying to
Ibn al-Hajj.

Our scholar repeatedly admonishes the Egyptian man, be it husband,
father, brother or religious scholar, to prevent anarchic behavior by
women on the street: he explains to them the rules of going out (*adab
al-khuruj*) according to the sunna. A woman should go out only for a
necessity, and if she does, she should go in long and unattractive
garments. If women walk in the streets, they should walk close to the
walls of houses, in order to make way for men. In accordance with
the Prophet's saying, Ibn al-Hajj admonishes men to make the road
difficult and narrow for women, and he exclaims: "Look how these
norms have been neglected in our days. . . . She goes out in the
streets as if she were a shining bride, walking in the middle of the

road and jostling men. They have a manner of walking that causes the pious men to withdraw closer to the walls, in order to make way for them. Other men, however, would jostle and humor them deliberately." Heedless of such warnings, women went to markets to purchase their needs, and they seem to have done that regularly on two important market days: the suq (market) of Cairo on Mondays, and the suq of Misr on Sundays. The favorite spots of women were the jeweler's shop, that of the cloth merchant, and that of the shoemaker. According to Ibn al-Hajj's description, women would sit in the shops for several hours, conversing and humoring the shop owners, hoping for a good bargain. . . .

To secure their household needs, women of the city also dealt with male peddlers who facilitated selling and buying transactions in residential areas distant from the market. Even though Ibn al-Hajj praises the peddler for transporting necessities to the women in their houses, thus protecting the *harim* (wives) of Muslims, he criticizes women's casual behavior in dealing with these peddlers. The transportation of such important items as water, milk, oil, flour, and flax entailed regular visits to homes, which in turn must have led to the development of some degree of familiarity between the peddler and his female client. Ibn al-Hajj insists that rules should be followed: women should not be alone with a peddler; should not come to the door unveiled, as was their custom; and should not get involved in long arguments over selling and buying. "And it is a great wonder that many of their men, who are supposed to be superior in mind and piety, arrive to their houses to find the peddler of flax, or whatever, discussing with their women matters regarding buying and selling. And the men do not forbid what is going on . . . and their answer to this is to say: 'I do not accuse my wife of anything, because I trust her and do not believe that infidelity crosses her mind.' " In defense of their casual behavior, middle- and upper-middle-class women produced a typical class argument: to those women, such men were of an inferior status and therefore ineligible as sexual partners. To this argument Ibn al-Hajj retorts: "They invent their own rules, arguing that men such as the flax seller and the water-carrier are not men to be ashamed of . . . they are not ashamed of slaves or commoners either, because they view them as being too inferior in status. This attitude has become widespread among many women nowadays.". . .

Female nudity in the public baths also upset Ibn al-Hajj: "When women performed their ablutions, Muslim, Jewish, Christian women pranced about the place naked, and women there are so bold as to scold the more timid females who wished to cover from the navel to the knees.". . .

Muslim prescriptive literature viewed the female body primarily as the repository of male sexual pleasure, and hence a source of *fitna* (temptation) that should be concealed; Ibn al-Hajj's treatise is no exception. Hence, female clothes were seen to serve the crucial function of concealment. Properly concealed, women might cease to be a threat to the social order. Yet female clothes were also viewed as serving the function of adornment for the husband's sexual pleasure. Thus, in contrast to men, women were legally permitted to use such luxurious items of adornment as gold, silver, and silk: "For it is as the *hadith* stated, they are deficient in mind and religion, and therefore, they are permitted to use silk, gold, silver and other such items because of their *nuqsan* [deficiency]. As for the man, he is the repository of perfection, God has perfected and adorned him, so he is not allowed to indulge in the adornment permitted to those who are deficient.". . . Ibn al-Hajj's descriptions of female modes of dress in Cairo give us an insight into how women actually dressed there, and to what extent Cairene women abided by the Islamic rules of female dress. The basic female dress in Cairo was the long and loose *thaub* or *qamis* (chemise), under which the long and baggy *sirwals* (baggy trousers) were worn; the head and neck were normally covered by long and ample headclothes. But Ibn al-Hajj tells us that instead of the wide and ample clothes that were designed to conceal the contours of the female body, Cairene women wore a tight and short chemise, which defined the body and was contrary to the prescribed shar'i dress. "Women wore the short and tight chemise which only reached the knees; as for the trousers, worn under the chemise, these were worn far below the navel, exposing that part to the eye, unless the upper garment was made of thick and ample material." But it seems that women wore their trousers only outside the house; at home they wore just the chemise. Ibn al-Hajj considered this to be defying the shar'ia, which prohibits the woman from exposing the forbidden parts of her body to anyone but her husband.

. . . Ibn al-Hajj criticized such practices of female adornment as

painting the eyebrows and tattooing the skin because they too interfered with the proper performance of rituals of ablution. As for the
removal of facial hair and splitting and filing teeth to render them
white, we are told that these should not be performed by a male
barber, as was normally done: "A strange man should not be permitted to touch the lips and face of a woman because it leads to corrupt-
ing behavior." Ibn al-Hajj did not criticize such practices because he
opposed female adornment, for he stressed the importance of the
wife's duty to adorn herself for her husband. Alas, this was not the
case among most Cairene women: "At home she usually dresses in
her worst clothes, pays no attention to her looks, and leaves her hair
uncombed. She allows herself to be in such a state of dirt and sweat
that her husband shuns her. . . . But when she goes out she dresses in
her best clothes. Adorned and perfumed, she puts on her jewelry,
wearing her ankle-bracelet over her sirwal." Competition in female
adornment was most intense when women went to the public bath.
There women would take their expensive clothes and jewelry to
show off after they were finished with their bath. Ibn al-Hajj complains bitterly because of the numerous problems that ensued between husband and wife—she demanding that he should buy her
expensive clothes to match those of her female friends. . . .

The common but significant event of childbirth was and still is a
cause of much celebration among Egyptian families and particularly
among women. In medieval Egyptian society, where female fertility
was highly prized and child mortality was often acute, a successful
delivery was naturally celebrated with the utmost joy and publicity.
The event inspired a host of rituals, all aimed to bring good health
and fortune to the baby and the mother, as well as joy to the whole
family. Typically, Ibn al-Hajj launched severe attacks on these female innovations, which he found to be meaningless, extravagant,
and without precedent in the Muslim sunna. He was, therefore, unhappy to see men contributing to and participating in these wicked
rituals: "And men do not scold them, on the contrary, they seem to be
pleased with all this, and encourage it. This is also true of the religious scholars and mystics, they also celebrate this in their homes,
and invite people for the celebrations."

During the process of delivery and the festivities consequent on
the birth of the child, the midwife played a leading role. Ibn al-Hajj,

obsessed as he was with female impurities, warned husbands of the unshar'i practices of the midwife, who touches the baby and its clothes with hands soiled by the impure blood of delivery. "And they do worse than this, they smear the baby with the impure blood on their fingers, explaining that it is good for this and that." If the midwife was dealing with a difficult delivery, she would mix soft bread with mouse stools and stuff it into the mouth of the mother, claiming that this would help ease the pain.

When the baby was born, loud and long-drawn-out shrills were heard everywhere in the house, as a manifestation of female joy. Music, dancing, and an atmosphere of gaiety followed, and a variety of special dishes was served to the family and neighbors of the community. This, Ibn al-Hajj tells us, went on for seven days; every time a woman came to express her congratulations, the song and dance would start all over again. To publicize the happy event, trumpets and pipes were blown in front of the house door, inviting neighbors and friend to participate in the joyful atmosphere. Our scholar remarks that these practices were so ingrained in people's daily lives that they considered them as important as religious rituals. . . .

When death befell a family member, the women of the household, especially those closest to the dead person, confronted the event with rituals of rejection. Social and religious inhibitions were little regarded, and the women gave vent to their sorrow and pain in a most vehement way: "Women expose their faces and spread their hair, they blacken both face and body, and lament and wail in loud shrieking voices. They heap earth on their heads, and place chains around their necks, and stain their houses in black." The most important funerary ritual was the process of body purification. In the case of female corpses, this task was undertaken by a woman specialist (*al-ghasila*). Ibn al-Hajj describes the dramatic scenario that occurred when the women of the house saw the ghasila approaching the house: "When the ghasila enters the house, the women give vent to a loud scream (*al-saiha al-uzma*); they pour insults and beatings on her. The ghasila, aware of this female tradition, is on her guard, and tries to hide from them. They shout at her, 'you are the face of calamity,' and in response, she says, 'I have seen the calamity in your house.' Eventually, they allow her to perform the washing ritual, and in turn, she admonishes them, and reminds them that death is God's will." . . .

After the body was properly shrouded, it was moved from the house to the bier, and here another farewell female shriek was heard as members of the family stood by to see the corpse leave the house. The *imam* (prayer leader) of the closest mosque then usually led a collective prayer, in which men and women prayed for the comfort and peace of the dead soul. This was followed by a lengthy funeral procession, in which religious and Quranic chanting was performed. "Walking behind their men, women performed their usual ritual of collective wailing and shrieking. They walk about oblivious of proper female modesty, striking their faces in lamentation."

On the morning following the death, men and women of the family usually went for lengthy visits to the tomb of their dead relative, using the house inside the graveyard for lodging. Food offerings formed an important part of Egyptian funerary rituals, and women of the family cooked food for three consecutive nights after the death. On the third evening special rituals of commemoration took place around the tomb. Baffled by these feastlike practices, Ibn al-Hajj remarks that they seemed more like wedding celebrations than death rituals. Male and female relatives and friends congregated to feast on a large variety of food and to listen to the Quranic reciters and mystical chantings. In addition, male and female preachers were hired to relate admonishing stories to their audience.

A period of intensive mourning followed, and it was the women of the family who mourned most passionately. During the mourning period immediately after the death, close female relatives of the deceased stayed home to receive condolences from female relatives and friends. A *naiha* (professional wailer) was hired to intensify the atmosphere of mourning in the house: leading female relatives and friends to the beats of the tambourine, the wailer orchestrated a powerful scene of lamentation. Ibn al-Hajj informs us that women indulged in these scenes, in defiance of the shar'ia, for several days and nights after the death. Mourning continued for at least one year, during which the women of the family wore black, the color of sorrow, and abstained from all forms of adornment. After the year of mourning was over, women prepared for the period of dissolving sorrow *(fakk al-huzn)*. This meant that they could go to the public baths, apply henna stain, and use other female embellishments.

This did not mean that women forgot their dead. In the hope of finding comfort and relief from their daily problems, women spent a great deal of time visiting the tombs of their dead relatives and favorite saints. Tomb visiting was also an important aspect of religious festivities; on those occasions men and women spent all morning and most of the afternoon in the company of their dead relatives or favorite saints. Ibn al-Hajj denounced women's tomb visiting, and he quotes a Prophetic tradition supporting his view: "God curses women who visit tombs." Being opposed to women's crossing forbidden boundaries outside their homes, he viewed their frequent visiting of tombs as a cause of great evil and corruption. . . .

Ibn al-Hajj remarks that whereas the feminine nature inclines towards chaotic and corrupt behavior, men are expected to take corrective measures to control the behavior of their women. But Cairene men disappointed him repeatedly: "The strange thing is that the husband and other men see all this and know of it, but do little about it. Even though this female behavior entails the forbidden, all those people who watch are silent; they make no comments, and do not even display any Islamic jealousy *(ghaira islamiyya)*." In spite of threats of a pious husband, however, the wife insisted on having her own way. We are told that if the husband tried to stop his wife from visiting the tombs, she would refuse, threatening him with separation or denial of sexual pleasures. The dispute could lead to enmity and beating and ultimately reach the judge's court. . . .

When it came to sexual matters, Ibn al-Hajj placed the onus on the man, not the woman, for the female was viewed as a passive body that needed to be sexually satisfied by the man. Contrary to the common habit of sleeping in ordinary clothes, he advises both man and wife to sleep in the nude, as indicated in the sunna. This he argues gives pleasure to the woman and allows for greater sexual gratification. Ibn al-Hajj criticizes the sexual attitude of the Egyptian man, who commonly approaches his wife without warning and achieves his sexual satisfaction without paying attention to her sexual desires. Sunni precedent requires sensitivity in sexual matters from the husband. Ibn al-Hajj states that although female sexuality is stronger than that of the male, it is difficult for the man to sense her sexual desires because of her *haya* (modesty). But the wife's desire, he argues, can be sensed from her special adornments: her makeup, perfume and finery. Ibn al-Haji also severely condemned the common practice of anal sex. According to the sunna, this is almost equivalent to the sin of homosexuality. Moreover, anal sex gives no satisfaction to the wife, thus leaving her sexually ungratified, which in turn makes her a potential sexual threat. The main concern of Ibn al-Hajj here was that female sexuality left unsatisfied within the boundaries of marriage would result in sexual chaos in Muslim society; therefore, the women's sexual desires must be satisfied within the marriage.

Both husbands and wives apparently practiced the habit of conjuring the mental image of a beloved during the sexual act and imagining the beloved, and not their spouse, to be their sexual partner. Ibn al-Hajj believed this practice to be tantamount to adultery, which would inevitably lead to much sexual chaos. . . . He describes another sexual behavior that seems to have been commonly practiced by some Egyptian wives: "This is an ugly and base habit; when the wife comes to bed, she takes something from her husband, most probably in addition to her *nafaqa* (legal allowance), which varies according to his financial situation, and is paid as a bed fee.". . .

Of divorce practices prevalent in urban Egyptian society, Ibn al-Hajj mentions only those that violate the shar'ia. He severely criticizes the widespread practice of repeated divorces, exceeding the Islamic legal limit of three consecutive divorces permitted to the husband. He says that certain men performed the function of a *muhallil* (husband of convenience) for a fixed period and fee, after which the wife could go back to her former but real husband. According to Ibn al-Hajj, mother, daughter, and granddaughter solicited the services of the same muhallil in order to go back to their respective husbands, who had divorced them three consecutive times. "Here is yet another example of female chaotic behavior, which defies all the rules of the shar'ia, for how can it be that mother, daughter, and granddaughter are permitted to marry the same man." When disputes between husband and wife got too complicated, women resorted to the help of the judge, who held his court in the precincts of the quarter's mosque. Prior to the court hearing, women waited inside the mosque, discussing their cases with their agents and husbands. Here again, Ibn al-Hajj states that women overstepped their boundaries, "for the mosque is surely not a place for marital squabbles." Divorced or widowed women were more vulnerable, because of their repeated exploitation by the male witnesses testifying to their marriage contracts. Ibn al-Hajj tells us that a widow was often forced to pay the witness any sum he demanded so that he might agree to testify as to the correct sum of her deferred dowry.

Huda Lutfi, "Manners and Customs of Fourteenth-Century Cairene Women: Female Anarchy versus Male Shar'i Order in Muslim Prescriptive Treatises," in Nikkie R. Keddie and Beth Baron, eds., *Women in Middle Eastern History: Shifting Boundaries in Sex and Gender* (New Haven: Yale University Press, 1991), 103–15. © 1991 by Yale University.

Suggested Further Readings

The best general survey of women and gender in Islam from pre-Islamic societies to the present is found in Leila Ahmed, *Women and Gender in Islam: Historical Roots of a Modern Debate* (New Haven: Yale University Press, 1992). Written by a Muslim feminist, this book is required reading for anyone interested in the historical background of the topic. Nikki R. Keddie and Beth Baron have collected useful articles on *Women in Middle Eastern History: Shifting Boundaries in Sex and Gender* (New Haven: Yale University Press, 1991). These editors have chosen material that illustrates the changes in gender boundaries, family patterns, and women's attitudes in Middle Eastern history. Parts 1 and 2 are relevant to the period before 1500. For a comparison of the past with the modern, see Fatima Mernissi, *Beyond the Veil: Male-Female Dynamics in Modern Muslim Society* (Bloomington: Indiana University Press, 1987). Part 1 is a description of the traditional view of Muslim women's place in society. The author uses the Moroccan situation in the mid-1970s as a comparative benchmark.

–10–
CHINA AND JAPAN
The Patriarchal Ideal

Murasaki Shikibu, Japanese noblewoman and author of *The Tale of Genji*. This great work, written in the early eleventh century, is the first Japanese novel. (The Bettmann Archive.)

Traditional Chinese and Japanese societies have been seen as thoroughly patriarchal and always patriarchal. Critics frequently cite female seclusion, Confucian restraints, and footbinding as evidence for their condemnations. These practices varied in intensity in different periods and regions. Some, like footbinding, actually began not in antiquity but comparatively late in recorded history. Furthermore, women found ways of resisting or accommodating to patriarchy that allowed them to manipulate constraints creatively. Japanese aristocratic women living in a seclusion comparable to the most restrictive Middle Eastern harem wrote some of the classics of their national literature.

Historians before the 1960s believed Chinese society was a perfect example of unchanging patriarchy; since the 1960s researchers have discovered variations in women's rights and freedoms from dynasty to dynasty. For instance, the Tang dynasty (618–907) was a time when life was better. Its successor, the Song (960–1279), was not as good.

An empress again ruled China in the Tang era, and royal women of three generations contested with the male bureaucracy to exercise power. Empress Wu governed from 684 to 705 C.E. with strong support from the Buddhists whose monasteries she patronized. China's most famous woman ruler, Empress Wu, like her predecessor Empress Lu, tried unsuccessfully to replace her husband's dynasty with her own family. Her daughter-in-law, Empress Wei, subsequently failed to seize power as regent for her young son after poisoning her husband. Empress Wu's daughter, the Princess T'ai-p'ing, and her granddaughter, the Princess An-lo, who was the daughter of Empress Wei, led opposing factions in the imperial palace of Emperor Xuanzong during a third generation of women's visible power at the Tang court.

Although palace women's power was seldom exercised for the benefit of all their gender, China's flourishing economy in the Tang and early Song eras led to expansion of a wealthy urban class, whose women gained the legal right to seek divorce and the temporary lessening of their obligatory seclusion. For most women, however, the government attack on Buddhism in the late Tang dynasty under the growing influence of the male bureaucracy heralded a renewal of ideals of female inferiority.

The ascendancy of Neo-Confucian philosophers in the Song period reasserted ancient Chinese gender norms. The Neo-

Confucians revered traditional Chinese authors of the Han dynasty, who gained new popularity as printing spread. According to these Confucians, society should be organized hierarchically, based on age and gender and with women subordinate to men. This subordination began prenatally, with ceremonies seeking the birth of a boy instead of a girl. Family rituals throughout infancy and childhood confirmed the importance of sons to continuing patrilineal ancestry and the insignificance of daughters, whose names were not entered in familial temples. Pan Chao, a woman scholar whose "The Seven Feminine Virtues" was written in the first century C.E. for girls to copy so that they might learn proper behavior, said, "In ancient times a female infant, on the third day after her birth, was placed underneath her parents' bed and given a spindle to play with. Meanwhile her father would fast and do penance . . . on the arrival of a female child . . . ." Another version of this tale, which though old never lost its popularity in China, told of the male baby's being placed on top of the parents' bed with a piece of jade as his toy. Pan Chao pointed out that the ceremony was to show a baby girl "at the earliest possible moment" that her destiny was an inferior one of "diligence and hard work," in which she would be "the first to get up in the morning and the last to go to bed in the evening and should work every minute in her waking hours." Humility and meekness were the virtues enjoined upon the woman, who should "keep herself constantly in the background," "never speak of her own goodness or flinch from the performance of her assigned duties, however unpleasant," "endure all the humiliations and insults, from wherever they come," and never allow herself to indulge in unbecoming laughter or to speak more than necessary.*

In harsh circumstances such as famines, girls were starved to death or sold into slavery, and even in good times they were told that food was wasted in feeding them because they would eventually marry outside their ancestry and increase the size and wealth of their husbands' families, not their own. Once married, a woman entered her husband's family as an outsider also, who would need to bear a son to gain acceptance. Because Chinese

---

*Pan Chao, "The Seven Feminine Virtues," in Dun J. Li, ed. and trans., *The Civilization of China: From the Formative Period to the Coming of the West* (New York: Charles Scribner's Sons, 1975), 95–96.

inheritance was patrilineal within a male kin group, women were effectively excluded from accumulating land or other valuable property.

Some other Confucian objectives for the family can be summarized: One, children must respect and obey parents and grandparents. Two, the property of a kin group was held in common and ultimately controlled by the oldest male. Three, widows should respect their dead husbands and not remarry. Four, a woman's sexual purity must be protected at all costs, including her obligation to self-mutilation or suicide to prevent her rape.

In attacking the way of Confucius, Chen Tu-hsiu in 1919 used some of the most extreme quotations from the Chinese classics. Concerning the rules to protect women's sexual purity, he found: "Men and women do not sit on the same mat." "In giving or receiving anything, a man or woman should not touch the other's hand." "Brothers- and sisters-in-law do not exchange inquiries about each other." "Boys and girls seven years or older do not sit or eat together." And referring to the process of arranging a marriage, he found, "Men and women do not know each other's name except through a matchmaker and should have no social relations or show affection until after marriage presents have been exchanged."

On the proper role for a daughter or wife, Chen Tu-hsiu wrote: "To be a women means to submit." "A married woman is to obey" her husband. A woman "never should disobey or be lazy carrying out the orders of parents and parents-in-law." "If a man is very fond of his wife, but his parents do not like her, she should be divorced." "Unless told to retire to her own apartment, a woman does not do so, and if she has an errand to do, she must get permission from her parents-in-law." "A man does not talk about affairs inside [the household] and a woman does not talk about affairs outside [the household]."*

10.1 Confucian Mothers

The Biographies of Eminent Chinese Women, by Liu Hsiang, who lived in the first century B.C.E., contains 125 biographies. It was reprinted over the centuries with commentaries appropriate

---

*William Theodore De Bary, Wing-tsit Chan, and Burton Watson, eds., *Sources of Chinese Tradition* (New York: Columbia University Press, 1960), 815–8.

to each new generation. One of the best-known stories portrays the mother of Mencius (Meng K'o, or Meng-tzu), a philosopher notable for interpreting the ideas of Confucius. It focuses on a mother's proper guidance of her son's education. Careful reading of the story, here translated from a Song dynasty version of 1214 C.E., reveals important aspects of women's lives as well as the Confucian ideals.

She was the mother of Meng K'o of Tsou; her honorary title was "Meng Mu." She was living near a graveyard when Meng-tzu was small and he enjoyed going out to play as if he were working among the graves. He enthusiastically built up the graves and performed burials. His mother said, "This is not the place for me to keep my son." Then she departed and dwelt beside a market place. Since he enjoyed playing as if his business were that of the merchant and bargainer, his mother again said, "This is not the place for me to live with my son." She once more moved her abode and dwelt beside a schoolhouse. He [Meng-tzu] amused himself by setting up the instruments of worship and by bowing politely to those coming and going. Meng Mu said, "Truly my son can dwell here." Thereafter they dwelt there and as Meng-tzu grew up he learned the six liberal arts. In the end he attained fame as a great scholar. . . .

While Meng-tzu was young yet, he was studying at school. When he returned home, Meng Mu, who was weaving, asked him, saying, "How much have you learned?" Meng-tzu said, "About as usual." Meng Mu took up a knife and cut the web of her loom. Meng-tzu was frightened and asked the reason for her doing that. Meng Mu said, "Your being remiss in your studies is like my cutting the web of my loom. Now, the Superior Man learns that he may establish a reputation; he investigates that he may broaden his knowledge. Therefore if you remain inactive, you will be peaceful; if you arouse yourself, you will keep harm away. If you now abandon your studies, you will not avoid becoming a privy servant and will be without means of freeing yourself from your misfortune. What difference is there [in your studying] and my weaving? I spin thread that we may have food. If the woman abandons her weaving when she is half way through, how shall she clothe her husband and how shall he grow without grain to eat? Just as the woman who abandons what she has [to do in order to support her family will not be able] to eat, so the man who fails in his cultivation of virtue, if he does not become a thief or robber, will become a captive or slave." Meng-tzu, having become frightened, studied diligently morning and evening without respite. He served his teacher, Tzu-Ssu, and consequently became the famous scholar of the whole nation. . . .

After Meng-tzu had married, he was about to enter [his wife's] private room and saw her disrobed within. As Meng-tzu was displeased, he immediately departed without entering. His wife apologized to Meng Mu and asked to depart. She said, "I have learned about the state of matrimony and it does not include [the sharing of] one's private room. Today when I secretly yielded to laziness in my own room, my husband saw me. At once he became displeased and treated me as a guest concubine. The rules of conduct of the wife demand that she not stay over night as a guest. I ask to return to my father and mother." For this reason, Meng Mu summoned her son and said to him, "It is proper etiquette that when one is about to enter a door to ask who is within and thus one attains to a proper respect. When one is about to enter a hall, he should raise his voice so as to warn those within. If one is about to enter the door of a room, the glance should be cast down, lest one see another's fault. Today you did not observe the rules of etiquette and yet you found fault with the etiquette of your wife. Are you not far from right conduct?"

Meng-tzu thanked her and retained his wife. . . .

While Meng-tzu was living in Ch'i, he had an air of sadness about him. Meng Mu noticed it and said, "Son, how is it that you have an air of sadness about you?" Meng-tzu replied, "I have not." Another day when at leisure at home, he was leaning against a pillar and sighing. Meng Mu saw him and said, "The other day you seemed to have a sad appearance but you said you were not sad. Today you are leaning against a pillar and sighing. Why are you doing that?" Meng-tzu replied, "I, K'o, have learned that the Superior Man is first qualified and then receives his position. He does not attempt to attain it unfairly and then receive a reward nor does he covet honors and emoluments. If the nobles do not listen, he does not force himself upon his superiors; if they listen to his teachings but do not follow him, then he does not set foot in their court. Today, the Tao is not followed in the state of Ch'i and I desire to depart but my mother is old. That is why I am sad." Meng Mu said, "Now the proper conduct of a woman is found in her skill in preparing the five foods, fermenting wine, caring for her husband's parents, and making clothes and that is all. A woman's duty is to care for the household and she should have no desire to go abroad. The *Book of Changes* says, 'She provides sustenance and avoids going out.' *The Book of Songs* says: 'For her no decorations, no emblems; her only care is the wine and food.' This means that it does not belong to the woman to determine anything herself but she has the three obediences. Therefore, when young, she has to obey her parents; when married, she has to obey her husband; when her husband is dead, she obeys her son. This is proper etiquette. Now my son has reached maturity and I am old. Do you act according to righteousness and I shall act according to the rules of propriety."

Albert R. O'Hara, *The Position of Women in Early China: According to the Lieh Nu Chuan, "The Biographies of Eminent Chinese Women"* (Washington: Catholic University of America Press, 1945), 39–42.

Meng Mu was a strong-willed mother who spoiled her son. Her husband died when Meng K'o was young, and she raised him alone. It was not unusual for a mother and son to have a close relationship. Chinese mothers knew that when they reached old age their eldest son was expected to support them and their husbands.

Women produced silk cloth, a very valuable product. Not only did they clothe their families, but they, as Meng Mu did, used it to obtain food. Before the Chinese used money, they purchased goods with bolts of silk cloth and paid part of a family's taxes with silk. Some districts were so productive that all the taxes were collected in silk cloth. Considering the importance of silk weaving, its not surprising that Meng K'o was shocked when his mother ruined the silk on her loom. Chinese women were expected to feed and clothe both the men and the women of their families, which was a substantial contribution to the household economy, not to mention the family income from their surplus weaving.

While Chinese women usually could not own land, they, like Meng Mu, were in charge of the household budget, a wife's responsibility whether she had a husband or not. Scholars report that Chinese women were rarely literate; however, Meng Mu was familiar with the classics and could quote from them.

The point of the story is a mother's responsibility for teaching morality to her children. The Neo-Confucian authors of the Song dynasty (960–1279) gave lip service to women's contribution to social morality but were more concerned with repressing their sexuality. They harshly denied widows the chance for remarriage and honored those women who died resisting rape.

10.2 Footbinding in China

In either the late Song or the early Ming dynasty the Chinese began the now universally condemned practice of footbinding. The origins of footbinding have received little attention from scholars, yet the practice, which continued into the early twentieth century, had a significant social and economic impact on Chinese civilization. Sharon Sievers discusses footbinding in an essay written to advise history teachers:

The process of footbinding is, however, one of the things about women's lives routinely reported in introductory history classes; occasionally, students are presented with slides showing what happens to the feet of a five- or six-year-old girl when they are bound ever more tightly by her mother, until the soles and heels are in close proximity. Sometimes students are told that the practice began as an erotic fetish; occasionally it is reported that bound feet were devised to immobilize concubines in the women's quarters who might want to escape. There is some truth in both stories, of course: tiny three-inch "lotus petals" or "golden lilies" were prized by those who found them erotically stimulating, and bound feet certainly limited mobility—particularly the mobility of women in the cities whose feet were typically bound more tightly than those of women in the countryside. The problem is that too often the story of footbinding is left here; when it is, it is generally regarded as yet another example of exotic Asian behavior, with little connection to other historical developments, in China or elsewhere.

But footbinding, because it filtered down to affect virtually every social class, had enormous significance; the immobility of millions of women took them out of "outside" production at the same time it reinforced the Confucian prescription that they, as "inside" persons, did *no* outside work. In fact, Neo-Confucianism made this rule much more stringent, limiting the mobility of women so that they were not just "inside"; they were sequestered there.

It is significant that footbinding was not universally practiced in China: *hakka* women did not bind their feet, nor did women of most ethnic minorities, including Manchu women. Where rice culture dominated, as in southern China, the practice of footbinding was not always allowed to interfere with the productive lives of women. But John Buck's research (1937), suggesting that many peasant women did not work in the fields because of their lack of mobility, or that some women with bound feet worked, but often on their knees, has still not been superseded, and we are left with the strong impression that footbinding had a major economic impact on China's rice-growing regions.

How was it possible for such a practice to be built into the life cycle of most Chinese women, whatever their class—and whatever the impact on the economy? Perhaps the only plausible answer is that mothers bound the feet of their daughters because they felt they had little choice; over time, bound feet became as much a requirement as the dowry for a daughter whose marriage out of the family was a given. And, as wealth accumulated in the hands of a few, peasant families who found themselves in difficult circumstances could send a daughter off to serve in the home of a wealthy member of the gentry. In either case, bound feet were a requirement. Certainly, since "lotuses" were part of the gentry's aesthetic perception of women, a mother could never expect a daughter to marry up the social scale without them.

Beyond the requirements of the Chinese system, it is possible to see that the custom of footbinding was not only painful, and potentially dangerous to the health of children; it devalued and trivialized women to an extreme not often matched in history, though there are variations on this theme in many cultures. Footbinding was a practice that underscored the notion of women, and especially their sexuality, as a commodity; at the same time it seemed to suggest that they had little important productive work to perform. The devaluation of women's work is a universal issue in women's history, but there are few examples that demonstrate it as clearly as footbinding, largely because it affected women of virtually every class.

Finally there is the fact that because footbinding became such a pervasive part of Chinese life before the twentieth century, it became a rite of passage for nearly all Chinese women. As we know from twentieth-century interviews with Chinese women who lived through the experience, anyone who teaches about footbinding in China must be sensitive to the part it played in their lives. They did not always see themselves victimized by the practice; it was a part of becoming a woman in China. And even though there is now general agreement that it was an exploitative practice that caused enormous suffering, it is important to recognize the part it played in the daily lives of Chinese women who endured it, often because they felt, as their mothers did, that it would add to their prospects for a better life.

Sharon L. Sievers, "Women in China, Japan, and Korea," in Cheryl Johnson-Odim and Margaret Strobel, eds., *Restoring Women to History: Teaching Packets for Integrating Women's History into Courses on Africa, Asia, Latin America, the Caribbean, and the Middle East* (Bloomington, IN: Organization of American Historians, 1988), 80–2.

10.3 Women in the Japanese Emperor's Court

Footbinding was a form of seclusion, but it did not necessarily hide Chinese women from public gaze. Japanese aristocratic women lived in almost complete isolation from men. Yet they wrote novels and poetry that are among the classics of Japanese and world literature. The best authors in this period (the ninth through mid-thirteenth centuries) were women, who developed vernacular Japanese while men still wrote in Chinese. A measure of their accomplishments is the fact that one woman, Murasaki Shikibu, wrote *The Tale of Genji,* a novel ranked among the great works of world fiction.

It is almost unbelievable that Japanese women did this under the handicap of complete seclusion. The only adult male eyes that could see them were those of their fathers, husbands, and lovers. Sitting behind screens, curtains, blinds, or shutters was the only proper way to talk to any other male. Even while traveling on their infrequent excursions from their compounds, they remained behind the curtains of the ox carts.

Despite the restricted environment, some women were independent and self-confident. They displayed these characteristics in their writings and in their political activities. The authors were members of the imperial court located in Heian Kyo, then the capital; it is called Kyoto today. In the seventh century C.E., about half the emperors were female, and women frequently held bureaucratic offices. By the tenth century, aristocratic men filled the high government offices, which had become mostly powerless ceremonial posts. Power was in the hands of the Fujiwara family, who ruled in the name of the emperor. Wealthy members of the court spent their time amusing themselves and engaging in complex intrigues.

Girls who were expecting to become members of the court were carefully educated. Calligraphy was very important for success, because some people judged character from a person's handwriting. Music was another required subject, and mastery of an instrument, such as the seven-stringed zither, was normal. Finally it was essential that women have a thorough knowledge of poetry.

Both women and men were expected to have memorized an amazing number of poems, starting with the twenty books of collected poems called *Kokin Shu*. Everyone wrote poems almost on demand, with the thirty-one-syllable poem the most common. There were poetry contests involving just friends and national ones with thousands of entries. Lovers and friends exchanged original poems almost spontaneously.

As a group, the nobility was sexually active. Men not only had concubines but affairs with women of the court, occasionally including married women. Initiating casual affairs was the prerogative of the male; females only had the option of acceptance or rejection. A man would be warned that his career would suffer if he had only one wife. Unmarried women were rare among the court ladies, perhaps because of a belief that someone who remained a virgin was possessed by an evil spirit.

At the end of the tenth century, Sei Shonagon kept a journal that has become famous as *The Pillow Book*. Her comments suggest the spirit of these affairs. Normally a lover would spend the night and leave at daybreak. Sei explains the advantages of the different seasons of the year for lovers:

For secret meetings summer is best. It is true that the nights are terribly short and it begins to grow light before one has had a wink of sleep. But it is delightful to have all the shutters open, so that the cool air comes in and one can see into the garden. At last comes the time of parting, and just as lovers are trying to finish off all the small things that remain to be said, they are suddenly startled by a loud noise just outside the window. For a moment they make certain they are betrayed; but it turns out only to be a crow that cried as it flew past.

But it is pleasant, too, on very cold nights to lie with one's lover, buried under a great pile of bed-clothing. Noises such as the tolling of a bell sound so strange. It seems as though they came up from the bottom of a deep pit. Strange, too, is the first cry of the birds, sounding so muffled and distant that one feels sure their beaks are still tucked under their wings. Then each fresh note gets shriller and nearer.

Sei Shonagon, *The Pillow Book of Sei Shonagon*, trans. Arthur Waley (New York: Houghton Mifflin, 1929), 92–3.

Keeping assignations secret within the imperial compound was practically impossible because some walls were made of paper. After describing how careful the ladies-in-waiting had to be in the daytime to avoid having embarrassing conversations overheard, Sei remarks on the care that must be taken at night:

I like the feeling that one must always be on the alert. And if this is true during the day, how much more so at night, when one must be prepared for something to happen at any moment. All night long one hears the noise of footsteps in the corridor outside. Every now and then the sound will cease in front of some particular door, and there will be a gentle tapping, just with one finger; but one knows that the lady inside will have instantly recognized the knock. Sometimes, this soft tapping lasts a long while; the lady is no doubt pretending to be asleep. But at last comes the rustle of a dress or the sound of someone cautiously turning on her couch, and one knows that she has taken pity on him.

In summer, she can hear every movement of his fan, as he stands chafing outside; while in winter, stealthily though it be done, he will hear the sound of someone gently stirring the ashes in the brazier, and will at once begin knocking more resolutely, or even asking out loud for admittance. And while he does so, one can hear him squeezing up closer and closer against the door.

Sei Shonagon, *The Pillow Book of Sei Shonagon,* trans. Arthur Waley (New York: Houghton Mifflin, 1929), 126–7.

Convention required female passivity, so women could do little to encourage a lover, and in their enforced isolation they spent much of their time talking about the men. The disappointments they faced are shown in a poem by famous Ono no Komachi, who was active in the court in the middle of the ninth century:

> Did he come to me
> Because I fell asleep
> Longing for him?
> If I had known it was a dream,
> I would never have awakened!

The Thirty-Six Immortal Women Poets, trans. Andrew J. Pekarik (New York: George Braziller, 1991), 181.

To survive, women wrote poetry about their feelings. Izumi Shikibu (ca. 975–1027?) wrote of the pain she felt when she was reminded of her dead daughter. The empress, as a sign of sympathy, had continued to send robes in the name of the daughter as she had done for years in the past. The sight of the daughter's name on one such gift caused Izumi to write the following.

> This name of hers,
> Not buried together with her,
> And not decaying
> Underneath the moss, oh,
> Seeing it brings such sorrow!

The Thirty-Six Immortal Women Poets, trans. Andrew J. Pekarik (New York: George Braziller, 1991), 117.

Daughters, not sons, were the children most desired by these families. The importance of marriageable daughters is best understood by description of the so-called marriage politics that allowed the Fujiwara clan to maintain a dictatorship for two centuries even though the emperor remained on the throne. Remember that Japanese wives and grandmothers were responsible for determining promotions, marriage partners, and succession within their families. Visible political power was completely in male hands, but an extraordinary complex system disguised the invisible power of Fujiwara women.

Emperors in this period tended to resign when they were barely thirty. If an emperor was reluctant to become a Buddhist monk or simply resign, the Fujiwara chancellor would encourage him to do one or the other. The crown prince, heir to the emperor's post, was normally a minor when he ascended the throne, and the new emperor's powers would be exercised by a regent. The former emperor's empress or his grandmother traditionally were the most influential in choosing a regent, and since both of them were Fujiwaras, often daughters of the chancellor, the new regent was usually the old chancellor.

The underaged emperor married another Fujiwara consort, and when the first male child was born, the emperor's mother, grandmother, and the chancellor would have the infant declared crown prince. When the emperor reached maturity, the same group coerced him, if necessary, to make the Fujiwara regent his chancellor. And a new cycle would begin.

Through much of his life, the crown prince would actually be living with his mother's family. When the empress became pregnant she moved out of the emperor's compound to avoid causing the pollution pregnant women brought by their presence on sacred ground. She went to her parents' compound to have the baby, which was usually raised by her family. Given these traditions, it took a strong-willed emperor to defy Fujiwara control. Fujiwara marriage politics were unchallenged from the middle of the ninth century until the middle of the eleventh century. Then the emperors managed to regain control, although their power was much reduced.

Another reason Japanese aristocrats preferred daughters over sons was the much wider choice of marriage partners women enjoyed. Traditionally male aristocrats married women from their own or a slightly higher social level, but they could recognize any children of theirs who were born to women of any social level. In Murasaki's novel, her hero, Prince Genji, was the son of the emperor and a concubine. Even though his father was emperor, he could never become emperor, because his mother was not from a noble family. Yet Prince Genji's daughter, born to a commoner woman, eventually became empress after she was adopted by Genji's aristocratic wife.

Marriage created obligations for both parent families to support each other economically and politically. An awarded office included usage of designated land and a percentage of its farm production. At court, families sought to marry their children to government officials, and daughters could marry higher officials than could the sons.

Most noble writers had considerable wealth. Women such as Murasaki Shikibu and Sei Shonagon owned the separate houses in which they had lived before coming to the court. On the deaths of their fathers, such women received a share of the estate, and they may have had additional landholdings. Some empresses had so much property (land was given with the title) that they had to have an administrative council to manage it. Yet their seclusion prevented their hands-on administration, and they had to rely on trusted relatives to supervise the property and to protect it from dangers such as annexation by a neighbor.

Suggested Further Readings

The only female Chinese emperor, Wu Tse-tien (625–705 C.E.), is sympathetically portrayed by Diana Paul, "Empress Wu and the Historians: A Tyrant and Saint of Classical China," in Nancy Auer Falk and Rita M. Gross, eds., *Unspoken Worlds: Women's Religious Lives in Non-Western Cultures* (New York: Harper and Row, 1980). A theory of the causes of footbinding can be found in Joanna F. Handlin, "Lu Kun's New Audience: The Influence of Women's Literacy in Sixteenth-Century Thought," in Margery Wolf and Roxane Witke, eds., *Women in Chinese Society* (Stanford: Stanford University Press, 1975). Also see Mary Daly, *Gyn/Ecology: The Metaethics of Radical Feminism* (Boston: Beacon Press, 1978), for a view of footbinding as an epitome of patriarchal victimization of women; Patricia Ebrey, "Women, Marriage, and the Family in Chinese History," in Paul S. Ropp, ed., *Heritage of China: Contemporary Perspectives in Chinese*

Civilization (Berkeley: University of California Press, 1990), who explains the spread of footbinding in the Song dynasty as a gender characteristic that distinguished the southern elite from the northern Chinese; and C. Fred Blake, "Foot-binding in Neo-Confucian China and the Appropriation of Female Labor," *Signs* 19 (spring 1994): 676–712, for a complex argument that women voluntarily endured footbinding as an expression of female solidarity in a male-dominated culture, and for a comprehensive bibliography. Ivan Morris, *The World of the Shining Prince: Court Life in Ancient Japan* (New York: Alfred A. Knopf, 1969) was written to describe the court life in Murasaki Shikibu's *The Tale of Genji,* trans. Edward G. Seidensticker (New York: Alfred A. Knopf, 1987). It is equally applicable to Sei Shonagon's *The Pillow Book of Sei Shonagon,* 2 vols., trans. and ed. Ivan Morris (New York: Columbia University Press, 1967), which was written in the same period. The Morris edition of *The Pillow Book* contains notes and explanatory essays useful to students. The article by Hitomi Tonomura, "Black Hair and Red Trousers: Gendering the Flesh in Medieval Japan," *American Historical Review* 99 (1994): 129–54, analyzes gender in twelfth-century Japanese literature. She explains some of the changes that took place from the sixth century, when matrilocal and matrilineal marriages were the usual practice, to the fifteenth century, when patriarchy was the norm.

–11–
AFRICA
Traders, Slaves, Sorcerers, and Queen Mothers

A cast metal commemorative head of a royal woman, kingdom of Benin, Nigeria. It was probably made in the 1500s. (The Bettmann Archive.)

In Egypt, where the African continent abuts the Arabian penin-
sula, women's lives have been documented since the days of the
Old Kingdom. For Roman North Africa, Cleopatra and Perpetua
illustrate facets of women's lives. Religious records of Jews and
Muslims in North Africa, and of Christians in Ethiopia expose the
rituals of daily life at the beginning of the second millennium C.E.
About that time, Muslim men began writing in Arabic about the
West African societies they visited in the region south of the
Sahara Desert, in a band of savannah lands stretching from the
Atlantic to Ethiopia they called the Sudan. Indigenous histories
transmitted orally for centuries by professionals, who memorized
their narratives and are often called *griots* in West Africa, confirm
and amplify aspects of the Arabic written accounts. These
sources focus on the cities that flourished on the routes that
caravans took to carry West African goods to the ports of the
Mediterranean; the sources also concentrate on the great empires
of the Sudan: Ghana and Mali.

Male Muslim traders, scholars, or travelers often had little opportunity to observe the private life of the Sudanic peoples, for
foreigners were usually lodged in separate districts outside African towns. Public ceremonies and political events seen by outsiders were easily misunderstood. But these observations can
confirm the antiquity of institutions such as female slavery or
queen mothers that are more fully explained in historical sources
of later centuries. For instance, strangers could see slave women
at work and free women selling goods in markets.

11.1 Female Slavery and Women's Work

Muhammad b. Yusuf al-Warraq lived in West Africa in the tenth
century, when Ghana was flourishing. His comments on the skill
of slave cooks in Awdaghust are preserved in "The Book of
Routes and Realms," a compilation of earlier accounts edited by
Abu Ubayd al-Bakri and published in Spain more than a hundred
years later.

There are Sudan women, good cooks, one being sold for 100
mithqals or more. They excel at cooking delicious confections such
as sugared nuts, honey doughnuts, various other kinds of sweetmeats,
and other delicacies.

Al-Bakri also described slave girls whose most important attributes were their beauty and sexuality, but these were second-hand accounts of what some traveler was told, rather than what he saw. His personal observations were of working women. Abu Abdallah Ibn Battuta also mentioned them often in his account of travel in Mali in the middle of the fourteenth century.

When one of them goes on a journey he is followed by his male and female slaves carrying his furnishings and the vessels from which he eats and drinks made of gourds.

According to Ibn Battuta, in both the capital city of Mali and in Walata, where people were "proud of the number of male and female slaves which they have," they were reluctant to sell "educated slave girls" (Levtzion and Hopkins, 301–2). This reluctance to sell skilled women is not surprising, for both within African societies and in the Muslim lands of North Africa and Western Asia, female slaves were more valuable and costly than male slaves. Although defeated African men could be enslaved to be soldiers, miners, farmers, and laborers, adult males were as likely to be killed in raids or in the aftermath of battles. Slaves who were women and children fit more easily into African households, where they assumed the lowest status among the family dependents.

The importance of slavery in Africa was closely related to the position of women, the nature of marriage, and the principles on which African societies were organized. Despite the rise and fall of some great empires, most of the continent was organized into smaller units of peoples who claimed common bonds of descent and language that distinguished them from neighboring peoples. Whether ancestry was traced through patrilineal or matrilineal ties, elder men usually dominated women and younger men. Older women or wives or sisters of senior men might exercise significant power. Age and gender were not the only determinants of inequality within family units. Marriages between equal lineages required the payment of bridewealth by the prospective groom and his family to the parents of the bride, who lost the services of one of their productive dependents when she moved to her new home. But when such a bride came into her new home as the first, or senior, wife, she and her children acquired superior status within the household. Ranked below them were subsequent wives, sometimes acquired as pawns when families paid off their debts by offering a daughter. At the bottom of the hierarchy were slave concubines and their children. Within these inequalities, kinship mattered. After a slave woman had borne children within the household, she was unlikely to be sold but was also unlikely to be freed. However, her children, if born to any free male of the household, were recognized as relatives, rather than slaves. Her grandchildren were likely to be fully incorporated into the family. In this situation, the slave woman was doubly valuable: she *reproduced* the lineage by bearing heirs for it; at the same time she *produced* goods for consumption or trade in her daily work.

Everywhere in Africa work was divided by gender. Free and slave women were valued as workers because it was they who, more often than not, were responsible for growing food crops. The assignment of tasks varied from culture to culture. Men might weave in one place, while a neighboring people believed that only women could do this job. Building houses could be regarded as women's work in one place, as men's in another, and as a cooperative endeavor in yet another. Free individuals did not cross rigid gender boundaries within their own culture, yet slaves could be assigned to do any task regardless of gender. Women did the laborious work of grinding grains and cooking, but they also sold their surpluses in local markets.

Ibn Battuta, while traveling through rural Mali, observed a man weaving on a loom set in the trunk of a large baobab tree. He commented on the crops, familiar and strange. The "elegantly" carved calabashes and foods he describes can be found still, more than 600 years later, in the region:

Gourds grow very big in the land of the Sudan. They make bowls of them, cutting each in half so as to make two bowls, and carve them elegantly. . . . The traveler in this country does not carry any supplies, [whether staple food] or condiment nor any money, but carries only pieces of salt and the glass trinkets which people call *nazm* [beads] and a few spicy commodities. What pleases them most is cloves, mastic, and . . . incense. When he reaches a village the women of the Sudan bring *anili* [a plant] and milk and chickens and *nabq* flour and rice and *funi* (which is like mustard seed . . .) and cowpea meal and he buys from them what he wants.

From N. Levtzion and J.F.P. Hopkins, eds., *Corpus of Early Arabic Sources for West African History*, trans. J.F.P. Hopkins (Cambridge, UK: Cambridge University Press, 1981), 287. © 1981 by University of Ghana, International Academic Union, Cambridge University Press. Reprinted with the permission of Cambridge University Press.

Women worked hard on their farms, in their houses, and at their market stalls. Though they were obligated to feed themselves, their children, and their husband, each wife expected to have her own space within the family compound, to control her own children's behavior, and to keep the profits of her own work.

Furthermore, West African women moved freely about their villages or cities (except for their exclusion from spaces or buildings privileged to men only), since they, unlike North African women, were not secluded.

11.2 Women's Friendship with Men

As Ibn Battuta, a Moroccan, crossed much of the fourteenth-century Islamic world from the Straits of Gibraltar to China, he found many societies whose women's behavior shocked a North African Muslim man. Few were as disturbing as the women of Mali. Ibn Battuta's first experience with Sudanese women occurred in the Saharan border town of Walata.

Most of the inhabitants there belong to the Masufa [a Berber people], whose women are of surpassing beauty and have a higher status than the men. . . . As for their men, they feel no jealousy. . . . These are Muslims who observe the prayer and study *fiqh* [religious laws] and memorize the Koran. As for their women, they have no modesty in the presence of men and do not veil themselves in spite of their assiduity in prayer. . . .

The women there have friends and companions among the foreign men, just as the men have companions from among the foreign women. One of them may enter his house and find his wife with her man friend without making any objection.

One day I went into the presence of the *qadi* [chief justice] of Walata, after asking his permission to enter, and found him with a young and remarkably beautiful woman. When I saw her I hesitated and wished to withdraw, but she laughed at me and experienced no shyness. The *qadi* said to me: "Why are you turning back? She is my friend." I was amazed at their behavior, for he was a *faqih* [religious scholar] and a pilgrim. I was informed that he had asked the sultan's permission to make the Pilgrimage [to Mecca] that year with his lady friend (I do not know whether it was this one or not) but he had not allowed him [to do so].

One day I went into the presence of Abu Muhammad Yandakan al-Masufi in whose company we had come and found him sitting on a carpet. In the courtyard of his house there was a canopied couch with a woman on it conversing with a man seated. I said to him: "Who is this woman?" He said: "She is my wife." I said: "What connection has the man with her?" He replied: "He is her friend." I said to him: "Do you acquiesce in this when you have lived in our country and become acquainted with the precepts of the *Shar'[ia]*?" He replied: "The association of women with men is agreeable to us and a part of good conduct, to which no suspicion attaches. They are not like the women of your country." I was astonished at his laxity. I left him, and did not return thereafter. He invited me several times but I did not accept.

From N. Levtzion and J.F.P. Hopkins, eds., *Corpus of Early Arabic Sources for West African History,* trans. J.F.P. Hopkins (Cambridge, UK: Cambridge University Press, 1981), 285–6. © 1981 by University of Ghana, International Academic Union, Cambridge University Press. Reprinted with the permission of Cambridge University Press. "Iwalatan" in the original has been changed to "Walata."

11.3 Sorcerers and Queens

Mali, which Ibn Battuta visited in 1352, had grown from an insignificant kingdom to a vast empire more than a century earlier, in the reign of Sundiata. The origins of this empire are recorded orally by the *griots* of Guinea. While the narrative is primarily the story of the rise to power of the warrior king Sundiata, or Mari Djata, his exploits depended upon the help of two women, his mother, Sogolon, and his half-sister Nana Triban. Their story begins with Sundiata's father, King Maghan Kon Fatta, and the competition among his three wives.

The king's first wife, called Sassouma Berete, had two children. Her son would succeed his father and be called King Dankaran Touman. Her daughter was Princess Nana Triban, whose timely help was crucial to Sundiata's success. The second wife, Sogolon Kedjou, had three children, Sundiata and two daughters, Princesses Sogolon Kolonkan and Sogolon Djamarou. The third wife was called Namandje, and she had one son, Manding Bory, who was Sundiata's best friend.

Sundiata's birth and early childhood were deeply influenced by sorcery and occult powers. When King Maghan had been ruling for some years, and his eldest son was already eight, Sundiata's birth was forecast by a hunter-sorcerer. The sorcerer told the king that his successor had not been born and foretold the arrival of the king's second wife, Sundiata's mother, Sogolon. She would be hideous, the sorcerer said, with an enormous hump on her back and bulging eyes. Now, the king was vainly handsome and, as king, expected to pick beautiful women as wives. The sorcerer predicted that Sogolon's son would immortalize Mali by his conquests, becoming more powerful than Alexander the Great. There was, however, one precondition; a powerful red bull should be sacrificed before the future wife could arrive. The sacrifice was made.

Eventually two hunters, carrying silver bows on their shoulders, appeared before the king. They brought as a present a woman whom they thought worthy to be his wife. As the girl knelt before the king, he could not see her veiled face but observed the hump on her back. King Maghan could not hide his revulsion at Sogolon's appearance and asked the hunters to explain. They told a strange tale of a distant land, where while hunting a prize buffalo the hunters encountered a starving, weep-ing old woman whom they fed. She told them that she was the wild buffalo and, because of their generosity, how to kill her. They should then cut off her tail of gold, carry it to the land's king, and collect the reward of the most beautiful maiden in the land. But rather than choosing the loveliest girl, she warned they must look for the ugliest, who would be sitting on a platform beside the crowd. This woman, Sogolon Kedjou, was the buffalo woman's double, or spirit, who would be "extraordinary" to the man who could make love to her. When one of the hunters carried out these instructions his reward was the mockery of the kingdom, whose people laughed him out of town in the company of Sogolon.

When she refused to make love with the hunters, they brought her to the king of Mali. Maghan decided he must carry out the prophecy and ordered preparations for a wedding, inviting people from all twelve villages of his small kingdom.

Belief in sorcery was as usual in Africa as in the rest of the world's medieval societies. Occult power offered causal explanations for what might otherwise be inexplicable. Power was often attributed to sorcery, whether it was that of the king, of the successful hunter, or of the blacksmith who could forge iron from red dirt. Women could also gain power through the mastery of magic. But as Sogolon's story shows, such powers did not spare her the human griefs that befell ordinary women.

While the king prepared a magnificent wedding, Sogolon lived in seclusion with his elderly aunt. Naturally, rumors about her were everywhere, especially since it was known that she was not beautiful. Most of the rumors came from the jealous first wife, Sassouma Berete.

At the home of the king's old aunt, the hairdresser of Nianiba was plaiting Sogolon Kedjou's hair. As she lay on her mat, her head resting on the hairdresser's legs, she wept softly, while the king's sisters came to chaff her, as was the custom.

"This is your last day of freedom; from now onwards you will be our woman."

"Say farewell to your youth," added another.

"You won't dance in the square any more and have yourself admired by the boys," added a third.

Sogolon never uttered a word and from time to time the old hairdresser said, "There, there, stop crying. It's a new life beginning, you know, more beautiful than you think. You will be a mother and you will know the joy of being a queen surrounded by your children. Come now, daughter, don't listen to the gibes of your sisters-in-law." In front of the house the poetesses who belonged to the king's sisters chanted the name of the young bride.

D.T. Niane, *Sundiata: An Epic of Old Mali,* trans. G.D. Pickett (London: Longman Group Limited, 1965), 10.

The wedding proceeded normally, celebrated by dancing and musicians and the king's distribution of expensive gifts to his subjects. The first problem occurred on the wedding night. King Maghan at first was no more able than the hunters to make love to Sogolon. The violence by which the king finally would have his way—in fact, marital rape—is masked in the *griot*'s story by elements of magic that blame Sogolon's female wraith. The morning after the wedding night, the exhausted king met the *griot.*

"What is the matter, my king?" asked the griot.

"I have been unable to possess her—and besides, she frightens me, this young girl. I even doubt whether she is a human being; when I drew close to her during the night her body became covered with long hairs and that scared me very much. All night long I called upon my wraith but he was unable to master Sogolon's." All that day the king did not emerge. . . .

D.T. Niane, *Sundiata: An Epic of Old Mali,* trans. G.D. Pickett (London: Longman Group Limited, 1965), 11.

After failing for seven nights King Maghan vainly consulted the greatest sorcerers of Mali. Finally he acted on his own plan.

One night, when everyone was asleep, Nare Maghan got up. He unhooked his hunter's bag from the wall and, sitting in the middle of the house, he spread on the ground the sand which the bag contained. The king began tracing mysterious signs in the sand. . . . Sogolon woke up. Nare Maghan stopped drawing signs and with his hand under his chin he seemed to be brooding on the signs. All of a sudden he jumped up, bounded after his sword which hung above his bed, and said, "Sogolon, Sogolon, wake up. A dream has awakened me out of my sleep and the protective spirit of the Mandingo kings has appeared to me. I was mistaken in the interpretation I put upon the words of the hunter who led me to you. . . . Sogolon, I must sacrifice you to the greatness of my house. The blood of a virgin of the tribe of Konde must be spilt, and you are the Konde virgin whom fate has brought under my roof. Forgive me, but I must accomplish my mission. Forgive the hand which is going to shed your blood."

"No, no—why me?—no, I don't want to die."

"It is useless," said the king. "It is not me who has decided."

He seized Sogolon by the hair with an iron grip, but so great had been her fright that she had already fainted. In this faint, she was congealed in her human body and her wraith was no longer in her, and when she woke up, she was already a wife. That very night, Sogolon conceived.

D.T. Niane, *Sundiata: An Epic of Old Mali*, trans. G.D. Pickett (London: Longman Group Limited, 1965), 11–12.

Sogolon's pregnancy assured her status at the court. Her only problem was the jealousy of the king's first wife, who feared that the new favorite's child might displace her eight-year-old son as heir. Sassouma Berete sought help from sorcerers to kill her new rival, but they feared Sogolon. When the baby was due, nine of Mali's greatest midwives were called to the palace to attend the delivery of her son, formally named Mari Djata. He was called, after his mother, Sogolon Djata. When spoken quickly this latter name sounded like "Sundiata."

The joy marking Sundiata's birth diminished as he grew, for he still crawled at three years, spoke few words, and displayed none of his father's beauty. The slow development of the child thrilled Sassouma Berete. She enjoyed taunting Sogolon, for each woman knew that her own future was linked to that of her son. Sogolon nearly despaired because neither her herbal medicines nor her sorcery strengthened Sundiata's weak legs. The king's estrangement increased when Sogolon's second child was a daughter, Kolonkan, who resembled her mother. Abandoning Sogolon, the king married his third wife, a legendary beauty whose father was an ally of Maghan's.

King Maghan died when Sogolon's son was seven. The council of elders chose Sassouma Berete's son as successor, with his mother serving as regent and queen mother. She avenged herself against her co-wives mercilessly. Sassouma encouraged gossip about Sundiata's still useless legs and taunted Sogolon until she lost her temper and scolded her child for causing her so much humiliation. Sundiata's response was miraculous: he seized an iron rod which bowed as he leaned on it to rise to his feet; then he strode out of the village to uproot a baobab tree which he presented to his mother. His triumph made Sundiata such a hero that his mother gained new respect.

. . . in conversation people were fond of contrasting Sogolon's modesty with the pride and malice of Sassouma Berete. It was because the former had been an exemplary wife and mother that God had granted strength to her son's legs for, it was said, the more a wife loves and respects her husband and the more she suffers for her child, the more valorous will the child be one day. Each is the child of his mother; the child is worth no more than the mother is worth.

D.T. Niane, *Sundiata: An Epic of Old Mali,* trans. G.D. Pickett (London: Longman Group Limited, 1965), 22.

———————————

Sogolon bore primary responsibility for educating her son in the lore of animals and plants. As Sundiata approached manhood, his prowess as a hunter enhanced his popularity. Sassouma's unceasing surreptitious attacks on the families of her co-wives finally prompted them to flee into exile. For seven years Sogolon and her family wandered in adjacent kingdoms where Sundiata learned about statesmanship, trade, and war. Sogolon died just as Mali was invaded and Sundiata was called to defend his people against the conquering King of Sosso, Soumaoro Kante. Sundiata raised an army and fought bravely, but Sundiata could not defeat the sorcerer king in battle. Another woman rescued Sundiata. This was his half-sister Nana Triban, the daughter of King Maghan's first wife, Sassouma Berete.

When Sundiata left Mali, his half-brother King Dankaran Touman forced Nana Triban into a marriage of alliance with the King of Sosso, Soumaoro. At first she cried often, but eventually she became resigned. She later told Sundiata, "I was nice to Soumaoro and was the chosen one among his numerous wives. I had my chamber in the great tower where he himself lived. I knew how to flatter him and make him jealous. Soon I became his confidante and I pretended to hate you, to share the hate which my mother bore you."* In reality, Nana Triban conspired with Sundiata's friends to find the key to Soumaro's power. Through flattery she cajoled the secret from the king. The *Tana,* or magic power, of Soumaoro had a corresponding secret weakness that negated it: the ergot in a chicken spur. She then fled from her husband to Sundiata's camp.

When Nana Triban revealed this taboo to Sundiata, he was able to vanquish the enemy king with an arrow tipped in ergot and claim his seat as king of Mali. The ability of a woman to subvert the most powerful man by tempting him to boast to her is shown in this African tale of Nana Triban and the king of Sosso, as it is in the Jewish story of Delilah and Samson.

11.4 Queens and Queen Mothers

Ibn Battuta arrived in Mali's capital at the end of July 1352, and during his seven months' stay there he had many opportunities to observe the customs of the king's court. He refers to the king by the Arabic word "sultan" or the Malinke word "Mansa." The rituals of the court were strict. No one spoke directly to the ruler, nor did he respond directly; instead, as Ibn Battuta explains, a speaker addressed an official, Dugha—also known as the *griot—* who repeated the words to the king and through whom the king's response was interpreted. This practice was common among West African rulers and is continued today at the courts of some traditional rulers. Anyone honored by the king's attention or wishing to show respect to the royal family would sprinkle dust on his or her head or back, "like one washing himself with water," Ibn Battuta noted. It was near the end of the reign of Mansa Sulayman that the events described below took place.

---

*Niane, *Sundiata,* 57.

It happened during my sojourn at Mali that the sultan was displeased with his chief wife, the daughter of his maternal uncle, called Qasa. The meaning of *qasa* with them is "queen." She was his partner in rule according to the custom of the Sudan, and her name was mentioned with his from the pulpit. He imprisoned her in the house of one of the *farariyya* [princes] and appointed in her place his other wife Banju, who was not of royal blood. People talked much about this and disapproved of his act. His female cousins [literally, daughters of his paternal uncle] went in to congratulate Banju on her queenship. They put ashes on their forearms and did not scatter dust on their heads. Then the sultan released Qasa from her confinement. His cousins went in to congratulate her on her release and scattered dust over themselves according to the custom. Banju complained about this to the sultan and he was angry with his cousins. They were afraid of him and sought sanctuary in the mosque. He pardoned them and summoned them into his presence. The women's custom when they go into the sultan's presence is that they divest themselves of their clothes and enter naked. This they did and he was pleased with them. They proceeded to come to the door of the sultan morning and evening for a period of seven days, this being the practice of anyone whom the sultan had pardoned.

Qasa began to ride every day with her slave girls and men with dust on their heads and to stand by the council place veiled, her face being invisible. The emirs [chiefs] talked much about her affair, so the sultan gathered them at the council place and said to them through Dugha [his *griot*]: "You have been talking a great deal about the affair of Qasa. She has committed a great crime." Then one of her slave girls was brought bound and shackled and he said to her: "Say what you have to say!" She informed them that Qasa had sent her to Jatil, the sultan's cousin [literally, son of his paternal uncle] who was in flight from him at Kanburni, and invited him to depose the sultan from his kingship, saying: "I and all the army are at your service!" When the emirs heard that they said: "Indeed, that is a great crime and for it she deserves to be killed!" Qasa was fearful at this and sought refuge at the house of the *khatib* [religious leader]. It is their custom there that they seek sanctuary in the mosque, or if that is not possible then in the house of the *khatib*.

From N. Levtzion and J.F.P. Hopkins, eds., *Corpus of Early Arabic Sources for West African History*, trans. J.F.P. Hopkins (Cambridge, UK: Cambridge University Press, 1981), 294–5. © 1981 by University of Ghana, International Academic Union, Cambridge University Press. Reprinted with the permission of Cambridge University Press.

Qasa's story reveals how aristocratic women could manipulate the opinions of others in the ruling elite and of the general public. Sulayman's imprisonment of her was unpopular and a threat to all of the royal family. Despite the king's anger, Qasa was released. In her retaliation, however, she went too far. Whether she merely sought to humiliate Sulayman publicly or actually plotted with his cousin in deposing the king, Mali's leaders were fearful of renewing the civil wars that had plagued the empire after Sundiata's reign. While no women ever ruled Mali, they were active players in the family politics of the empire.

Elsewhere on the African continent, women played Sundiata's role as mythic founders of states and cities. Legends and oral histories of both matrilineal and patrilineal peoples repeat common themes: a queen who chose the site for a city, who established the ruling family, who held the symbols of power, and who governed. Often she is perceived as having chosen to share power with a male stranger or with her son, from whom subsequent kings derived their power. Some of these legends are ancient but persistent. Ethiopia's medieval Christian kings invested their monarchy with the religious and political heritage of the Queen of Sheba, whose wealth had dazzled King Solomon. In Daura, Nigeria, medieval oral histories recall that this Hausa city-state was founded and ruled by a queen, or *magajiya,* named Kufuru. Eight queens succeeded her, but the last, Daura, shared her power with a Muslim stranger from Baghdad who managed to kill a sacred snake that had prevented her people from drawing water out of their only well. Thenceforth, Daura was ruled by men, and as Islam spread in its ruling class, women were subordinated to men. But in Daura, as in many other African states, women's power remained institutionalized through the office of the queen mother. The myth of Daura's origin remained significant until the Hausa were conquered by the Fulani in the nineteenth century. Here the fact that queens preceded kings justified the doctrine that the *magajiya* or queen mother was the only person who could countermand the king's orders and, when necessary, initiate action to remove him from the throne.

But African states did not require such ancestors to justify the institution of the queen mother, a unique means of restraining the power of a monarch and of allowing women to be represented at court. Tombs and archaeology from Meroe, a Nubian state south of Egypt, indicate that queen mothers exercised power beside kings when that state was at its peak between 170 B.C.E. and 330 C.E.

Royal genealogies name the queen mothers, as well as the kings, of medieval Christian Ethiopia. In the centuries after 1500 C.E. queen mothers could be found among many of Africa's states, including those of the Lovedu and Swazi peoples in southern Africa, the Bamileke of Cameroon's grassfields, and the Akan peoples of modern Ghana. In all of these societies, the queen mother constitutes a necessary office of state, sometimes filled by a woman whose son is king and sometimes by one who may not be related to the king but is of royal descent. Monarchy with a queen mother achieved a complementary balance of power, for the king was not absolute, and the separate realms of feminine and masculine were represented at court. Parallel concerns with balance might be symbolized by the appointment of officials of the right and left, north and south. In Ethiopia, the king's three key wives were called the queen of the right, the queen of the left, and the junior queen of the right. But none of them exercised as much power as the queen mother.

Queen mothers did not ordinarily rule, as did the regent queens of Europe or China. Usually a queen mother was appointed when the king ascended to office. As in Daura, her principal power was that of rebuking or criticizing the king (which no other person was allowed to do). The queen mother also usually presided over subsidiary courts, often hearing cases involving women; she had the power to pardon or offer sanctuary to criminals condemned by the king and to regulate the affairs of women in the kingdom. Contrary to those cases where politically astute female rulers who seized power were publicly gendered as male, the African queen mother's gender was *always* female.

Historical records also document the occasional activities of ruling African women, such as Queen Amina, whose conquests extended the borders of the Hausa city-state of Zazzau in the sixteenth century, or a queen who led her troops against the Ethiopian Christians in the tenth century C.E., when that country's monarchy was weakened by contesting claimants to its throne. This queen killed her male predecessor before assuming power for a reign of over thirty years. Her army killed Christians and demolished churches as she established her kingdom's independence and regional power.

11.5 The Meaning of Nudity

Ibn Battuta criticized African women's baring of their bodies, as would many subsequent travelers from other continents.

One of their disapproved acts is that their female servants and slave girls and little girls appear before men naked, with their privy parts uncovered. During Ramadan I saw many of them in this state, for it is the custom of the *farariyya* [princes] to break their fast in the house of the sultan, and each one brings his food carried by twenty or more of his slave girls, they all being naked. Another is that their women go into the sultan's presence naked and uncovered, and that his daughters go naked. On the night of 25 Ramadan I saw about 200 slave girls bringing out food from his palace naked, having with them two of his daughters with rounded breasts having no covering upon them.

From N. Levtzion and J.F.P. Hopkins, eds., *Corpus of Early Arabic Sources for West African History,* trans. J.F.P. Hopkins (Cambridge, UK: Cambridge University Press, 1981), 296–7. © 1981 by University of Ghana, International Academic Union, Cambridge University Press. Reprinted with the permission of Cambridge University Press.

Note that Ibn Battuta is describing ceremonial nudity at the king's palace, not everyday dress, but to an orthodox Muslim the nakedness on the holy day marking the end of fasting for Ramadan was extraordinarily shocking. Ibn Battuta's own account of the events following Queen Qasa's fall from favor tells of royal women who usually wore clothing, which they removed before the king as a sign of their submission. Casual misreading and reliance on sometimes uninformed foreign travelers' comments about female nakedness contributed significantly to stereotypes about "primitive" Africa. Tension between orthodox Islam, as interpreted by North African men like Ibn Battuta, and West African societies whose elite males had become Muslims would exist for many centuries until an African Muslim synthesis penetrated the culture beyond the courts. Much of this tension was gendered. Muslims, Jews, and Christians all believed God required men and women to cover their bodies, and in the medieval years this meant head coverings as well as clothes that reached from neck to hands and feet. One of the most pervasive symbols of social inferiority and lack of civilization for Christian, Jewish, and Islamic peoples was the sight of women with bare breasts, whether in Africa, Asia, the island Pacific, or the Americas.

Suggested Further Readings

Annie Lebeuf, "The Role of Women in the Political Organization of African Societies," in Denise Paulme, ed., *Women of Tropical Africa* (Berkeley: University of California Press, 1963) analyzes the roles of queens and queen mothers in African monarchies without attention to historical chronology. Like many scholars working from anthropological sources, she assumes that the "traditional" has been unchanging. M.G. Smith, in *The Affairs of Daura* (Berkeley: University of California Press, 1978), attempts to set legends within historical time. For Taddesse Tamrat, *Church and State in Ethiopia, 1270–1527* (Oxford: Oxford University Press, 1972), gender is a minor factor in the politics of East Africa's most powerful nation. Though most of Karen Sacks's examples are drawn from later periods, she analyzes women's roles, access to power, and subordination by kin groups in several types of African societies in *Sisters and Wives* (Westport, CT: Greenwood Press, 1979). Women's slavery is discussed in Paul Lovejoy, *Transformations in Slavery* (Cambridge: Cambridge University Press, 1983) and in Claire C. Robertson and Martin A. Klein, eds., *Women and Slavery in Africa* (Madison: University of Wisconsin Press, 1983).

–12–

SOUTHEAST ASIA
The Most Fortunate Women in the World

A fifteenth-century sculpture from Sukuh temple, Java. The figure on the right is a woman pounding rice. On the left is Ganesha, the elephant-headed Hindu god. (Photograph by Sarah Shaver Hughes.)

The environment of Southeast Asia's islands and peninsulas is one of lush tropical rain forests; volcanic soils; a frost-free, year-round growing season; and easy water transport. Straddling the waterways between India and China, the region has attracted merchants and missionaries since ancient times. Hindu, Buddhist, and Confucian beliefs accompanied these travelers. By the twelfth century C.E., sculpture and temple complexes in Thailand, Cambodia, Burma, and Indonesia were visible expressions of the influence of India. Except in Vietnam, China's impact (like that of the later waves of Muslims and Christians from the Middle East and Europe) was subtle. By 1600, all the world knew of the wealth to be claimed by the nations that vied for control of the spice trade in the East Indies. Until then, outside cultures influenced the peoples of Southeast Asia only selectively. Tales from the Hindu epic poem the *Ramayana* shaped Javanese ballet and puppet performances just as Hindu architectural forms shaped the temples of Prambanan and Anghor Wat, but the caste system was rejected.

12.1 Gender Autonomy

The extent to which Southeast Asians retained distinctive regional customs is nowhere clearer than in their gender relationships. Instead of the patriarchy of China or India, these peoples developed a remarkable pattern of female independence and achievement. Of all the ancient civilizations examined in this volume, the women of Southeast Asia were the most fortunate. But that fact is not generally known even among feminist historians. Few ancient sources concerning Southeast Asian women have been translated into English, and very little research on gender has been published. Anthony Reid's history of the region between 1450 and 1680 analyzes some aspects of these women's lives.

Relations between the sexes represented one aspect of the social system in which a distinctive Southeastern Asian pattern was especially evident. Even the gradual strengthening of the influence of Islam, Christianity, Buddhism, and Confucianism in their respective spheres over the last four centuries has by no means eliminated a common pattern of relatively high female autonomy and economic importance. In the sixteenth and seventeenth centuries the region probably represented one extreme of human experience on these issues. It would be wrong to say that women were *equal* to men—indeed, there were very few areas in which they competed directly. Women had different functions from men, but these included transplanting and harvesting rice, weaving, and marketing. Their reproductive role gave them magical and ritual powers which it was difficult for men to match. These factors may explain why the value of daughters was never questioned in Southeastern Asia as it was in China, India, and the Middle East; on the contrary, "the more daughters a man has, the richer he is."

Throughout Southeastern Asia wealth passed from the male to the female side in marriage—the reverse of European dowry. Vietnam in modern times has been the exception to this pattern as to many others, because of the progressive imposition of the sternly patriarchal Confucian system in the fifteenth century. Yet in southern Vietnam as late as the seventeenth century men continued what must have been an older Southeastern Asia pattern, giving bride-wealth at marriage and even residing with the families of their brides.

To some early Christian missionaries the practice of paying bride-wealth was disapproved as a form of buying a wife. Although the terminology of the market was occasionally used in this as in other transactions, the practice of bride-wealth in fact demonstrated the high economic value of women and contributed to their autonomy. In contrast to the other major area of bride-price, Africa, where the wealth went to the bride's father and was eventually inherited through the male line, Southeast Asian women benefited directly from the system. Tome Pires put it strongly for the Malays he knew: "The man must give the woman ten *tahil* and six *mas* of gold as dowry which must always be actually in her power." In other cases bride-wealth was paid to the bride's parents, who transferred some property to their daughter.

Anthony Reid, *Southeast Asia in the Age of Commerce, 1450–1680*, vol. 1, *The Lands below the Winds* (New Haven, CT: Yale University Press, 1988), 146–7. © 1988 by Yale University.

In Thailand, Burma, Cambodia, and Malaya, newlyweds usually moved to the bride's village to farm land donated by her mother.

The husband in these societies (in sharp contrast to the Chinese or Indian models) was the one who had to adjust to a new family of in-laws. On some islands, such as Bali, women could not own land. Laws in most of Southeast Asia, however, provided for joint ownership of property accumulated in marriage. Some legal codes, such as that of medieval Thailand, called for the distribution of common property in a divorce according to each spouse's economic contribution, with wives expecting to receive the larger share. Equal inheritance for all children, regardless of gender, was customary, even in regions influenced by Islam, where the principle of giving sons bequests twice as large as those given to daughters was ignored.

The relative autonomy enjoyed by women extended to sexual relations. Southeast Asian literature of the period leaves us in little doubt that women took a very active part in courtship and lovemaking, and demanded as much as they gave by way of sexual and emotional gratification. The literature describes the physical attractiveness of male heroes and their appeal to women as enthusiastically as it does the reverse. . . . "If Hang Tuah passed, married women tore themselves from the embraces of their husbands so that they could go out and see him." Romantic tales of love were as prominent as in any other of the world's literatures. . . .

Even more characteristic of an essentially Southeast Asian genius were (and are) the earthy rhyming quatrains known as *pantun* in Malay and *lam* in many of the Tai languages. They do not always deal with matters of love, but their most characteristic spontaneous expression was as a dialogue between man and woman or the two parties to a marriage negotiation, taking the form of a battle of the sexes in which each tried to outdo the other in wit and suggestive allusion. . . .

As usual, Chou Ta-kuan had a colourful way of describing the expectations the Cambodian women of his day [1297] had of their men. "If the husband is called away for more than ten days, the wife is apt to say, 'I am not a spirit; how am I supposed to sleep alone?'" . . . At Javanese marriages, according to Raffles, the groom was solemnly warned, "If you should happen to be absent from her for the space of seven months on shore, or one year at sea, without giving her any subsistence . . . your marriage shall be dissolved, if your wife desires it, without further form or process.". . .

The most graphic demonstration of the strong position women enjoyed in sexual matters was the painful surgery men endured on their penis to increase the erotic pleasure of women. Once again, this is a phenomenon whose dispersion throughout Southeastern Asia is very striking. . . . A careful recent survey of the ethnographic evidence suggests that the phenomenon may best be understood as a symptom of the power and autonomy enjoyed by Southeast Asian women. The authors show . . . that some women also undergo a clitoral circumcision kept secret from men and purported to enhance female sexual pleasure. The early Southeast Asian pattern appears to be the opposite of that in parts of Africa, where surgery was designed either to enhance sexual gratification in men or to decrease it in women.

The most draconian surgery was the insertion of a metal pin, complemented by a variety of wheels, spurs, or studs, in the central and southern Philippines and parts of Borneo. Pigafetta was the first of the astonished Europeans to describe [in 1524] the practice:

> The males, large and small, have their penis pierced from one side to the other near the head with a gold or tin bolt as large as a goose quill. In both ends of the same bolt some have what resembles a spur, with points upon the ends; other are like the head of a cart nail. I very often asked many, both old and young, to see their penis because I could not credit it. In the middle of the bolt is a hole, through which they urinate. . . . They say their women wish it so, and that if they did otherwise they would not have communication with them. When men wish to have communication with their women, the latter themselves take the penis not in the regular way and commence very gently to introduce it, with the spur on top first, and then the other part. When it is inside it takes its regular position; and thus the penis always stays inside until it gets soft, for otherwise they could not pull it out. . . .

The same result was obtained in other parts of Southeast Asia by the less painful but probably more delicate operation of inserting small balls or bells under the loose skin of the penis. The earliest report [1433] is from the Chinese Muslim Ma Huan. He reported in Siam,

> when a man has attained his twentieth year, they take the skin which surrounds the *membrum virile,* and with a fine knife . . . they

open it up and insert a dozen tin beads inside the skin; they close it up and protect it with medicinal herbs. . . . The beads look like a cluster of grapes . . . If it is the king . . . or a great chief or a wealthy man, they use gold to make hollow beads, inside which a grain of sand is placed. . . . They make a tinkling sound, and this is regarded as beautiful.

Numerous European writers note the same phenomenon in Pegu during the fifteenth and sixteenth centuries. . . . The primary purpose seems again the pleasure of the female. When the Dutch admiral Jacob van Neck asked in some astonishment what purpose was served by the sweet-sounding little golden bells the wealthy Thais of Patani carried in their penises, they replied that "the women obtain inexpressible pleasure from it."

Anthony Reid, *Southeast Asia in the Age of Commerce, 1450–1680*, vol. 1, *The Lands below the Winds* (New Haven, CT: Yale University Press, 1988), 147–50. © 1988 by Yale University.

12.2 Marriage

The average marriage was monogamous, although rulers had multiple wives and wealthy men had casual sexual relations with their slaves. Premarital sex was considered normal, but once married the couple commonly remained faithful. Adultery was a serious crime in many communities. Anthony Reid thinks the ease of divorce was an important factor in maintaining widespread monogamy.

Among the overwhelming majority of ordinary people, the pattern of monogamy was reinforced by the ease of divorce, the preferred means of ending an unsatisfactory union. In the Philippines, "marriages last only so long as harmony prevails, for at the slightest cause in the world they divorce one another." In Siam, similarly, "Husband and Wife may part again at pleasure, dealing their goods and children without further circumstance, and may re-marry if they think good, without fear of shame or punishment." . . . Throughout the island world the rule appeared to be that the wife (or her parents) kept the bride-wealth if the husband took the initiative to end the marriage, but had to repay it if she was primarily responsible. At least in the Philippines and Siam the children of a marriage were divided at divorce, the first going to the mother, the second to the father, and so on. . . .

That the majority Muslim population of Indonesia and Malaysia had divorce rates in excess of 50 percent as late as the 1960s is sometimes attributed to the influence of Islam in sanctioning easy divorce for men. Much more important, however, was the pan-Southeast-Asian pattern of female autonomy, which meant that divorce did not markedly reduce a woman's livelihood, status, or network of kin support. In noting the acceptance the Javanese gave to women of twenty-two or twenty-three living with their fourth or fifth husband, Earl [1837] attributed this attitude entirely to the freedom and economic independence enjoyed by women.

Christian Europe was until the eighteenth century a very "chaste" society in comparative terms, with an exceptionally late average age of marriage (in the twenties), with high proportions never marrying and with a low rate of extramarital conceptions by later standards. (In England this rate rose from only 12 percent of births in 1680 to 50 percent by 1800.) Southeast Asia was in many respects the complete antithesis of that chaste pattern, and it seemed to European observers of the time that its inhabitants were preoccupied with sex. The Portuguese liked to say that the Malays were "fond of music and given to love," while Javanese, like Burmese, Thais, and Filipinos, were characterized as "very lasciviously given, both men and women." What this meant was that pre-marital sexual relations were regarded indulgently, and virginity at marriage was not expected of either party. If pregnancy resulted from these pre-marital activities, the couple were expected to marry, and failing that, resort might be had to abortion or (at least in the Philippines) to infanticide.

Within marriage, on the other hand, the fidelity and devotedness of Southeast Asian couples appears to have surprised Europeans. The women of Banjarmasin, for example, were "very constant when married, but very loose when single." In pre-Islamic South Sulawesi fornication with an unmarried woman was overlooked, but with a married (upper class?) woman was punished with death. Even Spanish chroniclers who took a dim view of the sexual morality of Filipinos sometimes conceded that "the men treat their wives well, and love them according to their habits. . . ." The economic autonomy of women and their capacity to escape from unsatisfactory unions obliged husbands as well as wives to make some effort to keep the marriage intact. One example of how such a pattern operated to constrain foreign men accustomed to different patterns is given by Scott, who commented [in 1606] on a Chinese beating his Vietnamese wife in Banten that this could not have happened if the wife had been a local woman, "for the Javans will hardly suffer them to beat their women."

Curiously, when female virginity is mentioned as a major factor in marriage, it is as an impediment rather than an asset. In pre-Spanish Philippines, according to Morga, there were (ritual?) specialists whose function was to deflower virgins, "it being thought an obstacle and impediment to marriage for a girl to be a virgin.". . . The Western literature offers more titillation than explanation for such practices, generally suggesting that Southeast Asian men preferred their women experienced. It seems far more likely that the hymenal blood was considered dangerous or polluting to men, as is the case today with menstrual blood in many areas.

The pattern of premarital sexual activity and easy divorce, together with the commercial element potentially involved in the paying of bride-wealth, ensured that temporary marriage or concubinage rather than prostitution became the dominant means of coping with the vast annual influx of foreign traders to the major ports. The system in Patani was described as follows:

> When foreigners come there from other lands to do their business . . . men come and ask them whether they do not desire a woman; these young women and girls themselves also come and present themselves, from whom they may choose the one most agreeable to them, provided they agree what he shall pay for certain months. Once they agree about the money (which does not amount to much for so great a convenience), she comes to his house, and serves him by day as his maidservant and by night as his wedded wife. He is then not able to consort with other women or he will be in grave trouble with his wife, while she is similarly wholly forbidden to converse with other men, but the marriage lasts as long as he keeps his residence there, in good peace and unity. When he wants to

depart he gives her whatever is promised, and so they leave each other in friendship, and she may then look for another man as she wishes, in all propriety without scandal.

Exactly the same pattern is described for Javanese traders in Banda for the nutmeg season, for Europeans and others in Vietnam, Cambodia, Siam, and Burma. Hamilton related in affectionate detail how the system worked in Pegu, where a formal marriage ritual was held for these temporary relationships, to which both parties were bound by legal obligation. Like Chou Ta-kuan in Cambodia, he appreciated the double advantage of such local wives as not only bedmates but commercial partners. "If their Husbands have any goods to sell, they set up a shop and sell them by retail, to a much better account than they could be sold for by wholesale."

Prostitution was much rarer than temporary marriage or concubinage, but it began to appear in the major cities in the late sixteenth century. In every case the prostitutes were slave women belonging to the King or nobles. The Spanish described such women as offering themselves in small boats in the water city of Brunei in the 1570s; the Dutch described a similar phenomenon in Patani in 1602, though it was less common and less respectable than temporary marriage. . . . It seems probable that this type of slave prostitution in the major port cities of the region developed in response to a demand from Europeans and Chinese with different expectations. It may also have been stimulated by a growing sense, at least among Muslims, of the impropriety of temporary marriages with foreigners and unbelievers.

The broad pattern of sexual relations—relative premarital freedom, monogamy and fidelity within marriage (which was easily dissolved by divorce), and a strong female position in the sexual game—conflicted in different ways with the practices of all the world religions which were increasing their hold on Southeast Asia in the age of commerce. The sharpest conflict might have been expected with Islamic law, which made women both legally and economically dependent on their husbands and markedly restricted their rights to initiate divorce. . . .

The *talak* formula of Islamic law, whereby a man could divorce his wife (but not the reverse) by thrice repeating a simple repudiation, was also known in the cosmopolitan ports of the region. . . .

Since the economic and social position of the divorced Southeast Asia woman was at least as strong as that of the man, however, this religious prescription had little effect on the practice of divorce. As the great Arab navigator Ibn Majid complained, Malays "do not treat divorce as a religious act."

A Spanish observer in Brunei noted that husbands were entitled to divorce their wives for the most trivial reasons, but that in practice "they usually divorce voluntarily, both together wanting it; and they agree to return half the dowry and to divide the children if they have them."

Anthony Reid, *Southeast Asia in the Age of Commerce, 1450–1680,* vol. 1, *The Lands below the Winds* (New Haven, CT: Yale University Press, 1988), 152–8. © 1988 by Yale University.

The nineteenth-century Vietnamese poet Ho Xuan Huong succinctly expresses the Southeast Asian woman's contemptuous view of polygamy, a marriage practice introduced to her country by a thousand years of Chinese political domination (111 B.C.E. to 939 C.E.) and continued by the male Viet elite's admiration for Confucian values.

Sharing a Husband

One wife is covered by a quilted blanket, while one wife is left in the cold.

Cursed be this fate of sharing a common husband.

Seldom do you have an occasion to possess your husband,

Not even twice in one month.

You toil and endure hardships in order to earn your steamed rice, and then the rice is cold and tasteless.

It is like renting your services for hire, and then receiving no wages.

How is it that I have turned out this way,

I would rather suffer the fate of remaining unmarried and living alone by myself.

Ho Xuan Huong, "Sharing a Husband," in A. Woodside, ed., *Vietnam and the Chinese Model* (Cambridge, MA: Harvard University Press, 1971), 48.

12.3 Merchants, Diplomats, and Queens

In Southeast Asia, participation in public life by women was greater than in any other society discussed in this volume. Elite and ordinary women pursued opportunities beyond the household domain. Trade, diplomacy, statecraft, warfare, and literacy are activities chosen to illustrate the influential roles Southeast Asian women played. Because they owned property and earned their living, women had considerable freedom to live as they pleased.

In Bayon a Khmer temple has a carving from the twelfth century C.E. depicting two female Cambodian merchants dressed in fashionable sarongs with elaborate jewelry. The Chinese traveler Zhou Daguan described the milieu in 1297 C.E.:

In Cambodia it is the women who take charge of trade. For this reason a Chinese arriving in the country loses no time in getting himself a mate, for he will find her commercial instincts a great asset. Market is held every day from six o'clock until noon. There are no shops in which merchants live; instead, they display their goods on matting spread upon the ground.

Chou Ta-kuan (Zhou Daguan), *The Customs of Cambodia*, translated into English by Paul Pelliot from the French version that J. Gilman d'Arcy Paul translated from the original Chinese (Bangkok: Siam Society, 1987), 20.

This is the earliest written record of women in trade, but, Reid explains, numerous subsequent references testify to these practices continuing into the twentieth century:

Since marketing was a female domain par excellence, this is the place to start. Even today Southeast Asian countries top the comparative statistics assembled by Ester Boserup for female participation in trade and marketing. Fifty-six percent of those so listed in Thailand were women, 51 percent in the Philippines, 47 percent in Burma, and 46 percent in Cambodia. Although Indonesia has a lower rate, 31 percent, this still contrasted sharply with other Muslim countries, particularly in the Middle East (1 to 5 percent). In Bangkok at the time of the 1947 census, three times as many Thai women as men were registered as owners or managers of businesses. A famous Minangkabau poem first written down in the 1820s exhorted mothers to teach their daughters "to judge the rise and fall of prices." Southeast Asian women are still expected to show more commercially shrewd and thrifty attitudes than men, and male Chinese and European traders are apt to be derided for having the mean spirit of a woman on such matters.

Although the casual visitor to Southeast Asia today might not be aware of the female trading role, which is now restricted to rural and small-scale markets, this has not always been the case. Early European and Chinese traders were constantly surprised to find themselves dealing with women:

> . . . It is their [Siamese] custom that all affairs are managed by their wives . . . all trading transactions great and small [1433]. . . .

> The money-changers are here [Aceh], as at Tonkin, most women [1699]. . . .

> It is the women [of Maluku] who negotiate, do business, buy and sell [1544]. . . .

> It is usual for the husband to entrust his pecuniary affairs entirely to his wife. The women alone attend the markets, and conduct all the business of buying and selling. It is proverbial to say the Javanese men are fools in money concerns [1817].

The prominence of foreigners and of the ruling circle in the trade of most Southeast Asia cities ensured that most of the large-scale merchants and shipowners were male. A significant number of local women did, however, join this circle. A famous one was Nyai Gede Pinateh, a promoter of Islam and "foster-mother" of Sunan Giri, whose tomb is still honored at Gresik. She was a foreign-born Muslim. . . . Around 1500 she appears to have been acting as *shahbandar* (harbour master) of Gresik and reportedly sent her ships to trade in Bali, Maluku, and Cambodia. Some royal women used their access to capital to good effect. In the 1660s the wife of Sultan

Hasanuddin of Makassar, Lomo' Tombo, owned ships which she sent on very profitable trade missions to Johor. . . .

Besides these privileged royal women, the Dutch and English dealt with some formidable female traders. In Cochin-China [Vietnam] they haggled over pepper prices with "a great woman merchant *(coopvrouw)* of Sinoa [Hue]" who had made the journey to the capital of Cochin-China in order to check the market. She represented a firm comprising two sisters and a brother which could deliver much pepper, and although she travelled with a male companion, "the woman did the talking and the man listened and agreed." A woman of Mon descent, Soet Pegu, used her position as sexual partner and commercial partner to successive Dutch factors in Ayutthaya to virtually monopolize Dutch-Thai trade in the 1640s and thereby also gain great influence at court. . . .

From trade it was not a great step to diplomacy, especially for those who had been both commercial and sexual partners of foreign traders. Such women frequently became fluent in the languages needed in commerce. Thus the first Dutch mission to Cochin-China found that the king dealt with them through a Vietnamese woman who spoke excellent Portuguese and Malay and had long resided in Macao. She, along with another elderly woman who had had two Portuguese husbands as well as one Vietnamese, had been the principal translator for the Cochin-China court for thirty years. . . . Later the Sultan of Deli, in Sumatra, ordered "a most extraordinary and old eccentric woman" named Che Laut to accompany John Anderson on his embassy to various Sumatran states. She was "a prodigy of learning," spoke Chinese, Thai, Chuliah, Bengali, and Acehnese and knew the politics of all the Sumatran coastal states intimately.

Anthony Reid, *Southeast Asia in the Age of Commerce, 1450–1680*, vol. 1, *The Lands below the Winds* (New Haven, CT: Yale University Press, 1988), 163–6. © 1988 by Yale University.

Fernao Mendes Pinto traveled in Asia in the sixteenth century. His account, *The Travels of Mendes Pinto,* is a Portuguese classic. In Sunda, West Java, he was surprised that an ambassador of the emperor of Demark, the ruler of Java, Bali, and Madura, was an older woman, a widow about sixty years old. She was shown the highest honors by the local ruler, a vassal of Demark. He met her at the dock, took her to his palace, and lodged her with his queen, while he moved out to another apartment some distance away.

Pinto explained that even though the Javanese were Muslims, who generally did not allow women public roles, Southeast Asians ignored that Islamic tradition.

Now in order to understand why a woman, rather than a man, was sent to deliver this message, one must know that it was always a very ancient custom among the rulers of these kingdoms, ever since they began, for matters of great importance requiring peace and harmony to be handled through women. This is true not only for private messages that the lords send their vassals as in this particular instance, but also of public and general affairs that some kings handle with each other through their embassies.

Fernao Mendes Pinto, *The Travels of Mendes Pinto,* trans. Rebecca D. Catz (Chicago: University of Chicago Press, 1989), 383.

———————————

Reid interprets this practice as caused by the strong sense of personal honor of the men. In tense diplomatic encounters, male tempers might flare.

In some parts of the island world there appears to have been a positive preference for using women as envoys, particularly in the peacemaking process. . . . "If the King [in Banten in 1606] . . . send[s] a man [to fetch someone] the parties may refuse to come; but if he once send[s] a woman, he may not refuse nor make excuse. Moreover if any inferior bodie have a suit to a man of authoritie, if they come not themselves, they always send a woman.". . .

Of course men were also used as envoys, and overwhelmingly so as the international norms of Muslim and Christian states took greater effect in the seventeenth century. What the above comments suggest is that the preoccupation of elite males with ordering the political system in terms of hierarchies of status, and the obligation for them to avenge any infraction of that status (especially in Java), made them dangerous emissaries for those who really sought peace.

Men could not bargain as women were expected to, nor subordinate their sense of honour to the need for a settlement.

This peacemaking role is difficult to reconcile with the tradition of female warriors. Since warfare is normally an exclusively male business, every culture is probably inclined to romanticize and celebrate those exceptional women who emerge to save a desperate situation. Vietnam has no heroes more renowned than the Trung sisters, who rose up against the Chinese in A.D. 43. Thais remember two sisters who led the successful defence of Phuket in 1785: Queen Suriyothai, who was killed defending Ayutthaya in 1564; and Lady Mo, who rescued Khorat in 1826 after leading an escape by several hundred captive women. . . . If such militant heroines played a larger role in Southeast Asia than elsewhere, it is probably because status was more prominent than gender, and women were not excluded from taking the lead if the occasion required it. . . .

Anthony Reid, *Southeast Asia in the Age of Commerce, 1450–1680,* vol. 1, *The Lands below the Winds* (New Haven, CT: Yale University Press, 1988), 166–7. © 1988 by Yale University.

Mendes Pinto was also impressed with the military ardor of some women rulers and told the story of events that happened when he was in Malacca near the Sumatran kingdom of the queen of Aaru.

While the queen was outside the fortified stockade, it was overwhelmed by a superior force of Achinese and the king was killed, along with many of his followers. The enemy left a small force to occupy the captured fortification. The queen wanted to kill herself, but her people convinced her not to. Instead

. . . she mounted an elephant and rode off, accompanied by three hundred of her personal guards and many others who joined her later, swelling the ranks of her followers to seven hundred strong; and with them she headed straight for the city, determined to set it afire so as to prevent the enemy from gathering the spoils: she found about four hundred Achinese there engaged in plundering what was still left; and urging her men to turn themselves into *amucks,* reminding them, with tears streaming down her cheeks, of their obligation to do so, she fell upon the enemy so courageously that, according to what was said later in Malacca, not a single one of the four hundred escaped alive.

And when she realized that she was not powerful enough to do as much as she would have liked to, she withdrew once more into the forest.

Fernao Mendes Pinto, *The Travels of Mendes Pinto,* trans. Rebecca D. Catz (Chicago: University of Chicago Press, 1989), 49.

There she organized a guerilla war against the enemy before the rainy season ended military campaigns. She also sought help from other kingdoms. Finally she approached the king of Jantana in Malaya, an enemy of the Achinese. In response to her request for assistance, he offered to go to war with her enemies if she would marry him to give him an excuse for war. She made his promise a part of her dowry and married him. Her new husband did fight, and he won.

As Reid reports, in Southeast Asia not all queens were reluctant to rule alone. He finds an exceptional number of women monarchs in the region.

Female monarchy is anathema alike to the Hindu, Buddhist, Islamic, and Chinese traditions of statecraft. Austronesian societies, however, which include Polynesia and Madagascar as well as Indonesia and the Philippines, have been more inclined than any other major population group to place highborn women on the throne. Sulawesi, where birth always took priority over sex in succession, may be an extreme case. Six of the thirty-two rulers of Bone (the largest Bugis state) since its fourteenth-century origins have been women. . . .

Between the fifteenth and seventeenth centuries, however, there was a remarkable tendency for those states that participated most fully in the expanding commerce of the region to be governed by women. Many states raised women to the throne only when at the peak of their commercial importance. . . . The only woman on a Burmese throne in this period was Shinsawbu, who presided over the emergence of Pegu as a major entrepot in the Bay of Bengal. Japara, on Java's north coast, was a significant naval and commercial power only under its famous queen, Kali-nyamat, in the third quarter of the sixteenth century. . . .

Female rule was one of the few devices available to a commercially oriented aristocracy to limit the despotic power of kings and make the state safe for international commerce. Iskandar Muda had been a particularly frightening example of the dangers of absolutism, seeking to monopolize trade with the English and Dutch while killing, terrorizing, and dispossessing his own orangkaya (merchant-aristocrats). Having experimented with the female alternative, these aristocrats of Aceh and Patani sought to perpetuate it. In Patani the first queen "has reigned very peaceably with her councillors . . . so that all the subjects consider her government better than that of the dead king. For all necessities are very cheap here now, whereas in the king's time (so they say) they were dearer by half, because of the great exactions which then occurred." Similarly, Aceh in the time of its first queen was noted by its greatest chronicler to be frequented by international trade because of her just rule. The capital "was extremely prosperous at that time, foodstuffs were very cheap, and everybody lived in peace." In contrast, "the very name of a kinge is long since become nautious to them . . . through the Tyranical Government of theire last kinge." Theft was strictly punished under the queens, and property rights were respected. The orangkaya found they could govern collectively with the queen as sovereign and referee, and there was something of the quality of Elizabethan England in the way they vied for her favour but accepted her eventual judgement between them.

This was not simply a case of powerful males making use of a powerless female as a figurehead, for women were also active in both Aceh and Patani as traders and orangkaya. In Patani the level of official tribute was lowered under the fourth queen because she was said to have been independently wealthy from her inheritance and her extensive trade. In choosing to put women on the throne the orangkaya were opting not only for mild rule but for businesslike rule. As in other fields, men were expected to defend a high sense of status and honour on the battlefield but to be profligate with their wealth. It was women's business to understand market forces, to drive hard bargains, and to conserve their capital. In general, these expectations of women as rulers were not disappointed. Female rule failed only when Patani and Aceh ran out of credible candidates who still had the charisma of monarchy about them, and when the or-angkaya of the port capital began to lose their influence to forces less interested in trade.

Anthony Reid, *Southeast Asia in the Age of Commerce, 1450–1680,* vol. 1, *The Lands below the Winds* (New Haven, CT: Yale University Press, 1988), 169–72. © 1988 by Yale University.

12.4 Widespread Literacy

Southeast Asian women who were merchants were both numer-ate and literate. European observers in the seventeenth century commented on the high degree of literacy among both men and women in Southeastern Asia. A Spaniard wrote of the Philippine alphabetic symbols that "they use them a great deal, and the women much more than the men. The former write them and read them much more fluently than the latter" (Reid, 216). How-ever, in the censuses taken during the early twentieth century, literacy was lower. Anthony Reid concluded that:

Literacy in Southeast Asia declined between the sixteenth and early twentieth centuries. If this occurred in the island world, it can only have been because the more "modern" and universalist system of monastic education introduced by Islam and Christianity acted to suppress an older pattern of literacy of quite a different type.

The most striking evidence for such an interpretation comes from the 1930 Census of Netherlands India [Indonesia] and its less thor-ough predecessor of 1920. These recorded the highest literacy any-where in Indonesia not in those provinces where the modern school system was most widespread (North Sulawesi and Ambon) but in the Lampung districts of southern Sumatra. In 1930 45 percent of adult men and 34 percent of adult women could write. . . . The great major-ity of these literates could write, not in the roman script taught in the government schools, nor yet in the Arabic script learned for reciting the Koran, but in the old Indonesian *ka-ga-nga* alphabet. This was taught in no school and had no value either vocationally or in reading any established religious or secular literature. The explanation given for its persistence was the local custom of *manjau,* a courting game whereby young men and women would gather in the evenings and the youth would fling suggestive quatrains *(pantun)* written in the old script to the young women they fancied.

The sources do not reveal how young people learned the script, but since it was not taught in school there must have been a process of transmission in the home, probably from mothers or older siblings, with the very powerful incentive of participation in the mating game. Something of the sort was suggested for Bali by Jacobs, who remarked that the high literacy he observed there [in 1883] was achieved without any schools. "The Balinese learn this [writing] from each other in play, and already small toddlers teach each other to read the Balinese alphabet and to write it on *lontar* leaves."

The Philippines, the writing systems of which were probably derived from those of Sumatra, reveal a pattern strikingly similar to that of Lampung. The detailed Spanish accounts of the Philippines make no mention of schools. They insist that Filipino writing served no religious, judicial, or historical purposes, but was used only "to write missives and notes to one another. . . . "

The exceptionally high rates of female literacy reported for the Philippines, Bali, and Lampung now begin to take on more significance. In the absence of formal schools serving to perpetuate a religious elite, literacy was apparently transmitted by older relatives to children at home. . . . .

In the countries more influenced by Indian culture the transmission of literacy by male religious specialists through a monastic type school system is too clear to be denied. Yet even so, in Java and Bali the evidence of the pre-Islamic *kakawin* literature is that writing was also used on a grand scale for love letters and love poems written on palm leaves, pandanus petals, or strips of wood. At least among the court circle, who are the subjects of this classical literature, the skill in composing poems of love appears to have been an essential accomplishment for both sexes.

Virtually everywhere in Southeast Asia there was a strong tradition of contests in poetry, usually of the four-line pantun type, between men and women as part of the courtship process. . . .

What I am arguing for island Southeast Asia is that although the writing system must originally have been introduced from India in the first Christian millennium to serve a sacred literature, it spread to many parts of Sumatra, South Sulawesi, and the Philippines for different, everyday purposes. Prior to the sixteenth-century expansion of Islam and Christianity, writing was being adopted by largely animist cultures where women were more commercially and socially active than in other parts of the world. Women took up writing as actively as men, to use in exchanging notes and recording debts and other commercial matters which were in the female domain. The transmission of literacy was therefore a domestic matter, largely the responsibility of mothers and older siblings, and had nothing to do with an exclusive priestly class. Writing was facilitated by the relative simplicity of alphabets of only fourteen characters for consonantal syllables plus a few vowel markers. Equally important was the universal availability of writing materials suitable for short notes or accounts (but not for long compositions), in the form of palm-leaf and bamboo strips. On this basis we can accept levels of literacy in sixteenth-century Indonesia and the Philippines that were very high by any contemporary standards and as high as any in the world for women.

Anthony Reid, *Southeast Asia in the Age of Commerce, 1450–1680*, vol. 1, *The Lands below the Winds* (New Haven, CT: Yale University Press, 1988), 217–22. © 1988 by Yale University.

Suggested Further Readings

There is a considerable literature on Australian aboriginal peoples, mostly printed in Australia; for an example, see Wendy Beck and Lesley Head, "Women in Australian Prehistory," *Australian Feminist Studies* 11 (autumn 1990): 29–48. The problem of Chinese influence on Vietnamese women is discussed in Van Tai Ta, "The Status of Women in Traditional Vietnam: A Comparison of the Code of the Le Dynasty (1428–1788) with the Chinese Codes," *Journal of Asian History* 15 (1981): 97–145.

–13–
THE AMERICAS
Aztec, Inca, and Iroquois Women

Two women making a kind of paper from plant material. These clay figurines were crafted in western Mexico sometime between 300 and 950 C.E. (The Bettmann Archive.)

Human migration from northeastern Asia to the continents of the Western hemisphere began about 20,000 B.C.E. and continued for some ten millennia. Separated from the cultures of the Old World before the Neolithic age, the societies of the Americas created their own gendered cultures. Gender patterns varied as much among these societies of the Americas before 1500 C.E. as they did in the Old World. The European appellation of "Indian" to all the societies in the Western hemisphere belies their diversity.

Complex societies nearly as old as those of the Mediterranean or Asia developed in the Mesoamerican valley of Mexico and on the western edge of South America, where crops were first domesticated. The cultivation of corn, potatoes, squash, cotton, beans, and chili peppers spread gradually from these centers to other parts of North and South America and the Caribbean islands. Seasonal gathering of berries, acorns, and nuts, along with fishing and trapping and hunting animals, continued on these peripheries as farming spread, bringing with it the development of cultural complexes that influenced wide areas.

By 1400 C.E. the Iroquoian-speaking peoples of the eastern woodlands of North America were one such culture. Ranging from the Hurons, who lived north of Lake Ontario and the St. Lawrence River, to the Senecas, Mohawks, Onondagas, Oneidas, Cayugas, and Susquehannocks, who inhabited the region south of these waters, the peoples of Iroquoia shared gendered cultural traits, as well as deep enmities. These were egalitarian village societies in which women farmed while men hunted and waged war.

At the same time, the Aztecs dominated central Mexico, while the Inca empire ruled the peoples of the Peruvian Andes. Aztec and Inca societies were stratified by 1400, with nobilities whose men and women led privileged lives. Both of these relatively recent empires benefited from conquests of neighboring peoples who were then required to pay tribute in goods and human beings. Urbanity characterized the Incas of Cuzco and the Aztecs of Tenochtitlan, the latter perhaps the world's largest city before 1500 C.E.

13.1 Aztec Greetings to Newborn Babies

Aztec women lived in a patriarchal society, but one whose urban culture offered some noblewomen social power, and many free

women economic opportunities in trade or occupational special-
ization. These possibilities were not apparent in the Aztec gender
ideals starkly revealed by midwives' ritual chants to newborns.
When an Aztec baby was born, the midwife ceremonially
greeted it as she cut the umbilical cord. She told the baby what
to expect in its new life, using a different speech for boys and for
girls.

Because being a warrior was the most prestigious vocation for
boys, her speech emphasized that. Notice that the drink or food
given to the sun in the sacrifice of the "flowered death" was
blood spilled in battle or as priests killed captured warriors.

My precious son, my youngest one. . . . Heed, hearken: Thy home is
not here, for thou art an eagle, thou art an ocelot. . . . Thou art the
serpent, the bird of the lord of the near, of the nigh. Here is only the
place of thy nest. Thou hast only been hatched here; thou hast only
come, arrived. . . . Thou belongest out there. . . . Thou hast been sent
into warfare. War is thy desert, thy task. Thou shalt give drink,
nourishment, food to the sun, the lord of the earth. . . . Perhaps thou
wilt receive the gift, perhaps thou wilt merit death by the obsidian
knife, the flowered death by the obsidian knife.

Fr. Bernadino de Sahagun, *The Florentine Codex: General History of the Things of
New Spain,* vol. 6, trans. Arthur J.O. Anderson and Charles E. Dibble (Santa Fe,
NM: The School of American Research and the University of Utah Press, 1960),
171–2. Reprinted by permission of the publishers, the School of American Research and the University of Utah Press.

For girls, the midwife emphasized the home.

My beloved maiden. . . . Thou wilt be in the heart of the home, thou
wilt go nowhere, thou wilt nowhere become a wanderer, thou becom-
est the banked fire, the hearth stones. Here our Lord planteth thee,
burieth thee. And thou wilt become fatigued, thou wilt become tired;
thou art to provide water, to grind maize, to drudge; thou art to sweat
by the ashes, by the hearth.

Fr. Bernadino de Sahagun, *The Florentine Codex: General History of the Things of
New Spain,* vol. 6, trans. Arthur J.O. Anderson and Charles E. Dibble (Santa Fe,
NM: The School of American Research and the University of Utah Press, 1960),
172. Reprinted by permission of the publishers, the School of American Research
and the University of Utah Press.

13.2 Aztec Women's Careers and Character

The midwife aptly described the domestic drudgery of Aztec women. Grinding dried kernels of corn (maize) on a stone *metate* into smooth flour for tortillas was time-consuming and hard physical labor. Keeping an adequate supply of water for the household involved the women's making trips to local springs or aqueducts while carrying heavy containers. But Aztec women were not forced into seclusion in their homes, nor did they work only there.

Women traders dominated the market places of Tenochtitlan and its surrounding villages. As a part of the marriage ceremony, the new bride was given five valuable cotton capes. The capes were her starting capital for market trading. Women owned the numerous food stalls whose income was their property. Some specialized in a commodity such as fish or salt, although these women probably were the retail outlet for their families' businesses. In some of these families, women manufactured the product, dyeing feathers, spinning rabbit fur into thread, or embroidering. Women invested in the merchant caravans that traveled not only to villages within the Aztec empire but outside it as well. Successful female merchants developed a network of feasting partners and dependents, for Aztecs enjoyed feasts and gave them for economic, political, and social reasons. These women were free to use their wealth for personal satisfaction or to endow their children.

Aztecs admired a woman described as "robust," "very tough," and "middle-aged," with sons and daughters, who was a skilled spinner, weaver, and seamstress, as well as an excellent cook.* With their love of feasting, sometimes for days, "preparer of good food" was high praise for a talent valued by the whole community. And since weaving was a sacred art, a person called a "skilled weaver" had high status.

To make sure that children were prepared to be warriors and wives, all children attended schools. There were two different types of schools. One was primarily for aristocratic children to train them to be priestesses or priests, from which high officials were chosen, and one was for commoners. Commoners went to the local House of Youth, where successful warriors trained the boys for war, but the sources are silent on what the girls studied.

---

*Sahagun, *The Florentine Codex*, vol. 10, 51.

Certainly they learned the ritual songs and dances that they practiced jointly with the boys, and some may have learned spinning and weaving, the most prestigious arts practiced by women. The girls were carefully chaperoned until they were married.

Aztecs had the same types of female slavery that were found in most of the ancient world. Subordinate kingdoms sent tribute slaves. Foreign slaves were bought and sold. Aztec men and women could enslave themselves and did so, especially in time of famine, when parents also sold their children. Some Aztecs were enslaved as punishment for crimes.

Prostitutes were reviled and exploited by free women and men. Schoolboys learned sexual mores from prostitutes in state-run brothels. The women condemned to work in these "houses of joy" were probably Aztec or foreign slaves. The free women who managed the brothels determined the fees charged. Independent prostitutes who solicited at the marketplace were identified by their clothing, their loose hair, and their red-stained teeth.

A Franciscan priest, Fr. Bernadino de Sahagun, compiled accounts of women of different classes and occupations from educated Aztec informants. Sahagun's research, done between 1547 and 1568 during the second generation of the Spanish occupation of Mexico, reflects the beliefs of Aztecs of earlier times.

The noblewoman [is] a woman ruler, governor, leader—a provider, and administrator.

The good woman ruler [is] a provider of good conditions, a corrector, a punisher, a chastiser, a reprimander. She is heeded, obeyed; she creates order; she establishes rules.

[Another] noblewoman [is] a protector, meritorious of obedience, revered, worthy of being obeyed; a taker of responsibilities, a bearer of burdens—famed, venerable, renowned.

The good noblewoman [is] patient, gentle, kind, benign, hardworking, resolute, firm of heart, willing as a worker, well disposed, careful of her estate. She governs, leads, provides for one, arranges well, administers peacefully.

Fr. Bernadino de Sahagun, *The Florentine Codex: General History of the Things of New Spain,* vol. 10, trans. Arthur J.O. Anderson and Charles E. Dibble (Santa Fe, NM: The School of American Research and the University of Utah Press, 1960), 46. Reprinted by permission of the publishers, the School of American Research and the University of Utah Press.

Noblewomen merited repeated description because of their importance to Aztec society. The empire was cemented by marriages of royal daughters from Tenochtitlan to local lords in subject towns. The latter lords married their own daughters to lower-ranking allies in villages. Acceptance of a higher-ranking wife by a male nobleman acknowledged his tributary status to her father. Polygyny existed among the nobility, with the highest-ranking wife and her children being privileged in status and inheritance over lesser wives and concubines. According to linguistic scholar Joyce Marcus, "An Aztec wife of high rank might bring along a retinue of women—some noble, some commoner—who became additional secondary wives or concubines of the ruler. A ruler who married sisters considered them 'joint wives,' although usually one main wife, or highest-ranking wife, was designated as the one who would provide the heirs."[*] A Nahuatl (Aztec language) manuscript records an early fifteenth-century war that allegedly began when Tecpaxochitl, daughter of the ruler of Azcapotzalco, was relegated to concubine instead of wife by the ruler of Texcoco, who chose to marry a daughter of the ruler of the more powerful city of Tenochtitlan. Though royal Aztec women were given lovely names—Turquoise Stone, Water Parakeet, Rain Flower—in written documents it was their birthplaces and lands, rather than their personal names, that were recorded. This practice emphasized an Aztec woman's role in linking two male rulers instead of her personal qualities. Her children, however, would emphasize her high lineage instead of their father's lower-ranking status. Despite their patrilineal customs, Aztec nobility calculated their ancestry bilaterally in such cases. A few Aztec women are shown as rulers of the empire in the pictographic manuscripts, and, as Fr. Sahagun's comments suggest, noblewomen exercised power over their own lands. Among the Mixtec, who controlled part of central Mexico in the eleventh century, the reign of a warrior queen named 6 Monkey is attested in four separate manuscripts. After she led her army to victory and had the hearts cut out of two lords she defeated, she was renamed War Quechquemitl.

Fr. Sahagun's descriptions of ordinary women were primarily

---

[*]Joyce Marcus, *Mesoamerican Writing Systems: Propaganda, Myth, and History in Four Ancient Civilizations* (Princeton, NJ: Princeton University Press, 1992), 225.

of their occupational skills. Only daughters of the nobility were pawned to rulers of subject towns; other women married men of their own class and village.

The good weaver of designs is skilled—a maker of varicolored capes, and outliner of designs, a blender of colors, a joiner of pieces, a matcher of pieces, a person of good memory. She does things dexterously. She weaves designs. She selects. She weaves tightly. She forms borders. She forms the neck. She uses an uncompressed weave. She makes capes with the ballcourt and tree design. She weaves loosely—a loose, thick thread. She provides a metal weft. She forms the design with the sun on it. . . .

The cook is one who makes sauces, who makes tortillas; who kneads [dough]; who makes thing acid, who leavens. [She is] wiry, energetic. [She is] a maker of tortillas; . . . she makes them disc shape, thin, long. . . . She makes them into balls; twisted tortillas— twisted about chili. . . . She makes tamales—meat tamales; She makes cylindrical tortillas; she makes thick, coarse ones. She dilutes sauces; she cooks; she fries; she makes juices.

The good cook is honest, discreet; [she is] one who likes good food—an epicure, a taster [of food. She is] clean, one who bathes herself; prudent; one who washes her hands. . . . who has good drink, good food.

Fr. Bernadino de Sahagun, *The Florentine Codex: General History of the Things of New Spain*, vol. 10, trans. Arthur J.O. Anderson and Charles E. Dibble (Santa Fe, NM: The School of American Research and the University of Utah Press, 1960), 51–3. Reprinted by permission of the publishers, the School of American Research and the University of Utah Press.

Feathers sewn by skilled women into a personal identifying design were an important part of a warrior's dress worn into battle. Noblemen could wear a shirt covered with feathers as part of their battle dress, and honored warriors wore feathers in their headbands daily.

The feather seller [is] a bird owner. She raises birds; she plucks them. She plucks feathers; she treats them with chalk. She plucks feathers from the back and the breast; she peels downy feathers. She spins split ones. She spins feathers—spins them into an even thread, trims them. She spins them loosely, she spins them firmly; she uses the spindle, turns them loosely about the spindle, turns them firmly about the spindle.

She sells soft, spun [feathers]; long, even thread—trimmed, loose, loosely woven; white feathers, tail feathers, chick feathers, back and breast feathers, darkened ones, brown ones; goose feathers, domestic duck feathers, Peru duck feathers, wild duck feathers, turkey feathers—black, white, yellow, bright red, tawny carmine colored. . . .

The seller of fine chocolate . . . provides people with drink, with repasts. She grinds cacao [beans]; she crushes, breaks, pulverizes them. She chooses, selects, separates them. She drenches, soaks, steeps them. She adds water sparingly, conservatively; aerates it, filters it, strains it, pours it back and forth, aerates it; she makes it form a head, makes it foam, she removes the head, makes it thicken, makes it dry, pours water in, stirs water into it.

She sells good, superior, potable [chocolate]; the privilege, the drink of nobles, of rulers—finely ground, soft, foamy, reddish, bitter; [with] chili water, with flowers, with *uei nacaztli,* with *teonacaztli,* with vanilla, with *mecaxochitl,* with wild bee honey, with powdered aromatic flowers. . . .

The physician [is] a knower of herbs, of roots, of trees, of stones; she is experienced in these. [She is] one who has [the results of] examinations; she is a woman of experience, of trust, of professional skill; a counselor.

The good physician is a restorer, a provider of health, a reviver, a relaxer—one who makes people feel well. . . . She cures people; she provides them health; she lances them, she bleeds them—bleeds them in various places, pierces them with an obsidian lancet. She gives them potions, purges them, gives them medicine. She cures disorders of the anus. She anoints them; she rubs, she massages them. She provides them splints; she sets their bones—she sets a number of bones. She makes incisions, treats one's festering, one's gout, one's eyes. She cuts [growths from] one's eyes.

Fr. Bernadino de Sahagun, *The Florentine Codex: General History of the Things of New Spain,* vol. 10, trans. Arthur J.O. Anderson and Charles E. Dibble (Santa Fe, NM: The School of American Research and the University of Utah Press, 1960), 53, 92, 93. Reprinted by permission of the publishers, the School of American Research and the University of Utah Press.

In his collected descriptions of ordinary women, Fr. Sahagun included comments about gender etiquette among the Aztecs. Chewing gum, called chicle, was a libidinous act associated with femininity and male homosexuality.

And the chewing of chicle [is] the preference, the privilege of the little girls, the small girls, the young women. Also the mature women, the unmarried women use it; and all the women who [are] unmarried chew chicle in public.

One's wife also chews chicle, but not in public. Also the widowed and the old women do not, in public. But the bad women, those called harlots, [show] no fine feelings; quite publicly they go about chewing chicle along the roads, in the market place, clacking like castanets. Other women who constantly chew chicle in public achieve the attributes of evil women.

For this reason the women chew chicle: because thereby they cause their saliva to flow and thereby the mouths are scented; the mouth is given a pleasing taste. With it they dispel the bad odor of their mouths, or the bad smell of their teeth. Thus they chew chicle in order not to be detested. The men also chew chicle to cause their saliva to flow and to clean the teeth, but this very secretly—never in public.

The chewing of chicle [is] the real privilege of the addicts termed "effeminates." [It is] as if it were their privilege, their birthright. And the men who publicly chew chicle achieve the status of sodomites; they equal the effeminates.

Fr. Bernadino de Sahagun, *The Florentine Codex: General History of the Things of New Spain*, vol. 10, trans. Arthur J.O. Anderson and Charles E. Dibble (Santa Fe, NM: The School of American Research and the University of Utah Press, 1960), 89–90. Reprinted by permission of the publishers, the School of American Research and the University of Utah Press.

13.3 The Aztec Ceremony of the Sweeping of the Roads, September 1–20

The Aztecs are well known for the practice of human sacrifice. One of their beliefs was that the sun would not rise unless it was supplied with human blood. The victims were usually captured male warriors, although there were rituals in which women were killed. On important occasions, the sources claim thousands were sacrificed. In a few ceremonies, a person was chosen to act out a role as a god-representative *(ixiptla)*. Such people were elaborately dressed to represent and act like the god or goddess before their sacrificial death. Inga Clendinnen argues that they were usually slaves who had been sent as tribute from a subordinate state.*

Aztec women knew that their sons and husbands might be killed in battle or sacrificed at some distant place. Widows, who must have been numerous, sometimes married slaves to have a husband who was exempt from war.

There were ceremonies every lunar month. Inga Clendinnen describes one of the few in which women, in this case the respected female physicians and midwives, played a prominent part.

The festival of the eleventh month, Ochpaniztli, the "Sweeping of the Roads" . . . was devoted to Toci, "Our Grandmother," perhaps the most inclusive of the many names given to the earth powers. The primary referent of the "sweeping" was to the rush of winds before the brief winter rains. The rains marked the end of the season of growth and the beginning of the agricultural harvest, and the first flowering of the season of war. . . .

The solemnity of Ochpaniztli was marked off from the earlier exuberance by a five-day lull in all ritual action. Then, late in the afternoon of the sixth day, in silence, and in carefully ordered ranks, the warriors performed a slow, formal march, their hands filled with flowering branches. . . . So they continued over eight days with that ordered silent marching in the last light of the Sun.

Then the pace changed with the eruption into action of the midwives and the women physicians, all the women wearing the sacred tobacco pouch. . . . Divided into two bands, women surged back and forth in a play-skirmish; pelting each other with flowers, reeds and mossy tree-parasites molded into balls. The group led by three major officebearers of the curers' association swept along with them the

---

*Inga Clendinnen, *Aztecs: An Interpretation* (New York: Cambridge University Press, 1991), 99–110.

bedecked ixiptla of Teteo Innan, "Mother of the Sacred Ones": pa-
troness of midwives, curers, the marketplace traders and of things
domestic, and closely allied with Chicomecoatl, or "Sustenance
Woman." The doomed woman was teased and diverted; should she
weep it was thought that many stillbirths and deaths of great warriors
would follow.

For four days the normally sedate women skirmished before the
House of Song in the main temple precinct. . . . (The victim so mercilessly played with must have been close to hysteria as exhaustion and
excitement mounted.) On the fifth day towards sundown Teteo Innan
was brought to the marketplace, her women still encircling her, to be
greeted by the priests of Chicomecoatl, and for the last time walked
through her marketplace. . . . For the last few hours of her life she
was then taken back to "her" temple, and there adorned and arrayed.
In the thick of the night, in silence and darkness, she was hurried to
the pyramid of the Maize Lord, and stretched on the back of a priest.
They were placed "shoulder to shoulder," we are told, so she was
probably looking up into the night sky when her head was struck off.
Then, still in darkness, silence, and urgent haste, her body was
flayed, and a naked priest, a "very strong man, very powerful, very
tall," struggled into the wet skin, with its slack breast, and pouched
genitalia; a double nakedness of layered, ambiguous sexuality. The
skin of one thigh was reserved to be fashioned into a face-mask for
the man impersonating Centeotl, Young Lord Maize Cob, son of
Toci.

From this point on the priest in his skin had become and was
named "Toci." "She" came swiftly and silently down the steps of the
pyramid, her priests pressing closely behind her, and flanked by four
"Huaxtec" attendants; young, male, near-naked wearing rope breech-
clouts: emblems of male sexuality. . . . At the foot of the pyramid
were the lords and chief warriors of the city. These men, who
scorned to turn their backs in battle, fled through the dark streets to
the temple of Huitzilopochtli, the only sound the thud of their run-
ning feet, as Toci and her followers pursued them with brooms, the
"domestic" female symbol par excellence . . . but now sodden with
human blood. This was no "as if" exercise in terror: as they ran, we
are told, "there was much fear; fear spread among the people; indeed
fear entered into the people."

Inga Clendinnen, *Aztecs: An Interpretation* (New York: Cambridge University Press, 1991), 200–2. © Cambridge University Press 1991. Reprinted with the permission of Cambridge University Press.

The ceremony continued for two more days. Captives were sacrificed, including four by Toci. At one point the priests threw squash seeds and maize down from the temple to the people below, signifying that the sacred seed corn for next year's crop was safely stored. The climax each day featured the distribution of weapons, shields, and protective apparel to groups of warriors. Once they were ready for battle, a challenge was sent to the enemy that had been chosen for that year's war. As the warriors paraded, a cry of lament arose from their female relatives who knew that some in their family might soon be dead.

13.4 The Politics of Iroquois Cooperation

In the eastern woodlands of North America, along what is today the border between Canada and the United States, the Iroquoian peoples lived in self-governing villages loosely allied into nations. No class distinctions divided their families into nobles and commoners. Iroquois culture at the time of first contact with Europeans in the early seventeenth century was distinguished by their method of social control. Community action was possible only with unanimous consent or, at a minimum, with the absence of public opposition. Because women were economically and politically vital factors in Iroquois society, women's input into community political decisions was essential. Nancy Bonvillain explains:

An important point to bear in mind is that, for the Iroquois, social roles were essentially non-competitive. That is, in contrast to our tendency to see individuals and aggregates of individuals as occupying positions of status and influence which compete with each other for prominence, the Iroquoian view focused on the interdependence and harmony among individuals and social groups. In many areas of life, women and men had separate roles, but each was accorded prestige. The fundamental non-competitiveness of their view of social functioning within the society was made explicit in political and religious ceremonies but was evident in daily life as well.

Nancy Bonvillain, "Iroquois Women," in Nancy Bonvillain, ed., *Studies in Iroquoian Culture* (Rindge, NH: Department of Anthropology, Franklin Pierce College, 1980), 48.

Bonvillain illustrates women's importance in providing at least half the food and all the clothing used by the Iroquois.

Among the Iroquoian peoples, the primary mode of subsistence was horticulture, mainly the corn-beans-squash complex typical of farming societies in North America. Here, the horticultural labor was predominantly done by women. The adult male role in farming was limited to cutting the trees when new land was prepared for planting. . . . In addition to horticultural tasks, women's subsistence activities consisted of preparing food, collecting firewood and all other domestic work. They also made pottery, bark bowls and baskets, wove mats and made and decorated all the clothing and ornaments worn by both men and women.

Nancy Bonvillain, "Iroquois Women," in Nancy Bonvillain, ed., *Studies in Iroquoian Culture* (Rindge, NH: Department of Anthropology, Franklin Pierce College, 1980), 49.

A revealing aspect of Iroquois life can be found in the long houses. The long, half-cylindrical houses, constructed of saplings and bark, were the common home of families of the same *ohwachira,* a lineage traced through the female line. Each housed from four to twenty families in rows on either side of a center aisle that contained a fireplace every twenty feet. Two families shared the same fireplace and were jointly responsible for providing firewood and maintaining the fire. They also shared food preparation, cooking in one pot and eating out of the same pot.

The women of the oldest generation living in the long house were the "matrons" who had the authority to allocate the farming land as needed among the families, as well as the meat killed by any of the husbands; some of the meat was given to each family in the long house. It was said that no one would go hungry in an Iroquois village until the last grain of corn was eaten. Women controlled the cleared fields, and men controlled the forest where they hunted, fished, and traded.

Because the Iroquois were matrilineal, a daughter or son was primarily affiliated with the mother's family. Unlike many matrilineal societies in which elder males monopolized public life, among the Iroquois the older women of the lineages chose the successors to the chiefs. Should the women become dissatisfied with the chief's performance, they could replace him with another.

Bonvillain explains that women had other political institutions.

Along with each chief was a group of assistants or "agoianders," both male and female, who advised him. These were chosen by the matrons of the matrilineage. Charlevoix [an early seventeenth-century European observer] says "Each family has a right to choose a counsellor of its own, and an assistant to the chief, who is to watch for their interest; and without whose consent the chief can undertake nothing. Amongst the Huron nations, the women name the counsellor, and often choose persons of their own sex." . . .

Charlevoix, too, says that in the [local] councils the women deliberate first and then inform the chiefs of their opinions, although he adds that ". . . in all probability this is done only for form's sake." . . .

Intertribal councils were attended by representatives from clan groups within each of the separate nations. These representatives were all men, although some of the men went to federal councils as representatives of the women. Specific individuals were selected as orators to make public speeches. The orators spoke for the chiefs and for other represented groups, i.e., the women and the warriors. Charlevoix mentions having attended a welcoming council where there was a male ". . . orator of the Huron women." . . . Lafitau [another early seventeenth-century European observer] says "The women have their orators who speak for them in public councils. Sometimes they also choose an orator among the men who speaks as if he were a woman and sustains that role but that is seldom done except in foreign affairs or meetings of the confederated tribes." . . .

Nancy Bonvillain, "Iroquois Women," in Nancy Bonvillain, ed., *Studies in Iroquoian Culture* (Rindge, NH: Department of Anthropology, Franklin Pierce College, 1980), 54–5.

13.5 Food and Power

Because Iroquois politics was consensual, women could veto a proposed action by continuing public opposition. There has been some disagreement over what the basis was for women's influence in the community decisions. Judith Brown argues that their leverage was based on control of the economy.

Iroquois women controlled the factors of agricultural production, for they had a right in the land which they cultivated, and in the implements, and the seeds. Iroquois agricultural activities, which yielded bountiful harvests, were highly organized under elected female leadership. Most important, Iroquois women maintained the right to distribute and dispense all food, even that procured by men. This was especially significant, as stored food constituted one of the major forms of wealth for the tribe. Through their control of the economic organization of the tribe, Iroquois matrons were able to make available or withhold food for meetings of the Council and for war parties, for the observance of religious festivals and for the daily meals of the household. These economic realities were institutionalized in the matrons' power to nominate Council Elders and to influence Council decisions. They had a voice in the conduct of war and the establishment of treaties. They elected "keepers of the faith" and served in that capacity. They controlled life in the longhouse.

The unusual role of Iroquois women in politics, religion, and domestic life cannot be dismissed simply as a historical curiosity. It cannot be explained by Iroquois kinship structure, nor can it be attributed to the size of the women's contribution to Iroquois subsistence. The powerful position of Iroquois women was the result of their control of the economic organization of their tribe.

Judith K. Brown, "Iroquois Women: An Ethnohistoric Note," in Rayna R. Reiter, ed., *Toward an Anthropology of Women* (New York: Monthly Review Press, 1975), 250–1.

An Iroquois woman's right to land depended on her family's need for its products and her continuous planting of it. In contrast to the situation in Europe, the Middle East, and much of Asia, there was no right to permanent private ownership of bounded tracts of land. Because they practiced swidden (slash and burn) farming, old fields were abandoned as new ones were cleared from forests. The matrons controlled the process of redividing old and new acreage, as they did the division of crops and game.

13.6 Pawns of the Inca

Periodic redistribution of village land was once thought to have been practiced by the Andean peoples conquered by the Incas in the middle of the fifteenth century. Recent research portrays a more complex society in which land redistribution was relatively unimportant. Instead of swidden horticulture practiced by females, the Andean people used remarkable irrigation systems to farm arid tracts whose cultivation was jointly controlled by couples. Protected-use rights to land tracts were owned by either an adult female or an adult male. Women inherited from their mothers and men inherited from their fathers. Both inherited land usage, offices, and occupations. A woman traced her lineage through her female ancestors; a term for this system is "dual inheritance." Occasionally someone died without an heir. In that situation the inheritance would be apportioned among the village population after a part was allotted to the spouse.

People primarily identified with a clan, called an *allyu,* whose members considered themselves descendants of the same notable ancestor. Members of the *allyu,* which was a complicated web of obligations and responsibilities, had an ethic of cooperation and sharing, especially of sharing labor. There was hierarchy within the *allyu,* with some receiving more labor and products than others. Thus someone might owe a woman a number of days of field labor and receive in return her invitation to a banquet. Marriage, however, involved interdependent and egalitarian shared labor between husband and wife. A Spanish priest, Father Bernabe Cobo, in 1653 observed but did not understand the Andean division of labor:

And among these people, women were so subjected and worked so in the service of their husbands. . . . [T]hey did not just perform domestic tasks, but also [labored] in the fields, in the cultivation of their lands, in building houses, and carrying burdens when their husbands were going away, in peace or war; and more than once I heard that while women were carrying these burdens, they would feel labor pains, and giving birth, they would go to a place where there was water and they would wash the baby and themselves, and putting the baby on top of the load they were carrying, they would continue walking as before they gave birth. In sum, there was nothing their husbands did, where their wives did not help.

Irene Silverblatt, *Moon, Sun, and Witches* (Princeton: Princeton University Press, 1987), 10.

Our culture shares Father Cobo's opinion that physical labor is demeaning. In contrast, the Andean population expected everyone who was physically capable to work—even the Inca ceremonially planted corn. Both women and men had prescribed roles during planting. Men used a type of stick hoe, and women handled the seeds. They were careful to pray to the "earth mother," make an offering of corn beer, and ask her for a good harvest. "Earth mother" had two daughters, "corn mother" and "potato mother." At harvest, women chose the ears of corn and potatoes to be saved for seed planting the next year. The seed corn and potatoes were dressed and placed in sacred storage. In the long run, the judgment of the women concerning which seeds were promising was responsible for increased yields and the development of new varieties.

Women's domestic labor was especially associated with spinning, weaving, and cooking—the processing of raw materials for human consumption. Weaving had been developed and had reached an extraordinary level of artistry more than two thousand years before in the Andean coastal communities and was still a very important activity. Ordinary women literally wove the clothes on their family's backs. Very fine pieces were worn by leaders during ceremonial occasions and given by them as prestige presents. These textiles included yarns of cotton grown in the coastal lowlands and fine wools from alpacas and vicunas that grazed on the high pastures. Some pieces included bright feathers from tropical birds that lived in the Amazonian basin across the Andes mountains.

The best weavers were found among priestesses called *acllas,* who were pledged to serve the Incan state. They were female pawns of the Inca rulers, who had developed a unusually well-organized system of subjugating conquered people by confiscating some of their daughters as property of the emperor (the Inca). When the Incas conquered a nation, they required its people to build a local temple to the sun, the Inca's personal god, and a residence for young women chosen from the vanquished to be "wives of the sun." The Incas selected virgin girls (usually before menarche) on the basis of their beauty and high family status. In their cloistered residence, *acllas* learned spinning, weaving, preparing food, and brewing ceremonial beer. Their seclusion and virginity were carefully guarded. These women's main responsibility was to administer the temple, dressing the sun-god figure and making sacrifices and offerings to it. The *acllas'* connection to their family clan *(allyu)* would cease. The Incas honored them for serving the sun god, but the *acllas'* families and friends thought of them as tribute whose normal lives had been sacrificed to the conquerors.

Those of each local temple who were exceptional were taken to the capital, Cuzco. Some were sacrificed, and a few became secondary wives of the Inca himself, while the Inca gave others as brides to men whom he favored. No man was permitted to practice polygyny except those given additional wives by the ruler. The *acllas* were valuable to their new husbands, as they came with fields and the labor obligated to work them for the husbands' benefit. The new wife's weaving could be given as gifts to other officials, putting them in debt to her husband. *Acllas* who remained serving their village temples might also be married off at the whim of the Inca, although some women in each residency never left and constituted a permanent staff.

Suggested Further Readings

Joyce Marcus is sensitive to gender and incorporates a discussion of elite women in comparing sources of information on Aztec, Mixtec, Zapotec, and Mayan cultures in *Mesoamerican Writing Systems: Propaganda, Myth, and History in Four Ancient Civilizations* (Princeton: Princeton University Press, 1992). Art and writing were closely linked in these societies, whose carvings and painted codices reveal both individual and social practices, as Anna C. Roosevelt explains in "Interpreting Certain Female

Images in Prehistoric Art," in *The Role of Gender in Precolumbian Art and Architecture,* edited by Virginia Miller (Lanham, MD: University Press of America, 1988). In two articles, Rosemary Joyce explores depictions of women's work: "Images of Gender and Labor Organization in Classic Maya Society," in *Exploring Gender through Archaeology,* edited by Cheryl Claassen (Madison, WI: Prehistory Press, 1992) and "Women's Work: Images of Production and Reproduction in Pre-Hispanic South Central America," *Current Anthropology* 34 (1993): 255–74. The social importance of women's food and/or textile production is also considered by Elizabeth M. Brumfiel in "Weaving and Cooking: Women's Production in Aztec Mexico," *Engendering Archaeology,* edited by Joan M. Gero and Margaret W. Conkey (London: Blackwell Publishers, 1991); Irene Silverblatt, "Andean Women in the Inca Empire," *Feminist Studies* 4 (October 1978): 36–61; Mary D. Pohl, "Women, Animal Rearing, and Social Status: The Case of the Formative Period Maya of Central America," *The Archaeology of Gender,* edited by Dale Walde and Noreen Willows (Calgary, Canada: Archaeological Association, University of Calgary, 1991); Cherri M. Pancake, "Gender Boundaries in the Production of Guatemalan Textiles," and Penny Dransart, "Pachamama: The Inka Earth Mother of the Long Sweeping Garment," both in *Dress and Gender,* edited by Ruth Barnes and Joanne B. Eicher (Providence, RI: Berg Publishers, 1992). California women are the topic of Thomas L. Jackson's, "Pounding Acorn: Women's Production as Social and Economic Focus," in Gero and Conkey, eds., *Engendering Archaeology.* Debate about the roles women played in Iroquois society began in the late nineteenth century; a contemporary viewpoint that is different from Judith Brown's is that of Elisabeth Tooker, "Women in Iroquois Society," in *Extending the Rafters: Interdisciplinary Approaches to Iroquoian Studies,* edited by Michael K. Foster, Jack Campist, and Marianne Mithun (Albany, NY: State University of New York Press, 1984).

GLOSSARY

Androcentric   Centered upon men; catering to men's desires or interests.

Agnate   A person related by patrilineal descent.

Bilateral kinship   Relatives traced through both father and mother.

Bride-price   See **Bridewealth.**

Bridewealth   Marriage payments from the groom and/or his family to the bride's family or to the bride.

Conjugal   Pertaining to the marital relationship.

Consanguineal   A relative by birth in contrast to one related by marriage.

Dowry   Property sent with the bride at her marriage, either as payment to the husband's kin or as the wife's share of her parent's estate.

Endogamy   A practice of marrying only within a specified group, such as an extended family, clan, village, caste, or class.

Exogamy   A practice in which marriage partners are sought outside a specified group, such as an extended family, clan, village, or class.

Extended family   A family unit making up one household, or related cooperating households, consisting of parents, grown siblings, their spouses and children, or other close relatives.

Levirate Marriage   Practice requiring a dead man's brother (or other close male relative) to marry his widow.

Matriarchy   Literally power exercised by mothers; also refers to female social dominance.

Matrilocal   Residence of a married couple with the wife's kin.

Matrilineal   Principle of descent from parent to child traced through the female line, with links to the mother conferring kin membership.

Misogyny   Male hatred or fear of women.

Monogamy   Marriage of one man and one woman only.

Natal   Relating to the family or place of one's birth.

Nuclear family   A family unit consisting of parents and their dependent children.

Patriarchy   Literally, power exercised by fathers; also refers to male social power or dominance.

Patrilocal   Residence of a married couple with the husband's kin.

Patrilineal   Principle of descent through the male line, with links to the father conferring kin membership.

Pawns   Those, especially women or children, whose individual lives are sacrificed to serve other's interests: a ruler's daughters married for purposes of state or family alliance; dependents sold into temporary slavery as collateral on a family debt; dependents given to a ruler as a sign of fealty.

Polyandry   Marriage of a woman to two or more husbands contemporaneously.

Polygyny/polygamy   Marriage of a man to two or more wives contemporaneously.

Uxorilocal   See **matrilocal.**

Virilocal   See **patrilocal.**

ABOUT THE EDITORS

Sarah Shaver Hughes and **Brady Hughes** have taught world history and women's history for many years. Brady Hughes retired in 1990 from the faculty of Hampton University, Virginia; Sarah Hughes teaches at Shippensburg University, Pennsylvania. Sarah Hughes received her doctorate from the College of William and Mary in 1975; Brady Hughes received his from the University of Wisconsin, Madison, in 1969.